THE
REVELATION
OF
GOD

PETER JENSEN

CONTOURS *of*

CHRISTIAN

THEOLOGY

GERALD BRAY
General Editor

InterVarsity Press
Downers Grove, Illinois

InterVarsity Press
P.O. Box 1400, Downers Grove, IL 60515-1426
World Wide Web: www.ivpress.com
E-mail: mail@ivpress.com

InterVarsity Press® is the book-publishing division of InterVarsity Christian Fellowship/USA®, a student movement active on campus at hundreds of universities, colleges and schools of nursing in the United States of America, and a member movement of the International Fellowship of Evangelical Students. For information about local and regional activities, write Public Relations Dept., InterVarsity Christian Fellowship/USA, 6400 Schroeder Rd., P.O. Box 7895, Madison, WI 53707-7895, or visit the IVCF website at <www.ivcf.org>.

ISBN 0-8308-1538-4

Printed in the United States of America ∞

Library of Congress Cataloging-in-Publication Data

Jensen, Peter.
  The revelation of God / Peter Jensen.
    p. cm.—(Contours of Christian theology)
  Includes bibliographical references and index.
  ISBN 0-8308-1538-4 (alk. paper)
    1. Revelation. 2. Bible—Evidences, authority, etc. 3. Jesus Christ—Person and offices.
I. Title. II. Series.
BT127.3 .J46 2002
231.7'4—dc21

                                     2002068529

P	17	16	15	14	13	12	11	10	9	8	7	6	5	4	3	2	1
Y	15	14	13	12	11	10	09	08	07	06	05	04	03	02			

To my beloved colleagues
on the Faculty of Moore College

Contents

Series preface

Contours of Christian Theology covers the main themes of Christian doctrine. The series offers a systematic presentation of most of the major doctrines in a way which complements the traditional textbooks but does not copy them. Top priority has been given to contemporary issues, some of which may not be dealt with elsewhere from an evangelical point of view. The series aims, however, not merely to answer current objections to evangelical Christianity, but also to rework the orthodox evangelical position in a fresh and compelling way. The overall thrust is therefore positive and evangelistic in the best sense.

The series is intended to be of value to theological students at all levels, whether at a Bible college, a seminary or a secular university. It should also appeal to ministers and educated laypeople. As far as possible, efforts have been made to make technical vocabulary accessible to the non-specialist reader, and the presentation has avoided the extremes of academic style. Occasionally this has meant that particular issues have been presented without a thorough argument, taking into account different positions, but when this has happened, authors have been encouraged to refer the reader to other works which take the discussion further. For this purpose adequate but not exhaustive notes have been produced.

The doctrines covered in the series are not exhaustive, but have been chosen in response to contemporary concerns. The title and presentation of each volume are at the discretion of the author, but the final editorial decisions have been taken by the Series Editor in consultation with IVP.

In offering this series to the public, the authors and the publishers hope that it will meet the needs of theological students in this generation, and bring honour and glory to God the Father, and to his Son, Jesus Christ, in whose service the work has been undertaken from the beginning.

Gerald Bray
Series Editor

Preface

A truly wise author or the publisher would never have begun this project. Both parties should have recognized that a slow writer burdened with the obligations of a college principal would be too tardy. In the event, the book has been so long in the preparation – over a decade – that the publisher has had every right to reassign the volume. Instead, there has been an extraordinary display of patience and courtesy, for which I am immensely grateful. Most recently Philip Duce has been the Theological Books Editor at Inter-Varsity Press and he has exhibited in abundance the same characteristics as his predecessors David Kingdon and Mark Smith.

Like all authors I have many other debts of gratitude. I wish to thank the students and Faculties of Moore Theological College in Sydney and Oak Hill Theological College in London, where various of my ideas were given their first hearing. A number of people gave their help, but Michael Ovey, Andrew Katay, Michael Jensen and Keith Mascord read and commented extensively. Mark Baddeley did sterling work in the final stages. I am especially grateful to Gerald Bray for his perceptive and encouraging remarks as editor of the series. The Council of Moore College has been both kind and generous with study leave.

I record, too, my deep admiration and my thanks to my wife Christine, a fellow worker in the service of the Lord Jesus, and an inspiration to me, to her family and to those among whom she ministers.

I am conscious of the defects of this book, but utterly convinced of the truth of its central thesis, that God has revealed himself definitively in the gospel of the Lord Jesus Christ. To him be all honour and praise.

November 2001   *Peter F. Jensen*

INTRODUCTION

I have beside me a book which, as far as I can remember, was the first critical work I ever read. It is Joseph McCabe's selection and translation of works by the great French rationalist of the eighteenth century, Voltaire.[1] What chiefly impressed me was the brilliance of Voltaire's attack on the Bible and Christianity. I had been brought up with a conventional respect for both, and it barely survived Voltaire's contempt.

> May the great God who hears me – a God who certainly could not be born of a girl, nor die on a gibbet, nor be eaten in a morsel of paste, nor have inspired this book with its contradictions, follies, and horrors – may this God, creator of all worlds, have pity on the sect of the Christians who blaspheme him.[2]

Voltaire was not content to excoriate Christian doctrine for its stupidity. With equal severity he also flayed the Scriptures, attacking not only their morality but also their credibility. 'I am not sufficiently versed in chemistry', he observed, 'to deal happily with the golden calf which, Exodus says, was made in a day, and which Moses reduced to ashes. Are they two miracles, or two possibilities of human art?'[3]

Encountering the Enlightenment

Although I did not know it at the time, I was being inducted into the wisdom of one of the great intellectual movements of modern history, the Enlightenment. At the hands of a literary master like Voltaire, I was experiencing the power of a critique that has interrogated belief in a hostile way for over two hundred years. Despite the many differences of opinion that characterized Christian doctrine by the time of Voltaire, there was fundamental agreement among Christians that the Bible was a special revelation from the one true God, and is rightly called the Word of God. It was also agreed that there exists a general revelation of God through the created world, though opinion differed about the extent to which it could be apprehended by sinful human beings. In any case, however, Christianity was thought to possess a singularly authoritative and saving capacity to bring sinners into a relationship with God.

For his part, Voltaire was no atheist. When he offered a proof for the existence of God, his reasoning was based not on revelation but on a sort of 'natural theology'. 'We speak here a strictly philosophical language; it is not our part even to glance at those who use the language of revelation.'[4] The questions posed by the Enlightenment were these: Does Christianity possess a special revelation from God? Would it not be best to keep religion within the bounds of human reason? What can we learn about God using human reason alone? Can we believe that the miracles of the Bible and of church history are authentic in the light of critical history? Can we give credence to the claim that the Bible is inspired, when it contains so many improbable stories and immoral teachings? The critical arguments of thinkers such as Voltaire have massively eroded the credibility of Christian teaching. Ironically, although we still call any authoritative textbook a 'bible', this usage merely reflects the vestigial remains of its former overwhelming authority. When it comes to the actual Bible, Voltaire's opinion has largely triumphed.

When, later, I turned to the study of theology, I was introduced to a powerful set of objections to the use of natural theology

14

itself. David Hume (1711–76) assailed both natural and revealed theology. He refused to allow that the argument for God from the world had any persuasive power. Far from leading to the conclusion that there is one sovereign creator of heaven and earth, it was more justifiable to conclude that polytheism is true, or that God's power is limited by infirmity. The world, he argued, may be understood as being

> ... very faulty and imperfect, compared to a superior standard; and was only the first rude essay of some infant deity, who afterwards abandoned it, ashamed of his lame performance: it is the work only of some dependent, inferior deity; and is the object of derision to his superiors: it is the production of old age and dotage in some superannuated deity; and ever since his death, has run on at adventures, from the first impulse and active force, which it received from him.[5]

Hume was even less satisfied with the claims for a revelation. He focused his assault on miracles, since they were an integral part both of the content of and the justification for revealed religion. So prevalent are the miracles of the Bible, and so frequent was the Christian appeal to miracles as the means of validating religion, that the choice of miracles for searching philosophical examination was especially telling. From Hume's point of view, miracles were fundamentally impossible because they broke the consistent laws of nature. He argued therefore that there could never be enough evidence via human testimony for a historian to believe a miracle. He concluded his discourse on miracles by advising Christians to stick to the notion that their religion was founded on faith, not reason. Any appeal to reason exposed religion to a test too hard for it to endure. With sharp irony he ends with these words:

> ... the Christian religion not only was at first attended with miracles, but even at this day cannot be believed by any reasonable person without one. Mere reason is insufficient to convince us of its veracity: And whoever is moved by *Faith* to assent to it, is conscious of a continued miracle in his own person, which subverts

all the principles of his understanding, and gives him a determination to believe what is most contrary to custom and experience.[6]

The triumph of the Enlightenment

The reason for commencing this discussion of revelation in such a personal way is that my experience illustrates in microcosm one of the major consequences of the Enlightenment and demonstrates its ongoing significance despite the many other cultural movements that have succeeded it. When Voltaire's writings came into my hands, and later, when I encountered Hume's thought, they were profoundly challenging. Voltaire made the Christian faith seem so ludicrous and constricting that it hardly seemed worth continuing any allegiance to it. It is no accident that both Voltaire and Hume were especially well known in their own day as historians. A new mood of anti-supernaturalism was entering the study of history, and, together with the critical investigations being undertaken into the origin and nature of the Bible, the old orthodoxy was being challenged at its very foundation. The Enlightenment arguments were sharpened, furthermore, by the perennially attractive message that man was the measure of all things. Human reason was the canon of judgment; human freedom was the chief virtue; human progress against superstition and unfounded authority was the programme. Modernity presupposes the truth of these assertions, and few contemporary western persons are entirely free from their fascinating coils.

The Enlightenment thinkers were involved in an intellectual struggle against church and state over the issue of human autonomy. Since both church and state appealed to the Bible to justify their own authority, it is not surprising that the Bible should have become contested ground. In the end, the whole movement (of which Voltaire and Hume are but two exponents) has achieved, among other things, a stunning victory over the Christian faith. Christianity lost its intellectual, social and spiritual authority, especially in Protestant Europe. In Bernard Ramm's judgment, 'the mortal wound inflicted by the Enlightenment on Protestant orthodoxy was a staggering one and one from which there has never been a full recovery,'[7] and Colin Gunton observes that 'salient aspects of modern culture are predicated on the denial of the Christian gospel'.[8]

The writings of Voltaire and Hume were two of the routes along which the radical thought of the eighteenth century reached me in the later twentieth century. They were, of course, part of a much wider history that included such great and diverse thinkers as Locke, Spinoza, Kant and Hegel. Even in the seventeenth century, philosophers and theologians had begun to take positions that would radically alter the place accorded to the Bible in the church and the culture. Also, the nineteenth century saw an encounter – some called it a war – between revelation and science, which was to have significant repercussions for the authority of revelation. Darwinism appeared to have dealt fatal blows to the biblical creation stories and to any concept of order in the creation; that is, to both special and general revelation. At the same time, the complexity and variety of the human world were being manifested in ways that immediately prompted questions about any system that claimed to be absolute or unique. In the end, such ideas as biblical revelation, general revelation and natural theology were confronted with hostility, not just from philosophy, but from the disciplined study of history, anthropology, religion and science as well. We need only think of such names as Marx, Darwin and Freud to recognize the extent of the cultural disenchantment with revelation.

Christian responses to the crisis of the Enlightenment

The assault on its claims to possess a unique revelation of God challenged the Christian faith at a most sensitive point. The usual response (among western intellectuals at least) has been to agree with the criticisms, leading to unbelief. The loss of the intellectual status of Christianity is a striking feature of the modern period. It is true that during the last two hundred years one of the greatest missionary expansions of the church has occurred. The translation, publication and dissemination of the Bible alone constitute an extraordinary historical phenomenon; so, too, is the continuing intense academic study of its pages. Far from the Bible's being completely discredited, it is the most frequently printed book in the world. Nevertheless, it must be said that the pressure brought to bear on the intellectual assertions of Christianity by secularism have been intense, and it is not surprising that they have contributed both to loss of membership and to significant tensions and strains within the Christian community itself. The divisions between denominations have become less significant than the divisions between those who have adopted different strategies for dealing with the challenge of modernity.[9] A central issue has been the theological estimate of the Bible. Some have continued to argue for the 'traditional' view that the Bible is inspired by God, and hence is God's direct self-revelation. As we have seen, Bernard Ramm speaks of a wound inflicted on Protestant orthodoxy 'from which there has never been a full recovery'; but he also makes the point that, as though by a miracle, 'it did manage to survive'.[10]

The most notable, but not the only, exponent of this position has been the North American theologian Carl F. H. Henry, whose magisterial six-volume work on revelation has continued to attract serious attention.[11] Such conservative Christians have not regarded themselves as bound to reproduce the exact thoughts of their predecessors; there has been development in the doctrine of Scripture, and in the understanding of its teaching. They have shown willingness to incorporate the wealth of information made available about the ancient world, its languages and its customs, which may be regarded as one of the positive fruits of the Enlightenment. In addition, such expositions of revelation have always defended a concept of general revelation. It has usually followed the lines laid down by John Calvin, namely that there is a revelation by God in nature and in the heart, but it is suppressed, rendering the recipient both ignorant and guilty.[12]

Most of those Protestants who have thought at a serious level about revelation have, however, chosen a different course. Naturally, they retain a deep respect for Scripture, especially the New Testament witness to Jesus Christ. Without such respect it is difficult for a religious system to remain Christian in any but the most nominal sense. However, there has been an overwhelming decision to move the chief locus of revelation away from the Bible. Emil Brunner, for example, referred to the 'fatal equation of revelation with the inspiration of the Scriptures',[13] and inspiration is now typically understood either in an attenuated way, or as

18

the illumination of the receiving agent. The fundamental purpose of these reinterpretations is twofold: to save the revelation of God and to save the witness of the Scriptures. If the Bible contains the moral and historical defects exposed by writers such as Voltaire, it cannot be too directly identified as revelation from God; it should not be called 'the inspired word of God'.

It would be wrong, however, to regard this reinterpretation as merely defensive. To its many proponents it has also given the opportunity to cut away what they regard as unfortunate elements of the traditional theory, and to replace them with features that do more justice to the nature of the human and divine persons involved. Thus they frequently reject propositional revelation as being intellectualist, and emphasize the experience of divine–human encounter.[14] They often favour a dynamic revelation focusing on God's historical deeds rather than on a static set of words. In addition, they regard the older theories as doing less than full justice to the multiform nature of Scripture. Likewise, they have considerable sympathy for the view that revelation is by no means confined to religion. They also have more sympathy than their predecessors for some time past with the positive possibilities for the Christian of general revelation and natural theology.

Naturally, there are significant differences between the types of revelation theology proposed. Broadly speaking, the nineteenth century may be said to have been dominated by Friedrich Schleiermacher, and the twentieth by Karl Barth. Some, following the lead of Schleiermacher, will find the locus of revelation in the human experience of God. Others, like Karl Barth, will react against this allegedly human-centred approach, and speak of Jesus Christ as the one Word of God, to whom the Scriptures bear witness. But there are notable alternatives, exemplified by scholars such as Wolfhart Pannenberg, who speaks of revelation in and through history and eschatology. The Roman Catholic theologian Avery Dulles has suggested a taxonomy of no fewer than five 'models' of revelation used in contemporary theology. He speaks of revelation as doctrine (in which he includes Carl Henry and other Protestant and Catholic writers), as history, as inner experience, as dialectical presence and as new awareness. Despite the variety, he suggests a definition that 'would probably be acceptable to many adherents of each model'. His suggestion runs as follows:

19

> Revelation is God's free action whereby he communic-
> ates saving truth to created minds, especially through
> Jesus Christ as accepted by the apostolic Church and
> attested by the Bible and by the continuing community
> of believers.[15]

His proposal successfully reflects a number of the emphases found in most treatments of revelation. Not surprisingly, given that Dulles writes as a Catholic, the account falls on the church more than it would in a corresponding Protestant account.[16] In Protestant systematic theology, especially that touched by the neo-orthodox movement of the twentieth century, there seem to be three emphases that remain fairly constant, as thinkers have laboured to justify and explain revelation. Some, but not all, of these are to be found in Dulles's summary. Each element has been forged in the conviction that we can no longer appeal to the Bible as such to be revelation, and hence reflects some of the reaction to that way of approach.

Revelation as event

First, in a conscious break with older views that identified revela-
tion with the words of the Bible, many modern theologians assert that revelation is an act of God, an event, an episode. Dulles seeks to capture this element by using the phrase 'free action'. In adopting this view of revelation, theologians are first of all protecting the freedom of God. Daniel L. Migliore speaks of the biblical episodes and adds, 'While God is truly disclosed in these events, the divine freedom or hiddenness is never dissolved. *God does not cease to be a mystery in the event of revelation*'.[17] Against the tendency of nineteenth-century theology to treat God as immanent, the later theologians have stressed his transcendence, and so his freedom to be God. Revelation must be regarded as a gift, arising from the free initiative of God, and thus consistent both with his grace and with human need. Revelation is in his hands, not ours; we cannot control it, demand it or organize it. If we identify a book – even the Bible – as revelation, we assert our authority over God, and adopt a pharisaic approach, valuing the letter and not the Spirit. By treating revelation as an event, we think about God and the Bible in a way that is more true to the Bible itself. Far from being a handbook of timeless truths,

20

the Bible is pre-eminently a narrative of the 'mighty deeds' of God through which he saved his people and identified himself to them.

Thinking of revelation as an event is said to have other advantages. It fits in well with the way the concept often occurs in the Bible, whether in its Greek or its Hebrew form.[18] The term is not used of the Bible as a book, for example, but rather of the encounter between God and human beings, by which God makes himself known to them. It frequently has an eschatological component, in which Christ's appearing at the end of the age is called a 'revelation'. It is also used to describe what God is doing in the world, whether the natural world or the world of human affairs. The individual may receive a revelation, or it may be something that all should possess. Furthermore, the idea that revelation is an event suits the need to think of it on a wider front than that found in the Bible. It raises the subject of the experience of revelation (for example, the sense of the presence of God felt by many people, both Christian and non-Christian), and enables us to explore the reports of revelation in other religions. It also allows for an emphasis on the present illuminating and inspiring work of God's Spirit that earlier theories of revelation obscured.

Revelation as self-giving

In contemporary theology much is also made of the truth that our knowledge of God is relational. At this point Dulles's concept that God 'communicates saving truth to created minds' would be regarded as unhelpful, because it reverts to what may be called a propositional or intellectualist view of revelation, in which faith is regarded as accepting of certain truths on the authority of someone else, and the revelation itself is pre-eminently thought of as a body of revealed truths. As far as modern Protestant theology is concerned, this is to misunderstand the true heart of the Christian faith. In essence, Christianity is concerned with relationship, and especially the encounter between God and human beings. The intellectualist account leaves God at arm's length, so to speak. What we need is not so much communication of truths as communion of persons. It is no accident, indeed, that the central point of revelation is a person, Jesus Christ. The essence of Christianity is our relationship with him, not fundamentally with a set of words about him. As Emil Brunner has written, 'We are here no longer concerned with a relationship in "word", but with a personal relation: no longer are we content to "believe *it*", but our concern is to come to *Him*, to trust Him, to be united with Him, to surrender to Him. Revelation and faith now mean a personal encounter, personal communion.'[19]

Revelation as Jesus Christ

The person of Jesus Christ has now taken the place of the Bible as the content of Christian revelation. In the words of Robert Morgan, 'from Barth's threefold form of the Word of God, only the Word incarnate can properly be called divine revelation'.[20] When revelation was thought to be a set of infallible truths in the Bible, there was a constant tendency to turn it into a textbook on all sorts of subjects. In particular, the Bible was a source of moral information; in lists such as the Decalogue and the Beatitudes it provided handy guides for living the good life. The Bible was also regarded as containing excellent science and history, and advances in either sphere were tested by its teaching. Likewise the Bible was ransacked for detailed information about the future. The devastation wrought by the Enlightenment was, in part, the legacy of this kind of abuse of the Bible. A wrong estimate of its nature led to abusing its words and neglecting its real significance. If there is one thing clear to modern mainstream Protestant theologians, it is that there is no way back to the reinstatement of the Bible as the inspired and infallible Word of God in a primary sense.

This conclusion, however, enables the real nature of revelation to become plain. It consists of what the Bible is in fact all about, namely Jesus Christ. He is the revelation of God. Some would wish to argue that he alone is the revelation of God, and that every other purported revelation of God takes its meaning (positively or negatively) solely from him. Others, as in Dulles's proposal, prefer to speak 'especially' of Jesus Christ. Thus, also, Keith Ward describes the incarnation of God in Jesus as 'the central revelatory act of God'.[21] In any case, it is clear that the epistemological weight once borne by the Bible, nature and the traditions of the church as sources of revelation is, in many accounts of revelation, now borne by Jesus Christ. He is the message, the Word of God – the very title accorded him in John 1:1–3 – by which all other words are to be tested.

22

There are perceived to be several advantages in this focus. First, it has the benefit of being consistent with what the Bible itself says and is about. The message of the first Christian preachers and of the New Testament can justifiably be summed up as 'Jesus Christ'. Furthermore, it makes Christ himself the mediator, as he must be if he is in truth the 'one mediator between God and men' (1 Tim. 2:5). He is not some subsidiary messenger, a mere prophet, but in himself is both God and human being, the Word of God who is the very point at which we may behold God and live. Secondly, it defends the Christian revelation by the best possible method. It puts it out of reach. If it is in fact true, it comes from the God who cannot himself be tested or tried. It must be self-authenticating, not dependent upon some lesser aid for its verification. In defending the Scriptures, for example, we at once betray our fear that they do not come from God. With regard to Jesus Christ, he may be preached, and the declaration itself will persuade, becoming the event of revelation, if the Spirit so enables.

One of the chief advantages perceived in locating revelation primarily or even exclusively in Jesus Christ is that it enables us to find the right way of talking about other claimants to revelation. Everything can be measured by our estimate of him. In particular, it enables us to be warmly positive about the Bible while at the same time doing justice to its real nature. Dulles is right in suggesting that the role of the Bible is to 'attest' the revelation who is Jesus Christ. The Bible is now most often thought of as a witness to the word of God. This means that although it is still possible to call the Bible the word of God, and so to honour the indispensable part it plays in leading us to Jesus Christ, we are not in peril of so identifying it with God that it is bound to take on the very character of God himself. It is judged that we thus avoid both bibliolatry and the danger that what is regarded as the Bible's antiquated history and science may prove an unnecessary stumbling-block to faith.

Assessment

We must first say that the account of revelation sketched in part above is a significant intellectual and theological achievement. There have been times when it seemed that the Christian faith itself, as an intellectual construct, would disappear. There appeared to be no way that the Bible, subject to the criticisms that it has undergone, could maintain any sort of authority at all; and any semblance of orthodoxy in relation to Christology or the Trinity seemed also to have gone. By asserting the centrality of Christ as testified to by the Bible, proponents of the views given above have been able to bring the doctrine of the Trinity back to the very centre of the Christian faith. When we receive the Christian revelation we know that it is the work of God himself, that Jesus Christ is the Word of God and that the act of revelation is especially the work of the Spirit of God. This means that when we are caught up in revelation we are necessarily involved with the triune God. Here indeed is a version of the Christian faith that may be preached. It is not about ourselves, but about God and the good news of who he is and what he has done. It honours God for who he is, and attempts to grapple with the criticisms of a Feuerbach that Christianity is simply anthropology writ large. And yet, even if revelation has been rehabilitated thus, is it entirely successful in doing justice to the knowledge of God?

I think not. There is a symptomatic vagueness at crucial points that leaves us without the sort of knowledge that the Bible leads us to expect. Theological thinkers have succeeded in bringing God back into the centre of things, but they have not done so in a way that reflects the nature of our relationship with God as found in the Bible. A Christian faith that is unable to accomplish a relationship with God on the same terms that we can see in the experience of the writers of Scripture must have questionable validity. We may test the reality of the modern reconstruction of revelation by asking, for example, whether it puts God into the same position of authority over the lives of believers that we see assumed and taught in the New Testament. Does the revelation spoken of in modern theology do that? Unless it satisfies this important test it can hardly be said to give a knowledge of God that stands in clear continuity with the knowledge of God referred to in Scripture. Is it not the case, however, that, like all modern thought, theology itself reflects the notion of human autonomy *vis-à-vis* God? Does the faith of modern theology correspond to the faith of the New Testament?

The modern account of revelation has so much in it that is true – particularly the stress on Jesus Christ – that to some extent this

24

question may be answered in the affirmative. But there is also a fundamental lack in the account, which leads to a different conclusion. The first believers did not regard Scripture as a witness to the word of God rather than as being the word of God, and hence faith itself must inevitably take on a form different from theirs. They used the word 'witness', but it was one of the qualifications of an apostle, and when we speak of apostles we are using a different and more authoritative category. The use some scholars make of John the Baptist as the model witness is interesting; he was not an apostle. In each of the three main elements of the reconstruction of revelation, an unwillingness to make Scripture the word of God is of key importance. This is the watershed; this shapes the nature of the conclusions reached.

Let me illustrate. Revelation, we are told, is an act of God, an event. So it is. But there is no need to limit the events in question by declaring *a priori* that the giving of speech does not constitute an event with lasting public consequences. The mighty deeds of God, in all the accounts from which we discover those acts to have been performed, included mighty deeds of speech, as at Mount Sinai. Furthermore, as has often been pointed out, God's deeds are unintelligible without the interpretative word that accompanies them. Even more fundamentally, there is no need to limit an event by deciding that its episodic nature confines its revelatory impact to the time at which it occurs. On the contrary, even if a particular revelation is a specific event (and we have not broached the possibility here that revelation may be not so much episodic as 'standing' – as are the sun, moon and stars), it may well continue to have an ongoing life through the words that describe it. A mystery once revealed remains a mystery revealed. In fact, if, as I will argue in due course, Christianity is essentially promissory in nature, then the idea that we have in revelation the elusive episodic speech-acts of God, intended though it is to preserve God's freedom of God, manages to compromise his faithfulness in speech.

Secondly, the account of revelation I have described favours the idea of self-giving. No-one can deny that the concept attempts to capture an important truth, namely the relational nature of the Christian faith, and that at times the faith has suffered from over-formalization and intellectualization. But the aim of this language is explicitly to distance revelation from its reliance on inspired language; to make faith in a person take the precedence over faith in words. Even in human relationships, however, trustworthy language is the essential route along which faith comes. We need to trust one another's words, and we draw no real distinction between trusting a person and trusting that person's words. A relationship without words is impoverished. How much more must this be so of a relationship with the invisible God? Is this not a case of over-realized eschatology? In this life, we walk by faith rather than by sight or experience, and the alleged self-giving of God speaks of an immediacy of relationship that is not yet ours. I suggest that it amounts to the hope that we can replace the enscripturated word of God with something that will do justice to our relationship with God, but which in fact is insubstantial. Are we not also living on theological and religious capital gathered from earlier generations, who had a different approach to the language of the Bible? For example, can we really arrive at the doctrine of the Trinity analysing revelation as suggested above, or does it in fact arise from the exact language of Scripture?

Thirdly, this account of revelation focuses on Jesus Christ. As I have already observed, a theology that does not have such a focus can hardly be Christian at all. In attempting to preserve the revelation from critical attack, however, a fundamental distinction is made between Christ and the words that witness to him. As Keith Ward writes, 'Scripture, at least in Christian faith, consists of a set of human witnesses to Divine revelation, rather than constituting the content of revelation itself.'[22] But the Christ in whom we put our trust must be the scriptural Jesus and no other; there is a special quality in our verbal access to him that is indispensable in origin and significance. The option that places the final revelatory burden on Jesus Christ, but gives access to him through something other than inspired words, leaves us once again in darkness where we can rightly expect light. This is all the more the case if we are committed to the view that revelation is an event. Is faith satisfied merely by the witness to this event? Has the (quite biblical and proper) language of Word and witness taken an unwarranted priority over the more fundamental language of gospel and apostle?

I have chosen to comment on only three of the themes of recent Protestant theology. A survey of this and other material leads to

26

a twofold conclusion. First, the problems posed for the Christian faith by the Enlightenment and its aftermath await resolution. Each element of this doctrine of revelation has within it an unfortunate and unsustainable division, born largely out of repudiating the idea that the words of Scripture can be, in any direct and revelatory sense, the word of God. As I have indicated already, the task of rehabilitating that position in a post-Enlightenment world is truly formidable. But the alternative has not succeeded.[23] Secondly, some progress has been made, not least in challenging those who brought the challenge in the first place. Marx, Freud, Voltaire, Hume and even Kant no longer look quite as daunting as once they did. It is true that the various fissures in the church, most notably the divide between those whose strategy is 'liberal' and those whose strategy is 'conservative', remain. But responsible writing on revelation has drawn back from the more radical death-of-God solutions of the 1960s. Some of the themes dispensed with by an earlier generation – such as propositional revelation – have begun to receive serious attention at last, and there is a recognition that the underlying principles of an Enlightenment culture are both deeply unchristian and profoundly inhuman.

Yet the hostility to Christian revelatory claims, when presented as in any way authoritative or unique, remains unabated. It is often observed that modernism has given way to postmodernism. Without doubt, claims for Christian revelation must cope with an exceptionally relativistic environment, coming to terms with the New Age, energetic cults, the new physics, the insights of post-Vatican II Roman Catholicism and the strongest face-to-face encounters between living and powerful religions in centuries. It competes to make its message heard, having lost its favoured status in the West; as far as many people are concerned, the choice between (say) Mormonism and Protestantism has far more to do with style than with truth. The question of revelation is more than ever of missionary concern, and if, on the one hand, the prevailing western culture is more accepting of faith claims, on the other it is less accepting of such claims posed in an exclusive way. Not surprisingly, much attention is being given to the whole question of the relation between Christian revelation and the revelations on which other faiths are based.[24]

The nature and authority of the Bible remain a contested area, but the debate now includes theories of literary criticism and hermeneutics in a way unknown before. The pluralism of current thought expects a corresponding pluralism in the use of the Bible. Some of the older debates about the historical sources of the Bible have been bypassed; new questions are being raised and answered about the literary nature of the text (or texts) as it now stands. Without doubt there have been advances in the understanding of Scripture, and these have been welcomed by conservative scholars as well as by more radical ones. There is some promise here for overcoming some of the sterile approaches that had come to characterize Scripture interpretation in all schools of thought. But there are also dangers for any claim to a revelatory status for the biblical material. In particular, the systematic theology of the church, including such great dogmas as the Trinity, are premised on a reading of Scripture that new approaches may endanger. In the Protestant world, the day of the national or confessing church seems to be passing, and with it the mechanism by which dogmatic understandings of the Christian faith were transmitted. Catholicism and Orthodoxy are options for some, but they, too, are no longer protected, as once they may have been, from the intellectual challenges of modernism and postmodernism. There remains a vital need for an understanding of revelation that will honour the word by which God rules his church and calls men and women to himself.

Protestant evangelicalism of the sort represented by this book continues to make much of its claim to know that God has revealed himself to us especially through his inspired word, the Bible. It deliberately places itself in the stream of faith that flows to us from the pre-enlightenment orthodoxy. Indeed, evangelicals say that men and women from all cultures may have, and ought to have, a relationship with God. We may know God through his word. They say, furthermore, that there is an exclusiveness about this claim that the focus of God's revelation is to be found in the Christ of the Bible. They agree that there is a general revelation of God through the natural world, but they continue to share with Calvin the view that this revelation is not a saving one, because of the incapacity of sinners to respond appropriately to it. Clearly, such assertions are in stark contrast to the thinking both of the culture and of much of the church. It is agreed that it is the duty of evangelical Christians, having made such assertions, to offer a

28

coherent and persuasive account of how we may know God, so that its adherents may be nourished and united, and its message effectively promoted in the church and in the world.

The present study, therefore, aims to state and justify the Protestant evangelical position in the contemporary world. My starting-point is the argument that, in choosing to talk about revelation as a response to the Enlightenment, we have chosen the wrong initial category. I am not suggesting, therefore, that we simply turn back again to Scripture as such and reinstate it as revelation forthwith. It is better to follow the more prominent biblical category of the knowledge of God, and the more crucial biblical category of the gospel by which this knowledge arises. To do so will give us the opportunity to reassess the nature and role of Scripture, and so to understand revelation, not in exactly the same way as they were used before the Enlightenment, but in a way that is true to Scripture and to the Christian faith.

To the task of following this suggestion I now turn. In chapters 1–6, the focus is on revelation as such, both 'special' and 'general', from the viewpoint of the knowledge of God through the gospel. Chapters 7–9 are a study of the scriptural revelation, its authority and nature, and our approach to reading it. In chapters 10–11 I turn to the revelatory work of the Holy Spirit through illumination.

1

THE GOSPEL AS
REVELATION

The gospel and mission

The knowledge of God depends upon the gospel of Jesus Christ: 'Revelation does not merely bring the gospel: the gospel *is* revelation.'[1] We may gauge the nature and impact of this claim to revelation historically by reading what Paul, the great Christian missionary, wrote to his recent converts at Thessalonica. He described the transformation that had occurred in their lives in these terms: 'you turned to God from idols to serve the living and true God, and to wait for his Son from heaven, whom he raised from the dead – Jesus, who rescues us from the coming wrath' (1 Thess. 1:9–10). He attributed this transformation to their reception of a message he explicitly called 'our gospel' (1:5) and also 'the word of God' (2:13). Clearly, his converts had already been religious people, but before they received the gospel they were among those 'who do not know God' (4:5), and were therefore in danger of 'the coming wrath'. Now their lives were marked by a new knowledge of God and his plans for the world, a knowledge also characterized by faith, trust and love directed towards the one true God and his Son Jesus Christ. Paul also attributed to the work

31

of the Holy Spirit the fact that they believed in this way (1:5).

Preaching the gospel and receiving the gospel were integral to the experience of the first Christians. Recognition of the role of the gospel remains vital both for the experience of knowing God and also for the missionary obligation of contemporary Christians. The gospel stands at the beginning of the story that explains why there are Christians at all, on the boundary between belief and unbelief – often, for the hearer, prior to a knowledge of the Bible itself. For the person entering from the outside, the gospel is the introduction to the faith, the starting-point for understanding. It then rightly becomes the touchstone of the faith. Since this is where faith begins, it is essential that faith continues to conform to it. We cannot begin with the gospel and then proceed in some other direction, or build inconsistently on it. Both integrity and common sense tell us this. So also do some of the earliest witnesses: 'But even if we or an angel from heaven should preach to you a gospel other than the one we preached to you, let him be eternally condemned!' (Gal. 1:8). To expound the gospel first is to lay a foundation upon which the building is to be faithfully erected (1 Cor. 3:10–15).

Contemporary theology has lost touch with the missionary impetus of the Christian faith precisely when this is needed more than ever. As a result, it has lost sight of the significance of the gospel for revelation. It is true, of course, that European and North American theology has been labouring in a threatening intellectual environment, and to that extent has been notably sensitive to its culture and to its apologetic task within the culture. But it has been on the defensive, and the shape of its theology shows this. The intellectual problems posed by modern thought have dominated the way theology has been created. The theoretical concept of revelation has become more important than the reality of the gospel way of knowing God. Some, for example, see the most vital current task as being to examine the idea of revelation among the religions of the world, and to encourage the growth of mutual tolerance, knowledge and acceptance. But this perspective distorts our reading of the Bible by undervaluing its missionary context and message, and offers little help for the pressing missionary challenge that is ours.

Christianity was born in an era of religious and philosophical pluralism, an era of knowledge about and participation in religion. When New Testament Christianity met the non-Christian world, whether Jewish or Gentile, its characteristic response was not to collaborate, but to preach the gospel of Jesus Christ as Lord, and thereby to seek a change in its hearers' allegiance. If we wish to follow the New Testament's precepts and to observe its patterns, we ought to accept its priorities. It is right that Christians sympathetically study the culture of this world, listen carefully to its myriad voices and seek to meet its physical and social needs. In the final analysis, however, the gospel is the treasure that has been committed to us, and the gospel is what we have to share with others. 'If we have understood that Jesus Christ is at the heart of God's redemptive plan and that the divine purposes find their fulfilment, climax and consummation in his saving work, then we who have come under his rule as Lord must be wholly committed to the furtherance of those saving purposes in which Gentiles, along with Jews, are brought into obedience to him.'[2]

Responsible theologians ought to order their teaching by the gospel, and also to ensure that whatever else their theologies may contain, the reader can see what the essence of the gospel is. The failure to make the subject of the gospel explicit in some theologies means that the reader may not know in the end what the heart of the Christian message is. It is by an exposition of the gospel that the theologian earns the right to proceed, since the gospel is the most significant revelation of all. This claim, and what it entails, is the theme of the first six chapters of this book. I shall begin to examine it in this chapter by discussing three basic issues: the gospel's content, function and credibility.

The content of the gospel

What is the gospel? The starting-point for an answer lies with the New Testament in its capacity as a historical witness. A very early account, such as that of 1 Thessalonians, gives us first-class evidence about the gospel as preached by Paul, one of its major ambassadors. We recognize, however, that the preachers (and the writers who reported them) have their own emphases, contexts and methods. Of some of the New Testament writers, such as Mark, we may come to the view that they are *writing* the gospel; of others, such as Luke in the Acts, that they are *reporting* it. In others, such as Paul, we may see the tradition of the gospel articulated at various points to a greater or lesser degree; in others, we may detect the gospel's impact. Despite this variety, however, an exposition of the Christian gospel for today must be demonstrably continuous with the gospel as it was originally preached. This connection with its origins is inherent in, and not incidental to, the nature of the gospel. Those who originally communicated it believed that they possessed unique access to and authorization from the person who was at its centre, and hence the authoritative version of it. We would need to have a good reason for claiming the right to assert a different gospel under these circumstances. To say what the gospel is, therefore, we must be able to give an account of the gospel preached by Jesus and the first Christians.[3]

In one sense, the content of the Christian gospel as believed and promulgated by the earliest Christians may be summarized simply. When Jesus began preaching 'the gospel', it announced the coming kingdom of God. Through his teaching about that subject, and through the events that occurred (especially his death and resurrection), it became clear that he was the king of this coming kingdom, and that in some way it had already entered the world in and through him (Luke 17:21). When his apostles preached, they did not entirely abandon the language of 'kingdom', but they announced that Jesus was the Christ, and hence the Lord of all. Like him, they sought repentance and faith in those who heard them. They preached 'the message of salvation through Jesus Christ'.[4] Thus, when Luke wished to characterize the evangelistic preaching of the early Christians in a few words, it was sufficient for him to say that they 'proclaimed the Christ' (Acts 8:5), or 'told ... the good news about Jesus' (8:35), or 'preached the kingdom of God and taught about the Lord Jesus Christ' (28:31). That the simple statement that 'Jesus Christ is Lord' summarizes the gospel is also clear from such Pauline passages as 2 Corinthians 4:1–6.

Such a basic summary is one thing; unpacking it is another. It is perfectly clear that the manner of preaching 'Jesus Christ as Lord' differed widely in the time of the New Testament. There are several reasons for that. First, the words used depend upon where the speaker is in history. The teaching of Jesus, which so often revolved around the kingdom of God and the Son of Man, prefigures the later preaching of his followers, and indeed becomes part of it. But it bears the marks of its historical origins, which lay before the crucial events that would in later times be regarded as the pith of the gospel.

Secondly, the nature of the gospel preaching depends very much on the nature of the audience being addressed. Most obviously we see a difference in the approach to Jews as opposed to Gentiles, and in particular those Gentiles whose knowledge of the Jewish Scriptures may be regarded as minimal. Luke demonstrates this by his records of the speeches made by Paul to Jewish and to Gentile audiences (compare Acts 13 and 17). Having noted this, however, it is of interest to see in the writings of the New Testament, whether from Paul, Luke, John or Peter, that mixed groups of Jew and Gentile Christians were expected to be readily familiar with the Old Testament.

The third reason for the variety of approaches that we can discern in the New Testament is that each writer had his own particular purpose in writing. It is instructive to compare the brief accounts of apostolic preaching found in the Acts, and their counterparts in the summaries that we can glean from the epistles (such as 1 Cor. 15:1–11; 2 Cor. 4:1–6; or 1 Thess. 1:9–10), with the full-scale Gospels with which the New Testament begins. It is true that only in the opening verse of Mark is there a specific mention of 'gospel' in a way that may justify our calling them gospel presentations, but there is no doubt that a primary purpose for writing, as given by John ('these are written that you may believe that Jesus is the Christ, the Son of God, and that believing you may have life in his name'; 20:31), is true of them all. Here, too, is the gospel. But what does it achieve?

The function of the gospel

The achievement of the gospel is that people come to know God through informative and hortatory words about him. Whatever else the gospel is, it is verbal, an announcement by way of speech. Hence the gospel is preached, heralded or proclaimed; that is what one does with a gospel. The noun *euangelion*, and its allied words such as the verbs *euangelizomai* and *kēryssō*, tell us as much.[5] It almost certainly has an Old Testament background; but, for us, it is Mark who brings the term into prominence by using it at the very beginning of his Gospel (1:1) and then by giving it programmatic significance in his first record of Jesus' preaching. In his crucial opening speech, Jesus used it in order to announce

35

the imminent coming of God's kingdom (Mark 1:14–15). In Jesus' teaching, God's kingdom was primarily a future event, the moment at which God's sovereignty would be openly and decisively reasserted over a nation and a world alienated from him. The purpose of the kingdom was God's glory and his people's good, and to bring to completion the great history of salvation that the Old Testament Scriptures record and promise.

The gospel was to function as an instrument of salvation by warning Jesus' audience of this coming crisis and exhorting them to prepare themselves for it: 'Repent and believe the good news!' The gospel would thus ensure that there was a saved people in the day of God's triumph. It would do so by communicating truth and appealing for action on the basis of it. By the end of Mark's Gospel we are introduced to two further points about the gospel: first, its close association with Jesus himself (8:35; 10:29; 14:9), and secondly, its universal scope (13:10; 14:9; cf. 16:15). We may say that Jesus is to be the Lord to whom the gospel of the coming kingdom points, and that his name is to be preached in all the world. The gospel is the means 'by which the risen Christ in the fullness of time asserts his rule over the new people of God'.[6]

Mark also introduces us to the terminology of 'the word' to describe the preaching of Jesus, and hence the gospel, as in the parable of the sower (4:1–20). 'Gospel' and 'word of God' become virtual synonyms in the rest of the New Testament. The parable warns that we are to be judged by our willingness to hear with understanding and obedience; even at this early stage it is evident that the perception that Jesus is the Lord of the kingdom is integral to that true understanding. The crisis introduced by the gospel preached by Jesus is to be an enduring factor in the Christian evangelism that followed his death. Thus, as we can see from the brief extract from his first letter to the Thessalonians (1:9–10), Paul regarded those whom he met as not truly knowing God, and therefore as being unprepared for the coming of God's wrath. He became the servant or slave of the gospel, entirely devoted to furthering its cause in the world, especially among the Gentiles, to whom he was called as their apostle (Gal. 2:7). He believed that the gospel 'is the power of God for the salvation of everyone who believes: first for the Jew, then for the Gentile' (Rom. 1:16).

In the graphic account of his gospel ministry in 2 Corinthians

4:1–6, Paul reveals what he regards as the essence of the gospel. He calls it 'the word of God', 'the truth', 'our gospel'. He defends his ministry, asserting strongly that it matched the nature of the gospel by being true, not involving deception or distortion. He regards his gospel as being aimed at those who are blind to the truth, bound by Satan and perishing under God's judgment. He tells us that the substance of the gospel is 'Jesus Christ as Lord'. He indicates that accepting the gospel results from an action by God akin to the initial creation of light. Finally, he reveals that the gospel's beneficent effect is a special knowledge, namely 'the light of the knowledge of the glory of God in the face of Christ'.

From this typical Pauline passage we can estimate the significance of the gospel. By God we learn God. The gospel is the very means by which God prosecutes his work in the world; it is the means he uses to inform the world of its central truth; it is the way he applies the salvation of the atoning death of Jesus to men and women. Since the gospel is about God's grace, the way to knowing God is a way of grace. It does depends for its initiation and closure not upon human merit or effort, but upon God's kindness. In the whole complex of events by which God reconciles the world to himself, the gospel plays an indispensable role: 'faith comes from hearing the message, and the message is heard through the word of Christ' (Rom. 10:17). Indeed, in the end it is God who is the evangelist, it is his call that is issued in the form of the gospel, and it is he who brings us to faith (2 Thess. 2:13–14). We may trace the same power attributed to the word of the gospel not only in Paul, but in Peter (1 Pet. 1:23–25), James (1:18–25), Hebrews (4:2, 12–13), Acts (6:7; 14:21) John (17:17, 20) and the Synoptics (Mark 4:20; 8:39). It is a given of the New Testament. In short, so fundamental to the knowledge of God is the gospel that we may properly regard it as the type or paradigm of true revelation. It teaches us what revelation is and what it achieves.

The credibility of the gospel

The proper thing to do with an announcement such as the gospel is to believe it – if it is true. Then you will know. But is the gospel true? Does the very question not suggest that it is not a revelation? For one of the elements of revelation as usually understood is its 'gift' appearance, or its 'episodic' factor. There are two related questions here. The first is the issue of grace: whether it is right to seek any grounds at all for believing in the gospel. Does this not pander to human pride and undercut the grace and authority to which the gospel bears witness? How is it possible for us mortals to judge a word that comes from God? What, apart from another word of God, has sufficient authority to declare this one valid? The second question is that of evidence: if we conclude that it is right to seek reasons for believing, on what grounds does the Christian gospel promote itself as the truth, and therefore worthy of credence? Why should we be persuaded by it?

To begin with the first problem: it is true that the gospel itself presupposes a sovereign God who is perfectly capable of making himself known without asking human reason to pass judgment. Furthermore, the gospel is a gospel of grace precisely because it regards human beings as unable on their own to seek and find God. Whatever the nature of Christian epistemology, it must reflect God's grace and human incapacity if it is to be consistent with the gospel.[7] God is known 'through himself'. But the problem raised by the question did not trouble the original preachers of the gospel. When we consider how the gospel was actually transmitted by Jesus and the apostles, we see that human effort, whether physical, personal or intellectual, is not bypassed. On the contrary, in accordance with the incarnation itself, the human is regarded as fit to communicate the divine message. In the words of Paul, 'we have this treasure in jars of clay' (2 Cor. 4:7).

How is this so? Consider the works of the evangelist (especially Paul himself) as described in the New Testament. He needed all the human qualities of endurance and commitment. 'We are hard pressed on every side, but not crushed; perplexed, but not in despair; persecuted, but not abandoned ...' (2 Cor. 4:8–9). We see the evangelist planning (Rom. 1:13), toiling (2 Cor. 11:27–29), suffering (2 Cor. 4:11), disputing (Gal. 2:14), travelling (2 Cor. 11:26). The testimony that Jesus is alive relied upon 'many convincing proofs' (Acts 1:3). When confronted with an audience, evangelists present their material in an orderly way, appealing to the hearers' existing knowledge and to their capacity to listen to a reasoned discourse (Acts 10:34–39). New factual information is communicated (Acts 10:39–41), and ways of verifying the information are suggested (Acts 10:42–43). On the evidence of the Acts of the Apostles, evangelists engage in teaching (5:21), speaking boldly (9:27), testifying (8:25), explaining and trying to convince (28:23), interpreting (13:15ff.), proclaiming (8:4), discoursing (24:25), admonishing (13:43), defending (19:33), reasoning and persuading (18:4). Where necessary, they debate, arguing and disputing (9:22), and appeal to their hearers' conscience (9:25). Correspondingly, therefore, the hearers are required to think, to reason, to consider, to compare, to remember, to judge. The sermonic conclusion is accompanied by exhortation based on the information and commentary presented by the evangelists.

The biblical writers, then, are not in the slightest embarrassed by the human involvement in the transmission of revelation. For them, God uses human nature without abusing it to accomplish his ends. The work of the gospel requires all the human energies that can be put at its disposal, and its appeal is to the recipient's mind, demanding a considered response. 'Now the Bereans were of more noble character than the Thessalonians, for they received the message with great eagerness and examined the Scriptures every day to see if what Paul said was true' (Acts 17:11). The writers did not think there was any inconsistency between this and the gospel of grace.

The problem of protecting the word of God from being judged by something less than itself is met in another way. In particular, the evangelists had the overwhelming conviction that if their words met with acceptance the only reason was that God had opened the hearer's mind by the Spirit's power to bring light and truth to bear. So it was when Peter recognized the truth about Jesus (Matt. 16:17); when the Lord opened the eyes of his disciples 'so they could understand the Scriptures' (Luke 24:45); when Paul's gospel came to the Thessalonians, 'not simply with words, but also with power, with the Holy Spirit and with deep conviction' (1 Thess. 1:5); and when the Gentiles at Pisidian Antioch believed (Acts 13:48). The evangelists toiled to bring the gospel; their hearers worked to understand it; but God brought the gospel by the evangelists, and God gave the hearers the wisdom to understand. God was the true evangelist. Without doubt it was all of grace. The gift of God's disclosure arrives via human effort. In the ministry of the gospel, 'I planted the seed, Apollos

39

watered it, but God made it grow. So neither he who plants nor he who waters is anything, but only God, who makes things grow' (1 Cor. 3:6–7).

The second major issue is the that of the grounds on which the gospel promotes itself as the truth. Why should we believe it? As we examine the grounds given by the original evangelists, we once again see why it is that the gospel is free from the difficulty of appealing to an authority higher than God himself for its vindication. The gospel supports its explicit claim to be the word of God in a threefold way. All three arguments require the active intellectual involvement of the hearer; none sets up a rival to the gospel, and none of them is put forward as decisive, rational 'proof', since that would imply that the knowledge granted in the gospel is merely the transmitted information rather than the knowledge that leads to relationship.

The first and fundamental ground for believing that the gospel is the word of God is the claim that Jesus is the Christ. This claim can be tested and established (or denied) only by comparing the Old Testament with the work and words of Jesus. It was the conviction of the first Christians that Jesus Christ is the one who has fulfilled the promises of the Old Testament, and that in him the whole history of Israel finds its unique and proper consummation. Of course, it was equally the conviction of those who remained Jews (in the religious sense) that Jesus did *not* fulfil the promise of the Old Testament. Basic to both responses was the belief that God identifies himself by making promises and keeping them. The Old Testament contains the record of such promises; indeed, the whole notion of the covenant that formed the substratum of the national life entailed promise. It was clearly inherent in the way all four evangelists presented their Gospels; it is a key feature of the Acts of the Apostles; and Paul writes that he is 'an apostle and set apart for the gospel of God – the gospel he promised beforehand through his prophets in the Holy Scriptures regarding his Son ...' (Rom. 1:1–3). So, from the very beginning of its life, and in a way that was integral to its existence, the gospel presumed that the Old Testament was the word of God. The gospel confirmed its status as 'word of God' from an existing 'word of God'. The moment of revelation to an individual may be an episode, but the old revelation and the new stand as the public words of God. That is why, when Christian teachers refuse to allow the Old Testament its status as inspired 'Holy Scripture' (the 'very words of God', as Paul also calls them; Rom. 3:2), the gospel itself is threatened. Its authenticity depends on the authority of what goes before.

The second ground for belief is in the testimony borne to Jesus by the witnesses and evangelists. As far as historical authenticity is concerned, we have no writing directly from Jesus himself. But we have the words of those who claimed to be in touch with him in his historical existence, or in touch with those who knew him. These are public records that invite our interrogation. In particular there is the intersection of history and eschatology constituted by the resurrection of Jesus, to which Paul pointed in preaching to the Gentiles, who did not have the same regard for the Old Testament as he did: 'He has given proof of this to all men by raising him from the dead' (Acts 17:31; cf. 1:3). It is a claim he regards as integral to the gospel, as we may see in 1 Corinthians 15:4–8, 11: 'that he was buried, that he was raised on the third day according to the Scriptures, and that he appeared to Peter, and then to the Twelve. After that, he appeared to more than five hundred of the brothers at the same time, most of whom are still living ... last of all, he appeared to me also, as to one abnormally born ... Whether, then, it was I or they, this is what we preach, and this is what you believed.' To become a Christian through this gospel is not to abandon historical reality, but to accept the testimony of those whom we regard as trustworthy; it is to put our trust in their words, or, rather, to trust the one to whom their words testify, through their words.

The third ground on which the gospel persuades of its truth is its power to offer an authentic interpretation of human experience, and especially of the experiences of evil, suffering, death, guilt and grace. The gospel does this in various ways, but its capacity to interpret is found especially in what Paul calls 'the face of Christ' (2 Cor. 4:6). It is no accident that the basic form of the Christian gospel turned out to be the telling of the story of Jesus Christ. It is his extraordinary words that strike the conscience, inform the mind and create faith. It is his character and his deeds that fascinate and draw people to him. It is his capacity to make sense of human experience that persuades people that he is not merely a teacher but the Lord. In the end, it is not that a resurrection had occurred, but that it was *his*

41

resurrection, that provides the vitality of the gospel message. Whether it is Paul, John or Peter among the New Testament writers, when they spoke of the love of God they did so in no bland or generalizing way. It was to Jesus that they turned in order to understand God's love, and in particular to Jesus' death. Their gospel preaching did not transmit a philosophy, but announced the words and deeds of God in and through the words and deeds of his Son, Jesus.

Knowledge given proceeds from knowledge already gained. We have already seen that the preaching of the gospel as recorded in the New Testament differed in accordance with the audience, the most notable division being that between the Jews and the Gentiles. But it is also notable that the Bible as a whole never sets out to prove to the sceptic that God exists. It is true that atheism was little known in the ancient world; yet Paul makes it clear that there is a general revelation from God that all people may be expected to acknowledge. We can say that the gospel assumes that human beings have an innate, though suppressed, knowledge about the God who is witnessed to in the natural world (Acts 14:14–18; Rom. 1:18–31) and whose law is familiar to their consciences (Rom. 2:14–15) (see chapter 4 below). On the basis of this knowledge, which is nevertheless incapable of leading anyone to a true knowledge of God, the gospel makes its appeal. It passes on information about the past, the present and the future, and about God, humanity and Christ; and it is used by the Spirit of God to break down the barriers we erect against the knowledge of God so that we may enter into communion with him. In the final analysis, whatever apologetic victories may be won, whatever initial bridge-building may occur, whatever innate knowledge it may appeal to, it is the gospel itself, and the gospel by itself, that carries and creates conviction. It is nothing other than 'the sword of the Spirit' (Eph. 6:17). It is true that human reason, or better, human experience, is fully engaged in its reception; it is not true that we can appeal to something higher than the word of God itself to provide its warrant. In the end, as we judge it for ourselves, it judges us (Heb. 4:12–13).

Conclusion

In short, the Christian revelation is a matter of gracious disclosure, not of human enquiry, and as a 'word from God' it cannot be subject to human interrogation. Yet the actual revelation in the gospel comes via human speech and human effort. That is the genius of the gospel as revelation. It is not part of the argument of this book to take further the question of the authenticity of the gospel. The gospel will be either received or not. I merely wish to establish that the earliest Christians regarded it as the power of God for salvation, the indispensable way to the knowledge of God. For them, it was the primary revelation, the initial and the fundamental way into the presence of God (Gal.1:8), and the fulfilment and completion of the Old Testament revelation. If this is the case, and if this continues to be the case, so that we regard the gospel as the basic pattern of revelation from God, what are the implications for a doctrine of revelation?

In the next two chapters I intend to advance the argument that the gospel is the most significant revelation of all, first by exploring further the nature of the gospel (chapter 2), and secondly by examining the nature of the knowledge the gospel claims to deliver (chapter 3). At every point I shall continue to show what this approach entails for the doctrine of revelation, especially what it entails for the concept of the 'word of God'.

2

THE NATURE OF
TIIE GOSPEL

The long history of Christendom has obscured a vital point about
how people become Christians. The missionary situation of the
Christian movement is now forcing us to rediscover it. It was
both the belief and the experience of the first Christians, as
recorded in the New Testament, that relationship with God is
instated through the gospel of Jesus Christ. For a person who, in
Christian terms, does not know God, the route to this knowledge
is the gospel. The gospel is, therefore, the paradigm or pattern of
revelation. It is clear that to begin with the gospel, and then to
change or even to deny the method by which the knowledge of
God has come, is an unsafe procedure. The aim of this chapter is
to examine more closely the nature of the gospel of Jesus Christ
and what it entails for the doctrine of revelation. I isolate five
features common to the apostolic preaching recorded in the New
Testament and integral to God's method of self-revelation. These
'revelationary features' are as follows.

The gospel is a word from the God who speaks, creates, judges and saves

Where a Jewish audience may be presupposed, there is little need to say much about the identity or character of God. Nor does such an audience need to be persuaded that there is a record of the words of God (Rom. 3.2). The gospel presupposes that this record is the speech of the God who has already made himself known in Israel through his word, as the Lord who creates, judges and saves. But where the hearers are pagans, as in Athens or Lystra, the evangelist is quick to point out the nature of the God of whom he speaks. He tells them, first, of God as Creator: 'turn from these worthless things to the living God, who made heaven and earth and sea and everything in them'. Secondly, he speaks of God as Judge; the fact that the judgment of God has not yet fallen on those who worship 'these worthless things' is due to his mercy in allowing 'all nations to go their own way'. Thirdly, he proclaims God as Saviour, because now they must find salvation by turning to 'the living God' (Acts 14:15–16; cf. 17:16–34). Because God is Creator, he has the right to judge and the power to save, and possesses and uses the capacity of speech.

Whether to Jews or to Gentiles, therefore, this message was regarded as 'the word of God'. Three aspects of this frequent phrase need to be noted. First, without doubt, the announcement was about God, and in that sense may be regarded as 'of God'. Secondly, however, its chief significance was that it was the word that came from God, the word that comes with his authority and expresses his power. It is an axiom of the gospel that God reveals God, that he is the one who makes himself known by words. Even if the world despises the gospel as weak and foolish, it is in fact the very power of God and the wisdom of God (1 Cor. 1:18–25). Thirdly, 'the word of God' means language. Thus Peter, having attributed the saving new birth of his readers to the 'living and enduring word of God', identifies this 'word' with the gospel that was proclaimed: 'this is the word that was preached to you' (1 Pet. 1:23, 25; cf. 1 Thess. 2:13; Acts 8:25; Heb. 4:12). There is no word without words.

The use of the singular 'word' is common enough as a means of summing up a verbal communication that comes from a single source and has a single theme. Like 'gospel', it is inevitably a verbal communication. The speech of God, recorded and transmitted in words and sentences, propositions, promises, assertions, narratives, questions, proverbs, laws, parables and covenants, is a marked feature of the Old Testament.[1] Whether we feel at ease with it or not, if the gospel is the prime revelation of God, it is likewise a verbal occurrence. It undoubtedly claims to give us access to Jesus Christ and his great acts on our behalf; it is a fact that it promises union with Christ and salvation through him. But it is nothing if it is not a properly verbal entity. Nonverbal revelations may well exist, but the Christian gospel is not one of them.

One particular use of 'word' in the New Testament is, on the surface, personal rather than linguistic. This is the *logos* language of the Johannine writings. This observation encourages the tendency of the modern theology of revelation to avoid the terms 'gospel' or 'word of God' in referring to God's definitive revelation, and to speak immediately of 'Jesus Christ' instead. 'The Christian apprehension of revelation is the response of man to the Word of God whose name is Jesus Christ.'[2] In one sense Barth here states a basic truth of incarnational religion, which conforms not only to John 1:1–18 but also to passages such as Hebrews 1:1–4. After all, to preach Jesus Christ is to preach the gospel. But this is a false route if it also aims to avoid describing as 'revelation' the words and sentences attributed to God.

John identifies this Word as the one through whom all things have come into existence; then, astonishingly, we read that 'the Word became flesh and made his dwelling among us ... full of grace and truth' (John 1:1–3, 14), and 'No-one has ever seen God, but God the One and Only, who is at the Father's side, has made him known' (1:18). Similar but not identical references to the Word are made in 1 John 1:1 and Revelation 19:13. This is extraordinary language, and, not surprisingly, it has secured a significant place in any discussion of Christology. Indeed, in the early years of Christian theology the *logos* was a key term in developing an account of Christ. Its popularity can be ascribed to its apparent links to the philosophical world.

It is understandable, furthermore, that *logos* was chosen to bear the weight that has been laid upon it in modern theology. First, it speaks immediately of revelation, of communication. Secondly, it gives Jesus Christ his due and proper place as the substance and norm of revelation. Thirdly, it enables us to see the significance of creation *vis-à-vis* Christ: all things were created through him. Fourthly, it relates Jesus Christ to God in a way that makes it absolutely plain that when we deal with him we deal with God himself and not with some secondary deity. Fifthly, it shows from the very start that revelation is a matter of God's drawing near to us in event, not of our seeking and finding God. Finally, it provides us with a term we can use to relate revelation to that which mediates revelation, as Karl Barth did in speaking of 'the Word of God in its threefold form'.[3]

These are considerable advantages. There is, nevertheless, a methodological difficulty in taking what amounts to a particular use of a word and insisting that it control the rest. For Barth, following John 1, the one Word of God is Jesus Christ, and this means that, however respectful we may be of the written word, it cannot be called the 'word of God' in a direct way. Scripture is only a witness to the Word. Wolfhart Pannenberg has remarked on Barth's over-reliance on John 1, noting that 'Barth's biblical support for the thesis that Jesus is directly the Word and revelation of God is surprisingly thin (*CD*, 1/1, 118–119) when we consider the fundamental importance of the thesis for his dogmatic approach'.[4] By making the reference in John 1 the controlling idea for the word of God he has reversed the biblical order, which begins, even in Genesis 1, with speech. Even as a commentary on Genesis 1, if John 1 is to make any sense it does so by derivation, by deepening, not supplanting, the ordinary usage. The result of disturbing this order is unfortunate for the proper connection between language and revelation.

Thus, in the Johannine corpus, the incarnate Word comes to us clothed in words. Even his deeds, so full of grace and truth, are now – and indeed were in his lifetime after the event – accessible only verbally. The necessary testimony that the Father bears concerning the Son – a testimony that is verbal and that the Son declines to give on his own behalf – includes that of Moses, for example (5:31–47). The same words even accuse and condemn Jesus' adversaries (5:45–47). When John portrays Jesus' relationship to the word, he says, 'For the one whom God has sent speaks the words of God, for God gives the Spirit without limit' (3:34). It is thus that he 'exegetes' God (1:18) by using words inspired by the Spirit of God. The result is that his apostles 'obeyed [the] word'; 'For I gave them the words you gave me and they accepted them' (17:6, 8). Throughout, John portrays Jesus as having the highest respect for the words of God; the Word may be the norm for the words, but this does not compromise their right to be regarded as the authoritative, truthful and revelatory word of God.

In the interests of the need to protect revelation from any unseemly questioning, some modern theologians turn it into Word, which then becomes a person: 'The light of God that shines in Jesus Christ', writes Migliore, 'is transmitted, first of all, through the prism of the biblical witness.'[5] Emil Brunner, likewise, writes: 'The fact that He Himself takes the place of the spoken word is precisely the category which distinguishes the Old Testament revelation – the revelation through speech – from the New Testament revelation, the revelation in Christ.'[6] Despite the apparent virtue of making God central to and in control of his own revelation, this has been a false step, and one that leaves us without a genuine revelation accessible by faith. It would not have occurred if we had been prepared to follow the route suggested by the Scriptures themselves, that we come into communion with God through the Word, who speaks the words of the gospel. The revelation is not the proper nouns 'Jesus Christ', but the proposition, 'Jesus is Christ, the Lord.' The divine word comes to us in, and not apart from, the words of this gospel.

The gospel contains a warning of judgment to come on rebellious humanity

According to Matthew, the first preaching of John the Baptist and of Jesus was identical: 'Repent, for the kingdom of heaven is near' (3:1; 4:17). This preaching is soon described by Matthew in terms of the gospel itself (4:23). As we have seen, Mark reports similar language: '"The time has come," he said. "The kingdom of God is near. Repent and believe the good news!"' (1:14–15). As the imperative indicates, the coming of the kingdom of God in the teaching of the Gospels is thought to involve the judgment of God both on Israel and on the whole world. Luke recounts the chastening words of Jesus to those who reported to him a massacre of Galileans by Pilate: 'unless you repent, you too will all perish' (Luke 13:5). The powerful theme of judgment to come in the preaching of Jesus can be ignored, or translated into tamer categories (as was so often done in the nineteenth century) only by suppressing the clear evidence.

In many and graphic ways all four Gospels portray Jesus as a preacher of eschatological judgment, warning his hearers of the wrath to come. The emphasis does not fall on judgment after death, though there are sufficient warnings about what lies beyond the grave; but the focus is on God's dealing with the whole world, his coming kingdom, in which all will be brought to judgment. 'When the Son of Man comes in his glory, and all the angels with him, he will sit on his throne in heavenly glory. All the nations will be gathered before him, and he will separate the people one from another as a shepherd separates the sheep from the goats' (Matt. 25:31–32). The ministry of warning exercised by Jesus is not that of the moralist who simply warns that unpleasant consequences follow evil deeds; rather, he is like the herald of terrible events that will come upon people as a natural catastrophe, and will overwhelm those who do not take instant and decisive action to remove themselves from peril. The fall of Jerusalem, which occurred so soon after his ministry, was clearly regarded by the Gospel writers as a fulfilment of his words; but it was not the final fulfilment of words that have in fact a cosmic and end-of-history significance.

The same eschatological framework for the gospel was present when the apostles preached after the death of Jesus. By now it was plainly Jesus who was at the centre of the gospel, not least as the one who was the appointed judge. This much is inherent in Peter's Pentecost sermon, in which he announces Jesus' exaltation to God's right hand, and his appointment as Lord and Christ. The age that has now dawned is one in which God purposes to bring all the enemies of his Christ to submission to him (Acts 2:33–36). When Peter speaks to his first Gentile audience at a crucial turning-point for the advance of the gospel, he makes the universal role of Jesus plain: 'he is the one whom God appointed as judge of the living and the dead' (Acts 10:42). Likewise, Paul tells the Athenians that God 'has set a day when he will judge the world with justice by the man he has appointed' (Acts 17:31). Not surprisingly, the gospel is called a 'message of salvation' addressed both to Jews and to Gentiles and demanding the same response from both (Acts 13:26). Paul's writings, as we have already seen, give first-hand evidence that 'the coming wrath' formed part of his presentation of the gospel (1 Thess.1:9–10; cf. Rom 2:16; 1 Cor. 1:18; 2 Cor. 4:3; 5:10). The same truth is present wherever we look in the New Testament (e.g. Heb. 2:1–4; John 5:22–30; 1 Pet. 4:1–7).

The future of God's dealing with the whole world – and especially his judgment – may be regarded as essential to the framework of the gospel, without which it cannot be properly understood. The gospel locates us in a time that God is unfolding: historical time, but with a present meaning revealed by the promised future. Thus the form of the gospel is eschatological. In accordance with the teaching of the New Testament we recognize that the gospel announces that the eschaton has arrived, although it awaits its consummation in a further decisive, universal revelation of Christ (2 Thess. 1:5–10). But that is precisely the problem with the 'demonstrable continuity' for which we look in an exposition of the gospel today. The hermeneutical difficulty is sharpest at this point. We have been examining the gospel as it was first preached, but integral to that gospel is an eschatology that contains an adverse view of universal human sinfulness and its eventual fate in God's judgment, together with a Christology that made Christ the one true Saviour and judge of the whole world. Inherent in this gospel is a claim for the uniqueness and universality of Christ as God's past and future revelation. Can this still be true of the gospel we believe and preach today?

In his classic study of the early preaching of the apostles, C. H. Dodd quotes Kirsopp Lake, to the effect that 'modern man does not believe in any form of salvation known to ancient Christianity'. He adds, 'We tried to believe that criticism could prune away from the New Testament those elements in which it seemed to us to be fantastic, and leave us with an original "essence of Christianity", to which the modern man could say, "This is what I have always thought." But the attempt has failed. At the centre of it all lies this alien, eschatological Gospel, completely out of touch, as it seems, with our ways of thought.' In Dodd's view, the New Testament writers, 'while they worked out bold, even daring ways of restating the original Gospel, were so possessed by its

51

fundamental convictions that their restatements are true to its first intention'. He warns us that the real problem for the student of the New Testament is 'whether the fundamental affirmations of the apostolic Preaching are true and relevant'.[7] Though these words were written over sixty years ago, the gist of Dodd's observation remains sound.

And yet Lake's remark must be challenged at one crucial point: is the modern need for salvation so different? Humanity, ancient or modern, remains doomed to die, and fearful of death. Sin has not disappeared, and the law still informs the conscience. The compressed Pauline remark, 'The sting of death is sin, and the power of sin is the law' (1 Cor. 15:56), refers to realities ready to haunt modern people, or people at any point in time or cultural development. The categories of sin and law may be unfamiliar in name, and the imagery of the Day of Judgment may be alien, but the facts to which such language points are familiar in daily experience. Evil and the judgment of evil in ourselves and others are not alien to us. The Bible speaks with its own type of 'eschatological language' about the end realities, and the actual form these realities take will doubtless surprise us all; but the realities themselves are bound to be very familiar to us. So, too, is forgiveness, the fundamental offer of the gospel. Thus the decisive revelation of the Saviour in the past is full of promise of the revelation of the Judge to come.

Dodd was conscious of the hermeneutical consequences of what he was describing. Under the impact of the earlier version of the 'God is love' gospel (the 'fatherhood of God and the brotherhood of man'), criticism pruned the New Testament, removing the parts that were at odds with modern thought in order to find the essence of the matter. The gospel determined the hermeneutic, and the gospel in this case was so far removed from the original gospel that the hermeneutic did violence to the New Testament itself. In particular, it assailed the universality and uniqueness of Christ and rendered him one saviour among many. As Dodd also observes, however, Paul's preaching of the eschatological gospel was no more attuned to his culture than it is to ours, and any attempt at reinterpretation is 'always in danger of becoming something quite different; what Paul called "preaching another Jesus and another Gospel"'.[8] The eschatological mode is not incidental to Christology, but integral to it, and hence to the gospel.

In short, the issue of eschatology of the gospel is crucial to its integrity. If the gospel cannot be communicated effectively in the modern context in genuine continuity with its eschatological framework, we must ask whether biblical Christianity has any place in the modern world at all. But if, as I have tried to indicate, the eschatological themes remain strikingly relevant, the nature of the apostolic gospel entails that Jesus Christ is the 'one mediator between God and men' (1 Tim. 2:5).

The gospel centres on Jesus Christ as Lord through his death, resurrection and exaltation

We have already noted that when Paul preached at Thessalonica his message centred on repentance from the worship of idols and hope in the coming of Jesus to deliver from the wrath to come. According to Luke, his enemies in Thessalonica spread the rumour that he was preaching 'another king, Jesus'. Given that Paul preached the kingdom of God and the lordship of Christ (Acts 28:30; see also his summary of the gospel in Rom. 1:1–6, in which Christ is named Son of God and Son of David), it is easy to see how his words could be taken in this political sense. Indeed, at one level they were and are political, since they called for a higher allegiance than to Caesar. In any case, both the evangelists and their enemies testify in this way that 'Jesus Christ as Lord' constituted the central thrust of the apostolic message, whether spoken by Paul or by Peter. Nor can there be any other conclusion when we turn to the works later called 'Gospels'. John's Gospel, for example, deliberately portrays Jesus as the King of the Jews, through whose death the present ruler of the world will be cast out and all people drawn to a new obedience (John 12:31–36; cf. Luke 23:42–43). In the final analysis, whatever else goes into the evangelistic sermon by way of bridge-building, apologetics or information, we must be able to summarize it in the phrase 'preaching Christ' (cf. Acts 8:4). The sermon at Athens portrayed in Acts 17 contained basic material about God and the world, started from the known fact of the hearers' commitment to idols and appealed to pagan authors to illustrate what was being said. But the opportunity arose only because Paul was preaching 'Jesus and the resurrection', and it closed when his audience 'heard about the resurrection of the dead'(17:18, 32).

This Christ-centred gospel has two major consequences for the study of revelation. First, the gospel is not about us, but about Christ. It is true that without human beings, without human sin and without the need for the human response of repentance and faith, there would be no gospel; and without the consequences of peace with God, joy and righteousness, the gospel would have failed in its purposes. Nevertheless, the gospel is first and foremost about Christ, and a genuine communication of the gospel focuses the hearer's attention on him rather than on themselves. It is pre-eminently the 'gospel of God's grace' (Acts 20:24; cf. 14:3). The Christian gospel is not, for example, a religious technique for gaining serenity or answers to prayer. Preaching the gospel is not the equivalent of 'telling your faith story', as has been recommended by some. Nor does it suggest that salvation is a joint human and divine effort. Such religious talk (from which, it is true, Christianity has never been exempt) does not do justice to the nature of the gospel as preached by the apostles and first witnesses. It both reveals and matches human sin and incapacity. In the words of James Denney, 'there are only two ways of being religious. One is to try to put God in our debt. The other is simply to acknowledge the greatness of our debt to God.'[9] The true gospel lifts us out of ourselves because it is the message that the helplessness of humanity has been met by the grace and strength of God. There is no room for boasting except to boast in the Lord (1 Cor. 1:26–31).

Secondly, not only must the gospel be about Jesus Christ; it must be about the real Jesus Christ and no other. We who depend on the witnesses for our knowledge of the first preaching of the gospel must focus on the Jesus of the apostolic gospel and no other. Already in Paul's day there were those who preached what he called 'a Jesus other than the Jesus we preached', and indeed 'a different gospel from the one you accepted'. So convinced was he of the dangers of this that he spoke of it as the seduction of a wife from her husband (2 Cor. 11:1–6). His words to the Galatians were equally strong: 'But even if we or an angel from heaven should preach a gospel other than the one we preached to you, let him be eternally condemned!' (Gal. 1:9).

The problem is to do with the identity of Jesus Christ. In the end, the Christology of the whole Bible must be summoned as an answer to the question, 'Who is Jesus?' We may, however, take our beginning once more from what we can see of the evangelists themselves, for the evangelists did not simply preach about Jesus as a private individual and tell the story of his life, death and resurrection. Nor did they simply preach 'Jesus Christ'. The words 'Jesus Christ' are not revelation; Jesus Christ is not without words. What the apostles preached, and what is revelatory, is that 'Jesus is the Christ', or that 'Jesus is the Lord'. They preached a sentence, not a name.

Integral to the apostolic gospel was the claim that 'This Jesus I am proclaiming to you is the Christ' (Acts 17:3); or, as Paul told his Corinthian readers when reminding them of the basic gospel, 'Christ died for our sins according to Scriptures' (1 Cor. 15:3). It was of key importance to analyse the name with the title, 'Jesus Christ', and to recognize that the name went with the title only if his life, death and resurrection had fulfilled the existing Scriptures. Hence the fame of the Bereans, 'who received the message with great eagerness and examined the Scriptures every day to see if what Paul said was true' (Acts 17:11). If faith in Christ is the central response to the gospel, the Christ to whom response is made must clearly be the true one. Important as the syllables 'Jesus of Nazareth' are, they will not achieve a relationship with God if they do not actually refer in some way to the particular Jesus who is the one mediator between God and human beings.

The New Testament authenticates the identity of Jesus in three ways, describing him in such terms that there can be no doubt about the subject of the preaching. He is identified by what he said, through what he experienced and through what was said of him. When these three converge in the preaching of the gospel, the evangelist is speaking of the true Jesus and not some other.

First, he is *the one by whom certain things were said*. The words of Jesus Christ were carefully recorded and transmitted; they formed an authoritative corpus of material by which the original Christians identified Jesus and ordered their lives. Included in these words were not simply moral instructions and insights, but key teaching about his own person in relation to the kingdom of God, as well as promises and exhortations. They formed the basis of the Christian relationship with Jesus after his death; they enabled him to continue to be the Lord of his disciples (Matt. 28:16–20). They are what may be called the 'word of the

Lord', the fresh word of God, the New Testament.

Secondly, he is *the one to whom certain things happened*. The Jesus Christ of whom we read in the gospel, and who is put forward as the Saviour of the world, is not, for example, the Jesus Christ of Islamic belief, who did not truly suffer on the cross. Nor is he the docetic Christ of the proto-gnostics, who taught that he did not come in the flesh. 'Every spirit that acknowledges that Jesus Christ has come in the flesh is from God, but every spirit that does not acknowledge Jesus is not from God' (1 John 4:2-3) Nor was Jesus Christ a woman or a Gentile. Nor is he merely the moral tutor of the human race, or even merely the incarnate one sent by his Father to be 'God with us'. It is even possible to confess that Jesus Christ is 'true God and true human' and yet to preach 'another Jesus' by failing to confess him also as Christ crucified, risen and ascended for our salvation. The Jesus Christ of whom the gospel speaks is the one who was truly God, was born truly human, lived among us, died, rose again and was exalted to the right hand of God, whence he sent his promised Holy Spirit. If we become convinced that these things cannot be said of Jesus, it is better to say so and to create another Jesus than to confuse that creation with the Jesus preached in the gospel.

That is not to say, of course, that it is satisfactory to divorce history from the gospel, the historical Jesus from the Christ of faith. On the contrary, since the identity of Jesus is what is at stake in this discussion, we cannot think that if the works of Jesus are not truly his works, or the words of Jesus not truly his words, we have access to the Jesus who was the subject of the first preaching, or that it is somehow worth knowing an abstracted 'preached but not historical' being. If that were true, we simply would not know who this being was, and we cannot put our faith in such a Jesus. Accepting the Christ preached by the apostles is accepting the historical Jesus; if this were not so, it would best to reach that conclusion before receiving the gospel: 'if Christ has not been raised, our preaching is useless and so is your faith. More than that, we are then found to be false witnesses about God, for we have testified about God that he raised Christ from the dead' (1 Cor. 15:14–15).

The third clue to the identification of Jesus lies in *what was said of him*. Naturally, the witness of those who knew him, and of those who met the ones who knew him, is of prime importance. It is their testimony we hear when the New Testament speaks, for example, of the resurrection of Jesus from the dead. They do not describe his stature, face, accent or childhood. But they enable us to stand with Peter when Jesus asked, 'Who do you say I am?' and to answer with him, 'You are the Christ, the Son of the living God' (Matt. 16:15–16). Without doubt they were greatly impressed by his deeds and his words. What made the most significant impact, however, was their recognition – and subsequently, therefore, their teaching – that he fulfilled the 'hope of Israel'. They came to this conclusion by identifying him as the one who fulfilled the patterns and promises of the Old Testament Scriptures. They 'examined the Scriptures' and found that they testified to Jesus in such a way as to identify him as the Christ. In fact, according to Luke, it was Jesus himself who 'opened their minds so that they could understand the Scriptures', saying, 'Everything must be fulfilled that is written about me in the Law of Moses, the Prophets and the Psalms' (Luke 24:45, 44). As the word 'must' reminds us, the testimony of the existing Scriptures is not merely the fortuitous pattern that fate may deal out; it is because the Scriptures were regarded as the very testimony of God himself that their verdict was final. God speaks here as definitively as in the ears of the disciples on the day that Jesus was baptized (Mark 1:11). Indeed, that voice quoted the Old Testament Scriptures in order to identify the person and mission of Jesus. According to Paul, in a passage in which he gives a plain account of his gospel, the gospel was 'promised beforehand through [God's] prophets in the Holy Scriptures, regarding his Son' (Rom. 1:1–3; cf. 15:8–12; 16:25–27).

Thus the authenticity of any alleged reproduction of the gospel depends upon the identity of the Christ who is preached in that gospel. It must not be assumed that, merely because the words 'Jesus Christ' are prominent, the gospel that is the power of God for salvation is thereby being communicated. We must know the identity of this Jesus; there needs to be a consistency, a demonstrable continuity, between ancient and modern gospels in the testimony they bear to what he said, what happened to him and what was said about him. In particular, if we are to answer the vital question whether it is right to confess that Jesus is the Christ, we must estimate whether he has fulfilled the expectations of the Old Testament Scriptures. When we say, 'Jesus Christ is Lord', we are referring to a specific person, who comes to us in specific words, who did specific things and who makes specific demands. He is no lonely religious genius who appeared by accident among the Jews, and could equally well have appeared among the Egyptians or the Aztecs. He can be estimated and understood only as part of a particular culture that was prepared for the preaching of the kingdom of God by the existing written word of God.

The gospel, therefore, depends for its very life, now as then, on the prior existence of a written word of God, and issues in the preached and then written words of Jesus. Even when Jesus as Christ was preached to those without the written word, the Gentiles, the activity itself was justified and explained by the promises of the Old Testament (Acts 15:15ff.; Gal. 3:6–9; Rom. 15:7–9); and the new converts were inducted into a congregation that regarded the Scriptures as God's word written, and written for them, both Jew and Gentile: 'These things happened to them as examples and were written down as warnings for us, on whom the fulfilment of the ages has come' (1 Cor. 10:11; cf. Rom. 15:4). As we shall see in due course, the method of this revelation is not accidental; it is precisely the method by which God has demonstrated his character from the first.

The gospel is a word of promise about God's love and mercy

One of the most striking features of the New Testament is the note of joy accompanying the reception of the gospel (as in the story of the Ethiopian eunuch; Acts 8:39). Without doubt this emotion sprang from two features of the gospel message: first, the disclosure of the love of God through the gospel, and secondly, the merciful blessings that God promised and gave through the gospel. God's love is seen as the motive behind his saving actions as recorded in the Old Testament, notably by Hosea. But the prophet is by no means alone in this. We can return to the defining moments of the revelation of God at Sinai, and the exposition of his name as 'the compassionate and gracious God, slow to anger, abounding in love and faithfulness, maintaining love to thousands' (Exod. 34:6–7). In the New Testament, however, it is Christ's dying for his people on the cross that is most typically seen as the proof and norm of love: 'This is love: not that we loved God, but that he loved us and sent his Son as an atoning sacrifice for our sins' (1 John 4:10). The grace of God towards his enemies demonstrates the certainty of his acceptance even though there is no ground in us for that acceptance (Rom. 5:1–11).

Different New Testament writers have different ways of expressing the mercies of the gospel. John speaks most often of eternal life, and Paul seems to prefer words such as 'righteousness' and 'reconciliation'. The Acts of the Apostles isolates forgiveness as the blessing that is conferred in the gospel, and, indeed, an analysis of the Synoptics shows that this is close to the teaching of Jesus. It was not for nothing that he was known as the friend of tax collectors and sinners, and his habit of eating with the outcasts of society was an acted parable of the pardoning welcome that the waiting Father would give to those who would turn to him. This reminds us that the blessings of the gospel are enjoyed corporately. Likewise, the Pauline 'reconciliation' and 'righteousness' language has forgiveness at its heart, as is shown by its intimate connection to references to Christ's taking away or bearing sin. Indeed, Paul characterized his whole gospel as 'the message of the cross' (1 Cor. 1:18), and declared solemnly: 'what I received I passed on to you as of first importance: that Christ died for our sins according to the Scriptures' (15:3).

Joy in response to God's love and mercy is particularly appropriate in those who, like the Ethiopian eunuch, are beyond the bounds of Israel and so condemned by exclusion from the covenant community. Their inclusion exemplifies the special significance for the doctrine of revelation of the fact that God made known his intention to accept both Jew and Gentile into salvation on equal terms. In a sense, this intention is the essence of revelation. Paul refers to it as 'the mystery of Christ, which was not made known to men in other generations as it has now been revealed by the Spirit to God's holy apostles and prophets' (Eph. 3:4–5). God's revolutionary intention has been made known in three ways: first, by the words and deeds of Jesus through his attitude to such matters as the food laws (Mark 7), and by his missionary commission (Luke 24:46–48); secondly, through the specific commissioning and labours of the apostle Paul, the 'minister of Christ Jesus to the Gentiles' (Rom. 15:16);

and thirdly, through the existing promises of God in the Old Testament, the significance of which remained hidden ('a mystery') until the coming of the gospel (Rom. 15:7–13). Indeed, Paul can say that this promise was the gospel that was announced beforehand to Abraham (Gal. 3:8). In its turn, the co-existence of Jews and Gentiles in the one church is a revelation to 'rulers and authorities in the heavenly realms'. The sheer wideness of God's mercies in accepting 'Gentile sinners', who have no call upon him, is a never-ending theme of thanksgiving (Eph. 3:20–21).

Why should the inclusion of the Gentiles be so close to the heart of the revelation that is the gospel? First, it relates to the exclusive Christian claim that, 'although there are many "gods" and many "lords" ... yet for us there is but one God, the Father, from whom all things came ... and there is but one Lord, Jesus Christ' (1 Cor. 8:5–6). Also, it demonstrates once again an aspect of the gospel particularly important for the authentic Christian faith: its promissory nature. The gospel both claims to fulfil the promises of God and generates further promises: 'For I tell you that Christ has become a servant of the Jews on behalf of God's truth, to confirm the promises made to the patriarchs so that the Gentiles may glorify God for his mercy' (Rom. 15:8–9). The inclusion of the Gentiles is integral to the confirmation of the gospel, because it shows that this God can and does keep his promises. Through this, we know that God is God.

The gospel therefore demonstrates a key element in God's revelation, namely the promissory structure of Scripture. Receiving the gospel of Jesus Christ depends upon and authenticates the promises of God, and brings the believer inescapably into the sphere of promises. The promises fulfil and indicate God's prior revelation; the promises yet to be fulfilled are accepted by faith against the day when Christ is revealed, when we 'shall understand fully' (1 Cor. 13:12).

About promises in general we may make the following four preliminary observations, to be developed later. First, promises are always to do with the future. Secondly, they are necessarily verbal. Thirdly, they can be fruitfully received only by faith. Fourthly, when received, they create relationships. It is not surprising, then, that eschatology and history play such significant roles in the Bible. Promises look forward and so create eschatology, and the delay in their fulfilment creates history. Nor is it surprising that faith plays such a significant role in the knowledge of God; the type of word God has given us especially calls for truth on his part and faith on ours. Faith rests solely on his word of promise. Where the promise is in doubt, faith languishes.

The gospel demands repentance and faith in its hearers

It is clear from what has been said so far that the gospel bears information about God, his person and plans, that would be obtained from no other source. It truly reveals things that have been hidden, to which human beings cannot be privy in their own strength. But the word is never mere information. One of the characteristics that distinguish the gospel from moral teaching is that the gospel provokes a crisis of decision in its hearers. It seeks a fundamental shift of allegiance and of hope. Moral instruction may seek change and issue in a call to repentance from dead works. But the gospel is more radical than that, as we may gather by thinking once again of the Markan version of the opening imperative of Jesus' ministry, 'Repent and believe the good news' (1:15).

The two responses sought by Jesus in this command may be distinguished, but not divided. They take their shape from the announcement of the kingdom of God, which is their foundation and their gospel. In his call for repentance, in line with the prophets (including John the Baptist), Jesus is doubtless calling his hearers to take the specific action needed in regard to actual sins. But the Bible attributes individual sins to an underlying attitude to God, to a false relationship with him. The call for repentance, then, additionally and more fundamentally involves the call to abandon a self-centred view of self and to turn, or 're-turn', to the living God. It is a matter not merely of purity but of relationship. The announcement of the coming kingdom of God reorientates the person to God and his rule. The call to repentance demands submission to God. As the gospel unfolds its message, it becomes clear that, unlike that of John the Baptist (who also preaches that the people should repent in the light of the coming kingdom), Jesus is at its centre. The repentance he seeks becomes the discipleship his followers experience. When Paul preaches that Jesus Christ is Lord, he is calling for the repentance that makes Christ Lord and lives to please him in all things.

Faith is also the submission of the person to God, and hence cannot be finally separated from repentance. It is a recognition of helplessness, and a turning to God for succour in the way modelled by Bartimaeus, the blind man of the gospel story (Mark 10.46–52), and many others. As with Bartimaeus, however, the gospel narrative shows that faith is truly exercised when it is directed towards Jesus himself. Indeed, a survey of the use of 'faith' and its cognates in the New Testament reveals that in an overwhelming number of cases faith is directed to Jesus Christ, not even to 'God' or the Father. What the New Testament values is not faith as such (which, in any case, is a common human attribute), but faith in Christ. Indeed, faith takes its saving strength entirely from its object. It does not need to be complete faith, or faith with no doubts; but it does need to be faith in the right object, and hence faith in the one who is the mediator between God and us. That is why the New Testament is so concerned about the purity of the gospel; 'another Jesus' cannot save, no matter how fervent the faith exercised towards him. The Jesus who is the Saviour is the one identified and described in the words of the gospel. Belief in Christ can also be described as belief in the gospel, or belief in the word of the Lord. These are not separable or even separate things; to believe in the gospel is to believe in Christ; to believe in the word is to trust him for salvation. Essential to our apprehension of Christ in the gospel, for example, is our hope in his return and triumph. This, like the whole gospel, is accessible only to faith in the promises of God. 'We enjoy Christ', observed John Calvin, 'only as we embrace Christ clad in his own promises.'[10] There is no other possibility of encountering him in a saving way.

The universal demand of the gospel, that we must turn to God in repentance and have faith in our Lord Jesus Christ, has never commended itself to fallen human beings. To accede to the demand is to return to the situation from which, in Adam, we recoiled in the beginning. Repentance and faith relate us effectively to God on his terms, namely in submission to him. Hence the core of the gospel is that Jesus Christ is Lord, and the New Testament language applied to believers includes the word 'slave' as a fitting description of our relationship to him (e.g. Rom. 6:18, 22).[11] This is especially repugnant in the contemporary world, where human independence has received so ringing a cultural endorsement. In this respect, indeed, autonomy is a thread that binds modernism and postmodernism together. Theology is not exempt from the pressures of the culture, and it is prey to powerful contemporary ideologies that encapsulate the desire for independence. In this situation there is a great temptation to 'change the subject' when God is speaking, or to find his revelation in places other than in his word. This temptation challenges both the very nature of the gospel itself and our willingness to submit to the lordship of Christ.[12]

Conclusion

I have undertaken this study of the gospel because the New Testament sets it forth as the starting-point for knowing God, and as a claimant to the title 'word of God'. If it is what it claims to be (its credibility was discussed in chapter 1), it is clearly the fundamental revelation. I have endeavoured to show, however, that the gospel has a definite shape, and furthermore that it retains its contemporary relevance as long as the eschatological framework is accepted. I have also argued that accepting the truth of the gospel entails important implications for a doctrine of revelation. Not least is the absoluteness of Jesus Christ as the Saviour, Judge and Word of God. In particular, the gospel relies upon the identification both of itself and of Scripture as 'word of God' – a point that will receive special attention as we proceed. My argument is that we cannot begin by accepting the gospel on a certain set of terms only to abandon those terms later. The consequence of this argument is pursued and summarized in the following chapters.

3

THE GOSPEL AND THE KNOWLEDGE OF GOD

Until this point I have focused most of our attention on the gospel itself. I now turn to the equally significant theme of that relational knowledge of God that is the fruit of the gospel. For revelation yields knowledge, and the gospel-revelation claims to yield, above all, the saving knowledge of God. 'Now this is eternal life: that they may know you, the only true God, and Jesus Christ, whom you have sent' (John 17:3). Thus, on the one hand, we have the gospel; on the other, we have the knowledge of God that results from the gospel. What did the gospel preachers mean when they offered the knowledge of God through the gospel? What does this demonstrate about the way God relates to us? After discussing these points, I shall return to the question: what does this show about the role played by words in the reception of the gospel? Further, what does it teach about the revelatory nature of the Bible?

Knowing God

Ignoring God and ignorant of him

Beginning at Pentecost, at least some Christians were involved in mission with the gospel. Their perspectives on evangelism are especially relevant to our current situation. The first evangelists were convinced that their hearers lacked a saving knowledge of God. The audience may have been intensely religious, with 'many gods' and many 'lords'" (1 Cor. 8.5), they may have been zealous Jews seeking to establish their own righteousness (Rom. 10:2–3); they may have been immoral pagans (1 Thess. 4:5); but they are all characterized as being unrelated to God. It is not that there is no knowledge of God to be had. On the contrary, both conscience (Rom. 2:14–15) and the created order (Rom. 1:19–20) bear witness to the reality of God and his requirements. Both the facts about God and the nature of the response that human beings should properly make are evident. Furthermore, the Jews have the 'very words of God' (Rom. 3:2). Rather, the fundamental problem lies in the relationships we human beings have with other spiritual powers, which afflict human consciences, blind our spiritual senses, engross our attention and dull our minds. Paul characterizes the Gentiles in these terms: 'They are darkened in their understanding and separated from the life of God because of the ignorance that is in them due to the hardening of their hearts' (Eph. 4:18). He also says that 'the god of this age has blinded the minds of unbelievers' (2 Cor. 4:4), that we are the enemies of God (Rom. 5:10), and that we are hostile to him (Rom. 8:7).

This account of the spiritual condition of humankind is crucial to any discussion of revelation. Without it, we may well expect revelation to be simply a matter of God's granting us certain information that we lack because of our creaturely status. The gospel assumes, however, that we are alienated from God and hostile to him. If we are going to come to know him, God must open our eyes to the truth; but the truth to which our eyes are open also needs to be appropriate, namely that Jesus Christ is Lord. The mere act of illumination would be useless in itself. The rule of the 'god of this world' needs to be replaced by the rule of Jesus Christ. Thus, when the evangelists offered the knowledge of God,

66

they were saying that the old bondage to forces that were not God could be broken and a new relationship with God could commence. Hostility, alienation and enmity could be laid to one side, and we could enter a filial fellowship with the living God. It is essential to notice, however, that the spirituality to which the gospel introduces us presupposes that the word of God will continue to function as a key point for our faith-response to God.

Knowing God in truth

To know God is to be reconciled to God, to be at peace with him, to be his adopted son (Rom. 5:1–11; Gal. 4:1–11). Adoption is initiated by him, accepted by faith in his word, shaped by his instructions and marked by our obedience. It yields true insights into ourselves and the world, and issues in salvation. As in all family relations, our knowledge includes an extensive range of truths about him. That is because relationship requires faith, and it is no accident that in the Bible faith is identified as the vital point of contact between God and his people. In this case, truths on which we base our faith arise from God's verbal self-disclosure, and include reports of what he has done, is doing and intends to do, as well as his promises and commands. Relationship prospers within the arena of truth; it is impossible to trust a liar, or even one who is habitually inaccurate. Language creates that personal union that incorporates without assimilating: 'Sanctify them by the truth; your word is truth … My prayer is not for them alone. I pray also for those who will believe in me through their message, that all of them may be one, Father, just as you are in me and I am in you' (John 17:17, 20–21).

It is this personal union that is the fruit of the gospel: not absorption into the divine, but the mutual indwelling that speaks and listens. It is friendship, fellowship, communion, in which words given and received play an integral role. Our knowledge is limited by our creaturely ignorance, and by our sinful distortion of the truth God has given us. It is limited, too, by our place in the history of salvation; we look in hope for the further revelation of Jesus Christ at the end of the age. 'Now I know in part; then I shall know fully, even as I am fully known' (1 Cor. 13:12). But the revelation we have, based on the work of Christ and the Spirit and mediated to us in words, is adequate for the gift of communion it bestows. Dr John Kleinig, in writing about meditation in the New Testament, observes,

> The notion of remaining in the Word of Jesus is developed further in John 15:7–10. Just as a branch remains in the stock of the vine, so the disciple must remain attached to Jesus and his love by keeping his commandments. As a result of this, the words of Jesus come to 'remain' in the disciple (15:7). They find their home in his heart and take up residence there. By the process of meditation the external word is internalized and appropriated, so that it can unite the disciple with Jesus and keep him in constant contact with him. Wherever the words of Jesus remain, there Jesus himself remains (15:4–5). So by letting the words of Jesus 'remain' in him, the disciple remains in Jesus. And this in turn lays the foundation for Christian prayer.[1]

Throughout the Bible, our speech directed to God is understood to be an essential part of this friendship with God. Prayer is virtually a universal human phenomenon, but Christian prayer takes its nature from what we know about God, including the invitations to prayer that he gives us. The prayers of the Bible, including those of Jesus, show that prayer responds to the revelation of God in his word. Its scope, content and assurance are based on the character of God as he reveals himself. Confident prayer is based on knowing God's name. As far as Christians are concerned, God is characteristically addressed as Father, in the name of the Son and in the power of the Spirit. This trinitarian intimacy arises from an encounter with the words God has spoken. The Bible does not regard those who are ignorant of God as lacking spiritual relationships, but considers that those relationships are sinister rather than helpful. What Israel in particular has been given is the name of God, by which God's people may address him with success, in that they may be confident of being heard. Without the name, relationship is impossible. Prayer moves within the ambit of revelation; praise becomes retelling the marvellous deeds of the Lord.

How God identifies himself

It is particularly important to notice the method by which God identifies himself and makes himself known as the true God. The name given to Moses, which seems at least to contain the promise 'I WILL BE WHAT I WILL BE' (Exod. 3:14, mg.),[2] points to this mode of operation. As in the New Testament, it assumes that the human problem is spiritual rather than intellectual; belief in spiritual forces, in gods or even in God is taken for granted. The problem concerns salvation, release from idols, identification and relationship between humans and the true God. The name indicates first the possibility of relationship through the name. It identifies the true God in the midst of the many false gods. But, as the meaning of the name suggests, the fact that the Lord is God will be demonstrated by his deeds. 'There is also implicit in this interpretation the thought of implementing promises: I am who I am always, ever alike, and consequently I am true to my word and fulfil it.'[3] The true God is not just 'God', but the God who released the people from Egypt in accordance with his promises and brought them to the promised land. He is that God and no other. Thus a significant strand of Old Testament thought identifies God by his deeds and defines him thus.

Of course, inherent in such passages is the thought that the mighty deeds of the Lord are impressive in themselves. But that is not the fundamental notion. When the mighty deeds of God lead to increased knowledge of the Lord, either in Israel or among the nations, it is characteristically because he has already indicated what he would do. The true prophet of God in Deuteronomy 18:9–22 can be identified because what he says comes to pass, in contrast to the false prophets of Israel and the soothsayers of the nations; so, more generally, the true God may be identified by the way his promises are fulfilled in reality. In particular, the prophet Ezekiel constantly predicts that the Lord will perform certain great deeds, such as the destruction of Tyre, with the result that 'Then they will know that I am the LORD' (e.g. 26:6). But Ezekiel is not alone in this. Isaiah shares it (41:21–29; 46:8–13), and we may trace it back to passages such as Deuteronomy 4:15–40 and beyond. It is not merely the power of what God does; it is his ability to do what he says he will do that identifies the Lord and shows that he is God indeed. Hence Isaiah's fierce polemic:

69

'Ignorant are those who carry about idols of wood,
      who pray to gods that cannot save.
Declare what is to be, present it –
      let them take counsel together.
Who foretold this long ago,
      who declared it from the distant past?
Was it not I, the LORD?
      And there is no God apart from me,
a righteous God and a Saviour;
      there is none but me.'

(42:20–21; cf. 48:3–5)

In other words, it is not the signs and wonders on their own, or the words of promise on their own, but the conjunction of the two that leads to the spread of the knowledge of the Lord. Both Israel and the nations come to know that 'the LORD – he is God!' (1 Kgs. 18:39). But the deeds may be separated from the words by a considerable amount of time; the promises may stand awaiting their fulfilment for centuries, just as the promise of Christ's coming again – and hence the promise of complete knowledge – remains something to be received and lived by in faith. The coming together of deed and word identifies the God who has done this as the Lord, the promise-keeping God.

Two significant points flow from these observations. First, the 'word of promise/fulfilment' motif is integral to the way God makes himself known. We have seen that it is a feature of the gospel; but it is a feature of the biblical structure itself. When the people of Israel became a nation, they did so as a covenant people, and the salvation that they experienced was said to emerge directly from the Lord's remembering his earlier covenant with their forebears and acting upon it (Exod. 2:24–25). Covenants are words of promise, and the true God manifests himself, or names himself, by being able to keep his promises. The whole business of the naming of God, and of his identification as the one true God as opposed to any other spiritual force whatever, virtually creates the storyline of the Bible. Because promises have to do with the future, the Bible is forced to become eschatological. By this means the Bible deals with time in a way that enables us to live with hope, faith and love in the midst of history.

Secondly, we return to the question of the identification of Jesus. We have seen already that the demonstration that Jesus is the Christ demands the fulfilment of the promises of God in the Old Testament. It is, of course, the specific claim of the New Testament that 'no matter how many promises God has made, they are "Yes" in Christ' (2 Cor. 1:20). Here, in other words, is not only the vindication of Christ, but the revelation and vindication of the God whose name signifies I WILL BE WHO I WILL BE. When his covenant is fulfilled, the knowledge of God will cover the earth as the waters cover the sea. The first coming of Jesus has already brought a great outpouring of the knowledge of God in the gospel. He has been shown as never before to be a promise keeping God, the God who makes history, the one true God as opposed to the idols worshipped by those who are alienated from him. The prior words combine with the deeds to vindicate both words and deeds. The task of the hearer is to examine both together, and to judge whether the deeds indeed fulfil the promise. If they do not – and, of course, to this day many Jews deny that they do – then the gospel is not true, and the Old Testament awaits its authenticating moment.

The connection between words and deeds is further clarified when we consider how the knowledge of God was disseminated, sustained and added to. The flow of time was not permitted to destroy it. It stood in memorial places, in memorial signs, in actions to be remembered and actions to be reiterated, in festivals, in the regularity of the Sabbath, in readings and rememberings, in instruction and learning in the home and through the cult, in the composing of songs and the tradition of proverbs. Since the characteristic attitude of biblical religion is faith, the word of God, which creates, sustains and nourishes faith, was intended to be the basis of the devout life. This is provided for in the law (Deut. 6:4–9) and demonstrated in the Psalms (e.g. 19; 119).

The predictive element of the Bible's religion arose chiefly from its foundation in promises. As the prophets interpreted the covenant for their own day, they were inevitably led to cast their oracles as warnings and encouragements about the future. Similarly, Paul constantly appeals to what his readers know, or should know, as the basis of their present actions and beliefs. They share an existing knowledge of God, expressed in words, to

71

which he can and does frequently appeal. In short, the Bible bears powerful witness to the fact that the knowledge of God is created and sustained through the words that recount the promises and the corresponding deeds of the Lord, and the ordinances that are intended to remind us of these words. The word is integral to the knowledge of God. In the next two sections of this chapter we look at how this highly verbal knowledge of God is stabilized, formalized and given a shape akin to that of the Scripture itself.

Gospel and kingdom

I have observed that the knowledge of God involves release from spiritual bondage. The essence of the gospel of the kingdom of God is that Jesus Christ is Lord, and that our relationship with him is based on deliverance from the powers of darkness. 'For he has rescued us from the dominion of darkness and brought us into the kingdom of the Son he loves, in whom we have redemption, the forgiveness of sins' (Col. 1:13–14). We are not only the Lord's servants but also his slaves, bound to please him in all things.

God rules creation by his word

The gospel notion of the kingdom of God is rooted in the Old Testament. In its pages God is frequently described as the king of the whole world. Where there is a king there must be a kingdom: that is to say, a sphere of kingly authority, or rather an exercise of kingly power. God's sovereignty is exercised first of all towards the creation. By describing him as the creator of all things from nothing by his word alone, Genesis conveys his sovereign power as no theological treatise could hope to do. 'Israel attests that Yahweh creates the world by speech – by royal utterance, a powerful decree that in its very utterance is eagerly and dutifully enacted.'[5] Other parts of the Bible give evidence of his capacity to rule not only the inanimate but the animal and the human as well; not only individuals but mighty nations are bent to do his will; not only the good but the evil is in his hand; not only kings and princes but the very evil spirits themselves must bend to his direction; not only all space but all time too is under his authority. Such observations of God's sovereignty are commonplace to the reader of Scripture.

As can be seen from the opening chapter of the Bible, one way of underlining the effortless sovereignty of God is to show how he accomplishes all things by word of command. Less powerful beings may need to use physical force. Like any king, however, the Lord accomplishes his rule through speech.

> Your word, O LORD, is eternal;
>   it stands firm in the heavens.
> Your faithfulness continues through all generations;
>   you established the earth, and it endures.
> Your laws endure to this day,
>   for all things serve you.
>
> (Ps. 119:89–91)

The concept of the word of God is not the Bible's only way of describing the relationship between God and the creation, but it is a highly significant one. In particular, it emphasizes his powerful rule, which transcends and yet pervades creation.

God rules human beings by his word

The opening chapters of the Bible also introduce us to the use of God's word in relationship to the human beings he had directly created. They were singled out from the other creatures, indicating that they would stand in a unique relation to God. To them, as to those created in his image, he committed the task of ruling the world; for them he created the possibility of history in his command to fill the earth and subdue it; he addressed them directly; from them he received verbal responses. The regal splendour of God was reflected by the regal bearing of humanity as the history of the world began. But there was no question but that God was King. His rule was expressed in his words of command and promise. The charter of human authority also limited their liberty; or, rather, their true liberty was to be found in the constitution under which they were put. They were ruled by the word of God. They were in the kingdom of God. From the very beginning, it is worth noting, the kingdom of God implied a people of God over whom God exercised his rule.

It is not surprising, then, that the rebellion of humans against their Lord took the form of deliberately repudiating his word. The serpent began with the question, 'Did God really say …?'

(Gen. 3:1). In place of faith came unbelief. The events that followed vindicated the word of God and left Adam and Eve with new and harder words of command and promise. The easy fellowship of the Garden was now replaced by the way of pain and penalty, cruelty and lust; and the murder of one brother by another stained the earth. Before the fall, Adam exercised his authority by naming the animals; after the fall, the human families became tragically divided in their speech, unable to communicate with one another except by means of arduous language-learning. Now the animals had different names, depending on the language used. Proper nouns were univocal no longer. The loss of God's ruling word was mirrored by the loss of the power of human speech, which became untruthful, cruel and divisive. Thus the most extraordinary of all paradoxes developed: in a world in which God reigned, the appointed vice-regent was in revolt against that reign.

The story of salvation, with which the rest of the Bible is occupied, tells how God re-establishes his kingdom through his word. That is why the gospel message is first announced in those terms: 'Repent, for the kingdom of heaven is near' (Matt. 4:17). One of the chief ways in which his ruling word is expressed is through 'covenant'. As we consider the significance of God's choice of this manifestation of his word, we shall notice important ramifications for his self-revelation in Scripture.

Kingdom and covenant

The nature of covenants

It has been argued by some that the arrangements between God and humankind in the Garden of Eden constituted a covenant.[6] Whether or not this is a valid description, it soon became apparent through the great stories of Noah, Abraham and Moses that, as God began to re-establish his kingdom by his word, the Lord's chosen form of relationship with his people was by royal covenant. There are covenants between equals, of course, but when the Lord entered into covenants, he did so as one who ruled over a people. For their part, they received his covenant with its blessings, curses, stipulations and signs, and so became bound to him as to a lord. Thus a characteristic form of the word of God is the covenant.

74

We may describe a covenant as a promise given under oath, accompanied by stipulations and sealed with a sign. The covenant binds parties together, and so is sometimes thought of as a league or agreement. All these elements may be found in various covenants of the Bible, whether between God and human beings or simply between people. But the chief element, without which it could not be thought of as a covenant at all, is the promise. Even when one party to the covenant is ignorant of it, as in a will, the promissory element is essential. It may be a threat or a commitment to bless; it may be conditional or unconditional. In any case, promise is the essence of a covenant and gives it its peculiar force. Two great aspects of biblical religion are founded on the promise-making nature of God's covenants with his people.

Covenants and time

First, there is the Bible's attitude to time. A promise seeks to bind, to control time. It seeks to provide a solid element in the midst of the flow of time. In the case of human beings, the control of time by promises is, at best, temporary. In a marriage, one of the most solemn of our oath-swearing ceremonies, we can promise to be faithful only 'till death us do part'. In the case of the promises of God, we are dealing with the one whose word never fails, and who cannot lie.[7] As Hebrews says, 'Because God wanted to make the unchanging nature of his purpose very clear to the heirs of what was promised, he confirmed it with an oath. God did this so that, by two unchangeable things in which it is impossible for God to lie, we who have fled to take hold of the hope offered to us may be greatly encouraged' (Heb. 6:17–18).

These words allude to the result of the control of time by God's promises, namely hope in the future. It is in the very nature of promises to look forward in time. They create hope or fear; they inspire confidence or despair. In the end, they create not merely history but eschatology. Our present situation may seem to contradict all too clearly the promises of God on which we are relying. The whole business may be a delusion; that is what many have concluded. But the alternative is that the promises have yet to reach their true conclusion, that something far better awaits. Faith that this is so may well be strengthened by what are seen as astonishing partial fulfilments of the promises. Thus, for example, the return from exile vindicated the promises of God;

and yet it challenged those promises by being far less magnificent than the prophets had led people to believe. In this case, hope in the promises may fail. Alternatively, the partial fulfilments can be looked on as earnests of what is to come. In this case, they may generate faith and hope. The various expected days of the Lord may then coalesce into one great Day, when all the promises will come true together, and when it may be said at last that the kingdom of God has come.

Covenants and the word

The second aspect of biblical religion that rests on its covenantal structure is the centrality of the word for the knowledge of God. Just as promises irresistibly look forward, so also they are characteristically verbal. It is possible to promise with a gesture, or to promise implicitly. But this is not typical of promises, for a promise, which seeks to bind the future and to provide certainty in the midst of the flux of time, needs to be appealed to, remembered and studied. It needs to be spoken. Many of the covenantal ceremonies of the Bible are accompanied by signs as a way of guaranteeing the occasion and reminding the participants. But the signs do not constitute the promises; they take all their efficacy from the words spoken in conjunction with them. The astonishing thing about the religion of Israel was the absence of images of God; instead, the Ark of the Covenant contained the Book of the Covenant, the written record of what God had said, and hence was still saying, to his people. For it is in the nature of promises, too, that they keep speaking to us throughout their lifetime; they are not silent. Many words in ordinary conversation have no importance beyond the moment; but promises need to be recalled, remembered, marked and signified, because they continue to address us. Thus it is with the promises of God. He has spoken, and in this speech he speaks still.

The centrality of the word determines the nature of the piety of the Bible. Words are first and foremost received by faith. This is especially true of words of promise. That is how they are assimilated; that is how they do their work of creating league, alliance and partnership. Through these words, addressed to us, we become the covenant partners of God. Because they are words of promise, this faith is also known as hope, for hope is not alien to faith, but is faith shaped by its object, namely the word of promise, of which faith has grasped hold. The only authentically biblical religion is one in which words constitute and give access to the object of faith. To cast doubt upon the word of God is to endanger the whole way in which God brings salvation to his people.

Because we are dealing with covenants that lay the groundwork of relationship, we see in them the development of language and literature, which take us beyond promises as such. A marriage is founded on covenant; covenant provides the indispensable framework for the communion of the two persons; but the language and literature of a marriage are not reducible to covenant. The strong covenantal base of the biblical religion helped to create both history and prophecy, as the covenant is tested against the events that time produces and is found to have held or to have failed. The biblical historians observe, record and interpret these developments. The prophets (some of whom are historians, since the division between prophecy and history does not reflect the sort of history found in the Bible) use the promises to interpret the present and to predict the future. The songs and wisdom of the Bible self-consciously take their starting-point from the covenant and are at liberty to explore the individual and national relationship with God on the basis of it.[8]

This remains true when the covenant promises are accompanied by stipulations such as the law. Faith comes first, for without faith it is not possible to receive the covenant at all. Some covenants are absolute, demanding nothing but faith in their recipients, as in the case of Abraham (Gen. 12:1–3; 15:6). In such a covenant the grace of the gospel is prefigured; indeed, Paul says that the Lord preached the gospel beforehand to Abraham when he approached him with a covenant (Gal. 3:8). Yet true faith binds us in a league of fellowship to God and is never unresponsive to the whole will of God. In the covenant of Sinai the Lord explicitly lays down his stipulations to a saved people in the form of his law. This does not contradict the principle of faith, but shows that the covenant is a relationship in which the Lord rules. 'Then [Moses] took the Book of the Covenant and read it to the people. They responded, "We will do everything the LORD has said; we will obey"' (Exod. 24:7). As Brueggemann observes, 'commandment is always, in Israel's faith, in the context of covenant, so that the commands of Yahweh are through and through covenantal commands'.[9]

77

The Sinai covenant re-established the kingdom of God; his people were to live under his rule in his land. But the Sinai covenant was part of a complex of covenants, looking back to the Lord's covenants with Abraham, Isaac and Jacob, and supplemented in due course by the covenant with David recorded in 2 Samuel 7. In the final analysis it is best to think of one covenant in different expressions: the one rule of the one God over his one people, with other elements varying with the circumstances. The Old Testament, which takes its name from God's covenant with Israel, even contains the promise of a new covenant (Jer. 31) which would supersede the Old, not in its basic aim or provisions, but in its effects. 'In some sense', writes P. R. Williamson, 'previous divine covenants culminate in the new covenant, for this future covenant encapsulates the key promises made throughout the Old Testament era.'[10] This new covenant is the gospel.

Jesus Christ and the covenant

Jesus fulfils and endorses the promises

From the opening page of the New Testament, namely the genealogy of Matthew's Gospel, it is clear that the writers wish us to understand that the multifarious expectations aroused by the Old Testament are fulfilled in Christ. To take but one example: the Lord's covenant with David, that his 'kingdom shall endure for ever' (2 Sam. 7:16), is applied to Jesus throughout the New Testament. He is thought to be the Son of David, and hence the rightful king of Israel – a royal title with potential for kingdom over the whole world (Amos 9:11–12). It is not merely the case, as is assumed by modern readers of the Bible, that some instances of predictive prophecy are literally fulfilled, interesting though such instances are in themselves. Rather, a whole structure of expectation, pattern of doing things and historical movement are claimed to vindicate the ministry of Jesus: 'This is what I told you while I was still with you: Everything must be fulfilled that is written about me in the Law of Moses, the Prophets and the Psalms' (Luke 24:44). The covenantal religion of Israel, the alliance between the Lord and his people, had produced a special culture, contained in the Old Testament, whose goal was reached in the coming of Jesus.

Not only does Jesus fulfil the expectations aroused by the covenant, but he and the gospel writers interpret his ministry in the categories provided by that culture. Son of Man, kingdom of God, Christ, new covenant, word of God, Son of God – these and a host of other expressions take their rise from the Old Testament. It is not only the language as such that provides the interpretative categories for assessing the person and work of Jesus, but also the story of what Jesus says and does. His temptations in the desert parallel the experience of Israel; his choice of twelve apostles is a reminder of the twelve tribes; the sufferings of the servant of Isaiah 53 illumine the sufferings of Jesus; his miracles are the expected signs of the presence of God in the eschaton. It is not possible to understand Jesus adequately without setting him firmly in that context.

In applying the words of the Old Testament to himself so emphatically, Jesus was endorsing the ongoing significance of the old revelation of God's purposes. Indeed, as a study of the whole New Testament demonstrates, it is almost the case that the Old Testament is the Bible of Christianity and the New Testament is an appendix. Certainly the abiding authority of the Old Testament is confirmed, since both Jesus and his apostles treated it as the word of God (as did the early church), and appealed to it constantly as the validation of what they were saying and doing. It was the constitution of the people of God, the ruling point by which God governed their existence. But the teaching of the Old Testament itself contained the promise of something new and more. The prophecy of Jeremiah was that there would be a new covenant with Israel, a covenant with the effect that

> 'I will put my law in their minds
>   and write it on their hearts.
> I will be their God,
>   and they will be my people ...
>   they will all know me,
>   from the least of them to the greatest ...
> For I will forgive their wickedness
>   and will remember their sins no more.'
>   (Jer. 31:33–34)

This is the covenant Jesus inaugurated in his death (Matt. 27:28).

79

Jesus and the new covenant

Hebrews tells us that 'Christ is the mediator of a new covenant, that those who are called may receive the promised eternal inheritance' (9:15). As the wording of Jeremiah indicates, it is new in its effectiveness rather than in its provisions, for the hope of Jeremiah was the same as the hope of Moses and Abraham. The law to be written on hearts was still the law; the hope was not for an existence outside the sphere of God's sovereignty, but for the true knowledge of God, the inner capacity to please him, based on the forgiveness of sins. Nor is this merely an individual covenant; it is a covenant with Israel, and if in the end we see that the boundaries of the people of God are extended far beyond Israel, it still remains the case that to enter the new covenant is to enter the people of God, who are ruled by the covenantal word of God. In setting up the community of his saved people, God provided for its life under his rule or constitution; in the coming of Jesus we see what may even be called a new constitution, although its goal and substance remain the same. But we do not see a new people of God, ruled by some new method. God provides a covenant for his enlarged people to live within; God continues to exercise his kingdom over his people through a covenant.

So great is the change that Jesus introduces that the epistle to the Hebrews speaks of the old covenant as 'obsolete', and observes that 'what is obsolete and ageing will soon disappear' (8:13). The author has in mind especially the Mosaic covenant, which, in terms of biblical theology, was a major subset of the fundamental covenant principle. Paul treats the Sinai covenant as a temporary jailer: 'Before this faith came, we were held prisoners by the law, locked up until faith should be revealed' (Gal. 3:23). Despite these negative remarks, however, neither Hebrews nor Paul is inclined to put the Old Testament itself away, or to suggest that its authority has by some means failed. Rather, its authority is now to be understood in and through the authority Christ has as the Lord of the gospel. Indeed, Hebrews is especially replete with Old Testament quotations which it clearly regards as part of the continuing word of God, intended to rule the life of God's new covenant people. Even the outward regulations of the law, such as the sacrifices and the temple furnishings, illustrated what was to come. We could not understand Hebrews without a thorough grasp of the Old Testament.

Nevertheless, with the coming of Jesus Christ the age of fulfilment has dawned, necessitating a major reinterpretation of the old covenant. From now on, everything must be interpreted through Christ, because he is the focal point of God's rule, the king in the kingdom of God, the mediator of the new covenant. This does not require the fanciful interpretations of the Old Testament that have found Christ on every page; rather, at the deepest level the whole covenantal structure, the promises and patterns of God's dealing with his people, are to be understood as pointing to him. This is what makes the identification of Jesus as the Word of God in John 1 so significant. We are introduced to the one through whom all things were made, and hence are reminded of the ruling principle of the created order, namely the word of God. John reminds us not only of the creative work of the Word, but also of the way in which he is constantly repudiated: 'the world did not recognise him' (1:10). As this ruling Word, he brings revelation; he incorporates all the words of God and speaks the words of God (John 3:33). It is this word of God who has become flesh and dwelt among us. Moses brought law; the Word brings grace and truth. At every point of the story of salvation, God relates to humankind through his word, with its structure of promise and fulfilment. When Jesus Christ came, the covenant principle was not abandoned. All who are Christians are in covenant relationship with God, as were his people of old. In our day, that covenant word has as its heart the gospel that Jesus Christ is Lord.

The nature of Scripture

Scripture as 'the Book of the Covenant'

Scripture serves the kingdom of God by encapsulating the covenant. In this sense the Bible as a whole may be called 'the Book of the Covenant', for in it the covenant of God is recorded, expounded and applied. Indeed, Paul gives the warrant for the titles we accord to the Old and New Testaments by calling the Torah 'the old covenant' (2 Cor. 3:14) and the gospel a 'new covenant' (2 Cor. 3:6). Clearly, for Paul, what you did with the old covenant was to read it. C. K. Barrett observes that, although Paul is

81

especially writing of the Sinaitic covenant, it 'implies what we call the Old Testament and could be so translated'.[11]

In so doing Paul follows some clues to be found in the Old Testament itself. Thus when the law was found in the temple in the days of Josiah, it was variously described as the 'Book of the Law of the LORD that had been given through Moses', 'the Book of the Law', 'the Law' and 'the Book of the Covenant'. The contents of the document are described as 'the words of the Law', 'all that is written in this book', 'the word of the LORD' 'his commands, regulations and decrees', and 'the words of the covenant written in this book' (2 Chr. 34:14–31). Whether, as is often supposed, this account concerns a copy of Deuteronomy, or whether the book included the whole Torah, it is interesting to see that the term 'Book of the Covenant', at first applied only to a small body of material (Exod. 24:7), has been widened very significantly. This phenomenon has created the category of material known as 'the word of God', in which we have God's written word, intended to mould the very life of his people. It has the authority of God himself as he rules them.

The authority of covenantal Scripture

The covenantal character of Scripture has two important implications for the doctrine of Scripture. In the first place, given the connection between kingdom and covenant, it indicates the nature of scriptural authority. God has used the covenant to re-establish his rule over his people through his word. The covenant is a characteristic form of the word of God, culminating in the gospel, the word of promise and demand that centres on Jesus Christ. The function of the Scripture is to record, expound and apply this authority of God. That is why it is called the Word of God, the oracles of God, and the Holy Scriptures. When we enter relationship with God on the basis of his covenant, we enter a relationship with one whose very words may be trusted completely. It means too, that the Bible functions as both gospel and covenant in that it is intended to create and sustain our relationship with the living God on the right basis, namely on our being his covenant partners, bound to him in loyalty and obedience and relating to him through the mediator, Jesus Christ. In other words, gospel, kingdom, covenant and Scripture are interlocking concepts, functioning to bring us into a saved relationship with God. In short, at least from the time of the patriarchs, God's people have been bound to him through the words of promise called covenants; they have never been without the word of God; they have never been without his rule through his word; and these words may be found in the Scriptures. To see the Bible as merely a human artefact, a testimony to the human experience of the divine, but without the authority of God, is to misunderstand its nature.

The function of covenantal Scripture

Secondly, the covenantal character of Scripture challenges the idea of the Bible as a textbook. 'For the Christian conception of God the Bible is our only textbook. In its pages we have the self-revelation of God.'[12] Without doubt, the Bible teaches us about God. It has a key didactic function: if we are to respond to God in the area of truth, we need to be instructed in the truth. But we also need to do justice to its covenantal nature, its function of finding us and holding us for God through its promises. The promissory nature of Scripture means that it gives us information about the plans and purposes of God. The Bible is God's many-sided provision for his covenant people. The psalms and proverbs of the Bible, its prophetic laments, its promises and covenants, its narratives – these and its other literary forms serve to sustain and direct obedient faith. We must be careful not to miss the didactic usefulness of the Psalms, for example, but we can see them also as the words that God has given us to use in the different circumstances of life. They are also God-given, God-authorized songs of faith.

Conclusion

Emil Brunner was aware of the implications of his doctrine of revelation for Christian faith. In rejecting verbal inspiration, he thought that he was saving the real nature of faith. For him, even the apostolic witness 'can never be the *basis and object* of faith, but only the *means* of faith'.[13] But if the argument of this chapter is correct, the relation between the person of Christ and the word about him is far more intimate than Brunner will allow, and authentic faith involves the capacity to trust and obey words, sentences and paragraphs. The issue is obviously significant, for the very nature of the Christian life itself is at stake.

4

THE GOSPEL AS A PATTERN OF REVELATION

Identifying the gospel of Jesus Christ as God's primary revelation shapes what we believe about revelation in general. It acts as a paradigm or pattern of revelation, and exercises a controlling influence over our approach to other claimants to this name. In this brief bridging chapter I shall set out the major implications of the investigation so far. The perception that the gospel is the form or pattern of revelation has four major consequences, and these will provide fundamental axioms for our consideration in the coming chapters of the knowledge of God available from other sources.

The gospel is the measure of all revelation

First, the gospel is the key element in coming to a saving knowledge of God. It is no part of my case to argue that the gospel is the only revelation of God. On the contrary, as even a word study of *apokalypsis* and other words for 'revelation' (let alone biblical accounts that do not use the word or its cognates, but clearly refer to revelatory events and experiences) demonstrates, the Bible itself refers to many revelations and to various experiences that may be called 'revelation': visual, inward, dream-related, verbal.[1] I have deliberately not begun with a word study because of the danger of merely fitting the gospel into such a category when the claims made for it in the New Testament are so much more significant.

Other revelations in the Bible have a far more limited function. Paul claims to have received various revelations: for example, one instructing him to go up to Jerusalem (Gal. 2:2), and others he described as 'visions and revelations from the Lord', and 'surpassingly great revelations' which were 'inexpressible' (2 Cor. 12:1, 7, 4). He was familiar, too, with the phenomenon of revelations to prophets in church (1 Cor. 14:30), and with the concept that truth about God is revealed in what has been made (Rom. 1:20). Paul prays that his readers may receive further revelation, asking that 'God ... the glorious Father, may give you the Spirit of wisdom and revelation so that you may know him better' (Eph. 1:17). He envisages this as occurring in conjunction with the ordinary processes of thought, as when he tells the Philippians, 'if on some point you think differently, that too God will make clear to you' (Phil. 3:15). Indeed, as has often been noted, the second coming of Christ is also described in terms of revelation, as in 2 Thessalonians 1:7: 'This will happen when the Lord Jesus is revealed from heaven in blazing fire with his powerful angels.'[2]

The purpose and content of the gospel, however, make it stand out as the foundational revelation of the Christian faith, and the one through which the rest are to be interpreted. 'In the past', begins the epistle to the Hebrews, 'God spoke to our forefathers through the prophets at many times and in various ways, but in these last days he has spoken to us by his Son, whom he appointed heir of all things, and through whom he made the universe' (1:1–2). The contrast between God's former revelation and his last one is sustained in what follows. The angels, by whom, it was believed, the most significant revelation of all was given at Mount Sinai, are inferior to the Son in honour. Their revelation was ignored only at the extreme peril of the hearers; how much more the revelation of the Son, which came, not through angels, but through the Lord, his apostles and God himself (2:1–4)? It was not that the old covenant had become null and void; rather, it is now to find its interpretative centre in the Son.

Likewise, Paul underlines the centrality of the gospel as revelation in the closing doxology of Romans, just as he had in the opening greeting: 'Now to him who is able to establish you by my gospel and the proclamation of Jesus Christ, according to the revelation of the mystery hidden for long ages past, but now revealed and made known through the prophetic writings by the command of the eternal God, so that all nations might believe and obey him – to the only wise God be glory for ever through Jesus Christ! Amen' (Rom. 16:25–27; cf. 1:1–6; 1 Pet. 1:10–12). For Paul, there was a universal, general revelation through the creation, but the wickedness of the human heart and the corruption of the human mind ensured that it was in no way a saving revelation (Rom. 1.18–31). Because the Bible is Christ-centred it is also gospel-centred: 'All things have been committed to me by my Father. No-one knows the Son except the Father, and no-one knows the Father except the Son and those to whom the Son chooses to reveal him' (Matt. 11:27).

Not surprisingly, then, the New Testament does not see Christians as starting with the gospel and then graduating to higher mysteries. Whether it speaks specifically of the gospel or of Christ, it strongly exhorts readers to live in accordance with the gospel, to advance its cause, to relate to other Christians in its terms and to find in it all wisdom and knowledge. Whether the problem be the Judaizing Christians, who try to add the law to the gospel, or the Colossian heresy with its intellectual additions, the gospel remains the standard for the truth. 'So then, just as you received Christ Jesus as Lord, continue to live in him, rooted and built up in him, strengthened in the faith as you were taught, and overflowing with thankfulness' (Col. 2:6–7).

Christian revelation is basically verbal

The second conclusion from a study of the gospel relates to the place of language in revelation. We have seen the unwillingness of modern theology directly to identify words with revelation. Propositional revelation has been attacked and the revelation of persons favoured; communion with the self-giving God is preferred to information from propositions. But if the gospel occupies the place in the economy of salvation that its first proponents suggested, and if it accomplishes what they claimed for it, the distinction between personal and propositional knowledge cannot be sustained. Their view of revelation certainly permits words and language to be identified with revelation. The description of the gospel as the word of God demonstrates that. To have some other theory is to depart radically from the fount of the Christian tradition.[3]

We must also note that the role of language in the divine–human relationship brought into being through the gospel is far more integral than is allowed for in modern accounts of revelation. It simply is not possible to call the gospel, as many wish to call the Bible, a witness to revelation (for example). The gospel is revelation, both in that it communicates truths about God, his actions and intentions, and also in that it communicates his person. For instance, it tells us that he has fixed a day on which he will judge the living and the dead. This assertion is intensely personal and self-involving. It constitutes both information and promise, and is received only by faith. It demands that we align our lives with its message. It is not in itself the day of judgment; language is not the thing for which it stands. But language can, and in this case does, convey the reality of which it speaks, so that we behave exactly as we should towards that reality (Heb. 4:12–13). To this extent we are judged by the very words themselves. Likewise, we behave towards these words as we behave towards God himself. They convey his person to us, since they are to be treated as we would treat him. When we obey his word, we obey him; when we trust his word, we trust him; when we study his word, we study him; when we preach his word, we preach him. He is not his word; and yet he is, for his word is the appointed place of our relationship, and he is supremely faithful to it. His word communicates his self to us: 'If you remain in me and my words remain in you, ask whatever you wish, and it will be given you' (John 15:7).

Similarly, it is not plausible to call the gospel an event, or simply an event. It contains, of course, an account of Jesus' words and works, the 'event' of Jesus. The gospel recounts the greatest of God's acts. Without these events the gospel would be void. It is also true that in the gospel there is a dynamic to coming to know Christ, which is by nature an event. From one point of view, these events are the gospel. But they are made accessible to us only by the words that recount them. The gospel is not only an event; it is a fixed word, a truth that stands, a word foundational to life, which contains the promise of things to come. As I noted in chapter 2, it is in the very nature of promises that they cannot be reduced to events or acts. They transcend the history of which they are part. They are verbal and constant. It is part of their faithfulness that they must stand, as a structure stands. A promise is given in an act; it may be reiterated in a further act; but between such acts it will exist to be referred to, acted upon and hoped in.

That is the nature of words, and that is what makes words so wonderfully fitting as an instrument of fellowship. In human relationships, deafness is a terrible affliction because it cruelly isolates people from others. The words we use are vital means of friendship and command, of intimacy and order. As memorials to acts past and reminders of acts still to come, they guide and control the present. When they come from a faithful source they are entirely trustworthy, and cause faith to blossom and love to grow. We are able to refer back to them at any time, confident that they will have the same force as they did originally. We can securely build our lives on these words and model ourselves on their requirements, because they are a standing and yet living revelation of the character and intentions of the one who speaks.

It may be objected that this approach intrudes into the mystery of God that remains despite revelatory events. We walk by faith, not by sight, and we ought not to seek the confidence that holding the word of the Lord in our hands may bring. Such confidence, it may be said, belongs only to the time to come, when we shall know as we are known. However, such an objection is based on a misunderstanding of the nature of faith. It is not right to say that faith's uncertainty in its object is of the essence of faith itself, and that to ask for sure words is to ask either for the eschaton or for the secrets of God. God does not lose his freedom or his 'hiddenness' by giving us genuine speech. Our endeavour to protect his transcendence can have the effect of questioning his power to reveal himself in a trustworthy way. The uncertainty of faith is, first, the uncertainty of the one who has faith, brought about by sin; secondly, it is the uncertainty of the one who as yet has only promises and not fulfilment. But the promises themselves are as secure as the one who made them. These limitations are sufficient to explain the tension that exists for faith. Faith does not, in order to be truly Christian, need to hear that its object too is insecure;

nor does faith need to know all about God. Christian faith is founded on the word of the God who never lies, and it cannot shift from that foundation without drastic damage.

A relationship with God is created through a verbal gospel that calls itself the word of God. From the beginning, then, trusting in words that come from God and that determine our relationship with him is set to be integral to that relationship. To start with such words and then to say that they cannot bear the trust that made us Christians in the first place is to go back on the gospel. It is to start in one way and to try to continue in another. This is the fate of much modern Christianity. Certainly there is no neutral ground here. After due consideration, a person may come to believe that the gospel is untrue, that its promises are false, that the Jesus it presents is not the Jesus of history and that its interpretation of life is implausible. That is the point at which to repudiate Christianity. But to start with words that lead to worship of the one the words describe, and then to perform that worship while casting the words in a different role, is fatally inconsistent. There is no access to God by the Christian route apart from this word of God and faith in it. In short, the category 'word of God' as applied to the language of the gospel of Jesus Christ is integral to Christianity. It is the central revelation of God. It cannot be abandoned without abandoning Christianity itself.

Revelation conveys both information and relationship

The third conclusion we may draw from the nature and place of the gospel concerns the relationship based on the Christian revelation. Revelation leads to knowledge; the gospel brings the knowledge of God. But what sort of knowledge is this? The summary of the gospel is that 'Jesus Christ is Lord'. This proposition contains both information about reality and an immediate challenge to conform to it by submitting to Christ's lordship through repentance and faith. We are to 'obey the gospel'. The apostle Paul is prepared to speak of this new relationship as that of a son to a father and of a slave to an owner. He stresses, as does the rest of the New Testament, the service we owe the Lord; we must seek to please him in all things, to be like him, to bring every thought captive to him, to trust him and to obey him.

In all this, the identity of the Jesus Christ who is Lord is established by what he said and did, and by what was said about him (see chapter 1). We cannot relate to him independently of the words by which his identity is known. These include the words by which he determined that his disciples should live, whether commands or promises: '... teaching them to obey everything I have commanded you. And surely I am with you always, to the very end of the age' (Matt. 28:20). Faith directed to an invisible Lord requires words it can trust implicitly; it cannot survive on words that *may* be true, or that contain the truth, or that witness to the truth, or that are true episodically. A faith directed towards promises (such as 'I am with you always') must be able to trust them to the same degree as it trusts the one who makes the promises; at this point the promise and the promise-maker are indistinguishable. Likewise, a faith committed to the discipleship that involves the sacrifice of self even to death is summoned to that commitment by words of command and exhortation that truly represent the Lord himself; our response to them is our response to him. We cannot bypass the words that speak of him in an attempt to find his will more securely or more plainly. The words are where we find him. 'Do not say in your heart, "Who will ascend into heaven?" (that is, to bring Christ down), or, "Who will descend into the deep?" (that is, to bring Christ up from the dead). But what does [the righteousness that is by faith] say? "The word is near you; it is in your mouth and in your heart," that is, the word of faith we are proclaiming: That if you confess with your mouth, "Jesus is Lord," and believe in your heart that God raised him from the dead, you will be saved' (Rom. 10:6–9).

Thus the nature of the gospel determines two important facts about the knowledge of God. First, this knowledge includes information from God and about God, his character and his intentions. The very category of promise, about which we have just been thinking, demonstrates these points. As the God who makes promises and keeps them, God has revealed himself to be the faithful one. At the same time, his promises reveal his intentions. Secondly, the knowledge of which the gospel speaks is relational. God's promises are received by faith; as we receive them, so we relate to him and enter into the knowledge of him that the New

Testament describes as salvation. Earlier views of revelation may have tended to over-stress the informational element of the word of God; but views of revelation responsive to the Enlightenment have tended to disconnect information and relationship. In Emil Brunner's view, for example, 'He Himself, Jesus Christ, is the "Word" of God; it is therefore impossible to equate any human words, any "speech-about Him" with the divine self communica tion.'[4] The result has been an account of the Christian life in which the Lord's servants have not been encouraged to respond with faith and obedience to the Lord's words. The great liberation theme of the Enlightenment has entered the Christian soul, and human autonomy has been preferred to Christ's lordship through his words. It is as if he has been rendered dumb.

Scripture is revelation

The fourth conclusion is inherent in the other three. If the fundamental Christian revelation of the gospel necessarily identifies that gospel as the word of God, the identification should be extended to the Bible. This is for two reasons. First, any objection to verbal revelation *per se* must either put the gospel aside or itself fall by the wayside. If we have received the gospel, we have already wholeheartedly accepted the category 'word of God'. The authority of this word is established as far as we are concerned. We believe that Jesus Christ is Lord, and our belief necessarily involves submission to his teaching as to the very word of God itself. The only other question is the extent of this word, which brings us to the second reason. Once again, the chief decisions on this score have already been taken in principle. The Jesus Christ of the gospel, in whom we have believed, is none other than the one the gospel identifies as fulfilling the existing word of God in the Scriptures. If Jesus does not fulfil the Scriptures, he is not the Christ, and the gospel is false. If he did fulfil the Scriptures, it is because God was acting in his life, death and resurrection in fulfilment of the divine word of promise given beforehand. It is not surprising that both Jesus and his apostles held that the Old Testament comprised the 'very words of God' (Rom. 3:2), which could not fail those who trusted in them. Naturally, the Old Testament was now seen in the light of the revelation of the gospel; but the Christian faith was founded on the conviction that God had revealed himself through the words of prophets and apostles, 'with Christ Jesus himself as the chief cornerstone' (Eph. 2:20).

By this route I have returned to the view that there is a category, 'Scripture', which is God's revelation. But the journey has not been typical of earlier evangelical approaches, and the consequences of adopting this way into the subject may be untypical too. In chapters 7–9 I shall continue to examine the issue of the word of God and the Bible, using some of the themes of earlier chapters to grasp the nature of the revelation God has given us in its pages. Although we may advance beyond earlier positions, however, it ought not to be at the expense of the place of the Bible in the economy of God. The loss of scriptural authority in the church has been a calamity for the Christian cause, not least in the missionary-founded churches. These, having joyfully accepted the gospel from the missionaries, and with it the Scriptures, have often experienced the diminution of the Bible and then of the gospel in the next generation. The extraordinary dissemination of the Bible in modern times needs to be matched by the re-establishment of its authority for the Christian mind.

Conclusion

The first four chapters have laid a theological basis for the doctrine of revelation. I have not attempted to start from a concept of revelation and then ask whether in fact the Christian religion possesses such a thing. Rather, if we follow the path provided by the gospel, we see that knowing God, his person and his plans comes from faith in the word of God. The gospel is a word that centres on Jesus Christ and proclaims that he is Lord. The word of the gospel itself reveals that God has always sought to rule his people by his word of covenant. The Christian revelation not only discloses information about God's character; it also reasserts his rule over a wayward and rebellious people. It is not a religious experience, although to receive the gospel by faith is to experience entering a new relationship. The revelation is verbal; it announces the word of God, centred on Jesus Christ but multifaceted in its expression. It is coterminous with Scripture, and it functions to re-establish God's rule by creating and nourishing faith.

God's central revelation of himself, therefore, is evangelical at heart, covenantal by nature and scriptural in form. Where this is still doubted, the issue must be fought out with regard to the gospel itself, and on no other prior ground. If it is accepted, we need to enquire what a revelation of this nature entails. There are, for example, other claimants to the title of revelation. If we start on the basis of the gospel revelation as established, what place do we assign them? In the next two chapters, therefore, I shall turn to the subject of other revelations through human and religious experience. A closer examination of the Bible as revelation will wait until chapters 7–9.

5

REVELATION AND HUMAN EXPERIENCE

The gospel of Jesus Christ is both the source and the measure of the knowledge of God. It is therefore the revelation by which anything else that claims to deliver knowledge of God must be assessed and interpreted. We have seen that accepting the gospel entails accepting the covenantal Scriptures as the word of God. But is knowledge of God available elsewhere?

Several possibilities exist. There may, for example, be a preliminary knowledge, which supports or leads to the gospel. Did the apostolic preachers appeal to or presuppose other revelations when they put forward the gospel? Human reason could perhaps work out truths about God unaided by revelation, or there may be revelations in other religions. Is there a 'general revelation' of God, accessible to all human beings, in addition to the special revelation of God's word? Theological and philosophical literature is full of discussions of such issues. My purpose, in the light of the discussion so far, is to enquire about the implication of the gospel for other sources of the knowledge of God.

Adopting the gospel approach set out in the last four chapters,

I shall explore what is entailed by the gospel and taught by the Scriptures on these issues. For this purpose, I have also adopted the broad idea of experience as the leading theme in this and the next chapter. Is there anything in human experience (chapter 5) and anything in specifically religious experience (chapter 6) that intimates, leads to or supports a knowledge of God?

In this chapter, I shall begin by briefly considering the implications of the gospel in these areas, and shall then discuss claims for a natural theology and a general revelation. After this, I shall return to the topic of human experience in the light of the gospel. To illustrate the possibilities of this approach, I shall conclude by considering a theology of nature rather than a natural theology.

The gospel and the testimony of experience

If, as we consider the subject of other paths to the knowledge of God, we accept the truth of the gospel as a starting-point, four boundary conditions follow. These are specific applications of the four axioms established in the previous chapter.

First, we are committed to the view that saving knowledge constitutes a relationship that is a gift of God's grace (see above, pp. 37–38). 'Now this is eternal life: that they may know you, the only true God, and Jesus Christ, whom you have sent' (John 17:3). The initiative, the content and the closure are his. Whatever we say of other possible routes to the knowledge of God, and even if we incorporate elements from them into our own view, they can never contradict or overwhelm the grace of the gospel method. God is thus known 'through himself'; that is, as he chooses to reveal himself – indeed to give himself – in a saving fellowship. Our coming to know God in the gospel entirely conforms to his method of saving us through the cross of Christ, and to the doctrine of justification by faith alone. It rescues us from bondage to false gods and leaves us exactly where we should be, serving the Lord who saved us. This must be axiomatic.

Secondly, the gospel way of knowledge is premised on the hopeless plight of the human race, which merits only judgment because of its sin (see above, pp. 66ff.). As a direct result of sin, we have no power of our own to come to know God. In the words of Paul, 'the world through its wisdom did not know him' (1 Cor.

1:21). The Bible portrays our reasoning powers as having been so corrupted by sin that we cannot know the truth of God. Worse, we do not want to know it. Because of our attitude towards our Maker, we have no right to be saved and no independent capacity to know him. Whatever may be known about God apart from the gospel is suppressed, and the idolatry that results serves only to condemn (Rom.1:28–32). Thus the gospel constitutes the essence of the saving grace of God towards us, showing that the initiative belongs to God, and that no human striving and effort will penetrate the mystery of his will towards us. There is no neutral platform on which we may stand while we investigate the reality or otherwise of God: in our desire to be independent of him we are committed to oppose him.

Thirdly, we must recognize that the knowledge of God through the gospel is both final and exclusive (see above, pp. 85–87). Jesus himself said, 'All things have been committed to me by my Father. No-one knows the Son except the Father, and no-one knows the Father except the Son and those to whom the Son chooses to reveal him' (Matt. 11:27). The eschatology of the New Testament makes the claims of Jesus paramount. If Jesus has been appointed to be the judge of the living and the dead on the day of judgment (Acts 10:42), he is the one with whom all men and women have to do. He is the last word as well as the first, and no other revelation can make the claim that he makes. But his paramount excellence does not exclude other possibilities: indeed, the claim that the gospel is the word of God rests in part on the recognition that the Old Testament, too, is the word of God. Whatever we may make of other claims to revelation and to knowledge, however, our conclusions must not transgress the boundary afforded by his exclusive and final claim.

Fourthly, knowledge of God through Christ does not bypass human faculties (see above, pp. 38–40). This truth is implicit in the incarnation. The Son of God came in human flesh and communicated with human words, actions and gestures. He appealed to human sympathy, wisdom, imagination and reason; he taught, argued, preached, exemplified; he invited discussion, response, love and insight. The strong scriptural emphasis on God's grace in making himself known is never at the expense of the reality of human response. When, in Galatians 4:9, the apostle Paul corrects himself to give priority to God's gift, he does not do so at the expense of human effort: 'But now that you know God – or rather are known by God ...' Repentance and faith are both gifts of God and human obligations. That is why human experience is not alien to the appeal of the gospel.

These are the boundaries imposed by the gospel itself. In the light of what the gospel thus offers, what are the other claimants to be sources of the knowledge of God? We begin with the claim that there is an accessible general revelation and a viable natural theology.

General revelation and natural theology

By 'general revelation' I mean a divine activity that provides a universally accessible knowledge of God. It could take the form of a universal God-given inner understanding of the truth, or of his observable providential actions in history, or of inference from the construction of the natural order. The proffered knowledge may or may not be comprehended by human beings. For scholars, the most obvious way of judging whether such a revelation exists is to treat the enquiry as part of the human activity usually known as natural theology.

There are several definitions of 'natural theology'. Mine is: 'a human activity directed towards discovering the truth about the existence of a god or gods and the character of such a being or beings'. The term can also refer to the results of this activity: the theology that is so arrived at. In this sense, natural theology is characteristically exercised free of any supernatural aid through verbal communications from God, which would answer its questions. As the word 'natural' suggests, its conclusions may be reached by humans on their own. Revealed theology, by contrast, comes from a 'supernatural' source such as the Bible. Natural theology does not presuppose that any evidence for God is an intentional manifestation of the divine. Indeed, it may conclude that there is no god, or that there are a number of gods, or that God does not reveal himself intentionally, or that he reveals himself intentionally and universally. As we shall see, however, it may not be as easy to distinguish general revelation from natural theology as the discussion so far may suggest.

The existence of the divine is the first subject on the agenda of natural theology. Natural theologians usually adopt one of two courses as they work on this issue. First, they proffer rational proofs (or even disproofs) for the existence of God. Some arguments are purely deductive, such as the ontological proof associated with Anselm of Canterbury (1033–1109) and René Descartes (1596–1650). Others begin from observations about the nature of the world, as in the case of the teleological proof and the other demonstrations associated with Thomas Aquinas (1225–74). But the natural theologian may also wish to say something about the character of God, and again the evidence provided by the cosmos may well be the source of such information. For example, the mystery and awe evoked by the immensity of the universe may lead to conclusions about the omnipotence of its Creator. Likewise, its order and intricacy speak powerfully about the God who plans and constructs. Indeed, natural theology may go further and include the flow of history in its scrutiny of the world. The theologian may ask whether, in the events of history or in the developments of nations and ideologies, something of the plans and purposes of God can be discerned. In addition, the reality of God may be discussed with the aid of the testimony of the world's religious phenomena.

Natural theology has had periods of great success as well as periods of virtual eclipse. During the seventeenth and eighteenth centuries, for example, much English theological thought was dedicated to the tasks of natural theology. Works of the quality of William Paley's *A View of the Evidences of Christianity* (1794) and his *Natural Theology* (1802), and Bishop Joseph Butler's *Analogy of Religion Natural and Revealed to the Constitution and Course of Nature* (1736), were widely read and deeply influential. Certainly, in their prolegomena to the knowledge of God Reformed scholars of the nineteenth century, such as E. A. Litton, R. L. Dabney and Charles Hodge, took for granted the support they thought natural theology offered.[1] Likewise, the nineteenth century saw a renewal of Thomistic philosophy in the Roman Catholic Church, as thinkers from that communion looked for philosophical tools with which to confront the challenge of the Enlightenment. Despite the somewhat negative philosophical and theological climate of the twentieth century, there has been a recent revival of natural theology, with authors such as Richard Swinburne of Oxford[2] paying significant philosophical attention to the proofs for the existence of God and other traditional themes of natural theology. Some would judge that such efforts make important progress.

Much is at stake in the continuing effort to provide a positive natural theology. If the existence of God could be demonstrated, and if something of his character could be known, without appeal to revelation, the long-lasting scepticism of western culture could be challenged at a fundamental point. An apparently neutral ground could be established for evangelism and apologetics – one that would enable the seeker to investigate without fearing that special pleading is being used to establish the Christian cause. Once the existence of God was demonstrated, the seeker could be introduced to the more specific doctrines of the Bible. At the very least, a successful natural theology could connect the Christian claims with the general life of humanity, and could enable Christianity to relate to human experience in a way that a fideistic version of the faith fails to do. Furthermore, by the very fact that it is not specifically Christian as such, natural theology helps to provide a bridge to the beliefs and experience of others. It is open in thrust, rather than exclusive.

Notwithstanding all this, however, there are considerable difficulties with the whole enterprise. Two lines of attack have developed: the philosophical and the theological.

First, powerful *philosophical* critiques of natural theology exist. It is true that the wonders of the world as revealed by the early modern scientists seemed increasingly to support the view that God was the great Creator. But the triumph of such natural theology was not to last. Alongside the work of such apologists as William Paley (1743–1805), and even pre-dating it, came the strictures of David Hume (1711–76) and the philosophy of Immanuel Kant (1724–1804), and later the science of Charles Darwin (1809–82). Hume showed that, far from bearing the marks of its Creator, the world was an ambiguous place that could be read in different ways. Kant demonstrated the inadequacy of the standard arguments for the existence of God – in particular the ontological argument – and put the realm of God effectively beyond our reach, except as a matter of 'practical reason' in support of his ethical system. In the end, however, it was the evolutionary theory of Charles Darwin that rendered the old natural theology untenable by concluding that the idea of divine purpose was no longer necessary. If Hume demonstrated that the alleged evidence for God was ambiguous, Darwin appeared to show that there was no need for a divine being at all.

Much work has been done to meet the challenges posed by Hume, Kant and Darwin, and on their side, too, fresh champions of scepticism have arisen. Hume's views did not pass without critical comment in the eighteenth century, and theologians and philosophers could be found confidently asserting that his philosophy had been answered decisively.[3] Likewise, considerable intellectual effort was exerted in responding in various ways to Darwin and Kant. Neither was universally regarded as an enemy of natural theology; Kant had a natural theology of his own, which he expounded in his *Religion within the Bounds of Reason Alone* (1793). In fact, as has already been noted, even the proofs for the existence of God continue to attract very serious philosophical interest, as is evident from the writings of Richard Swinburne and Alvin Plantinga,[4] to name but two scholars. Furthermore, as we shall see, there are contemporary scientists who wish to advance arguments for the existence of God in the light of their own research. Nevertheless, as with all such human efforts, there is little decisive to show for all this effort, and little that is not as hotly disputed as it is confidently advanced.

But the enemies of natural theology are not all philosophers. There are, secondly, powerful *theological* objections to the enterprise as well. Theologians have observed that there is a tendency for a 'successful' natural theology to dominate revealed theology. This is clearly perceptible in the deistic movement of the seventeenth and eighteenth centuries, whose works of natural theology – notably that of John Toland (1670–1722), *Christianity Not Mysterious* (1696) – stripped Christianity of its miraculous elements and conformed it to the simple religion of rationalism. Under the impact of such an argument, the gospel of Jesus Christ becomes the outward trappings, necessary perhaps for the weak, of a religion that may be arrived at by reason alone. Understandably, the tendency of such reduced 'religion' is distinctly moralistic, being based on too optimistic an account of human nature and its capacity to reason its way to the truth.

But the case does not have to be so extreme. The need for apologetics in the early church led to claims of common ground between the God of the Bible and ideas of God in Greek philosophy. Professor Jaroslav Pelikan reports that 'at the hands of

101

such thinkers as the Cappadocians ... natural theology underwent a fundamental *metamorphosis*. It became not only an apologetic but also a presupposition for systematic, dogmatic theology.' He observes that it has been frequently argued that 'concessions and adjustments made to the natural theology of the Greek culture made in the name of apologetics came back to haunt the church's doctrines in their positive formulations'.[5] Likewise, in Thomistic theology the philosophical portals undoubtedly lead via special revelation to a full trinitarian faith. But the fact that natural theology is the chronological starting point gives it an unfortunate influence over the way revealed faith is set out. Since the findings of natural theology must be regarded as certain, the Bible is read through the eyes of the natural theologian with a tendency to mould the special to the shape of the natural. Most important of all, in order for human reason to be capable of discerning the truth by natural theology, the effect of the fall on the image of God in humankind is held not to involve the corruption of the mind.[6]

The same criticism may be made of the great nineteenth-century Reformed theologian Friedrich Schleiermacher (1768–1834), who accepted the method of Immanuel Kant, if not his conclusions, and made religious experience the source and the test of Christian doctrine. As Alan Torrance observes, 'Just as Kant by his transcendental method deduced that "every event has a cause" is a necessary category of all coherent experience, Schleiermacher had deduced by a similar analysis of the structure of conscious experience that God-consciousness is a necessary category of all spontaneous, conscious human experience ... It binds human experience as a unity. It is the synthetic origin or ground undergirding human conscious experience.'[7] The result was still a religion, and still one that focused on Jesus Christ. But Schleiermacher modified Christian doctrine to make it conform with his starting-point in consciousness, whether that doctrine concerned the Old Testament, Christology, the devil or even the Trinity: '... the assumption of an eternal distinction in the Supreme Being is not an utterance concerning the religious consciousness, for there it could never emerge. Who would venture to say that the impression made by the divine Christ obliges us to conceive of such an eternal distinction as its basis?'[8]

There have always been those – not least among earlier evangelical preachers of the gospel such as George Whitefield and Charles Simeon – who have opposed the method of putting natural theology first. In Karl Barth, however, the Protestant criticism of natural theology had its most formidable proponent. Accepting the negative verdict on natural theology by the culture in which he lived, and appealing both to Paul and to Calvin, he made a virtue of it, and declared war on every species of natural theology that he detected. To his mind, natural theology succeeded only in encouraging the hubris of the human race, without bringing us into contact with God. It was exactly alien to the doctrine of God's grace by which he justifies us. 'We can set ourselves against the recognition of grace in Jesus Christ, for that is a bitter recognition indeed. We can wish we were something other and better than mere objects of divine compassion and that alone. In that case it is open to us to glory in revelations. Some natural theology or other may easily be found to take up the tale with greater or lesser noise and effect. But once we have arrived at the recognition that we have received grace and stand in need of grace, such a course is impossible. Rather the confession becomes inevitable that Jesus Christ *alone* is the revelation.'[9] The revelation of God in Jesus Christ showed by its mere existence, *pace* Kant, that revelation was possible. This real revelation had to be accepted and studied, as the actuality that it is. Human beings were not even capable of receiving revelation until the revelation created its own audience and its own language.

The Barthian assault on natural theology arises from the gospel, and so concurs fundamentally with the first and second boundary conditions set out above. The presupposition of human neutrality, or at least of human capacity to investigate the things of God, is wrong to start with, and the result is an account of the situation that allows for the human contribution at an unfortunate point. It conforms to a semi-Pelagian or even Pelagian model of our relationship with God, in which there exists some movement from humankind to God as well as the movement from God to humankind. The gospel assumes, and the Bible teaches, that it is impossible for human beings to find God or to have clear ideas about him by intellectual effort. Those who say that natural theology does not work on philosophical grounds are (at one level) confirming the biblical judgment, and those who point to the deleterious results of natural theology for the gospel are likewise correct. Natural theology mixes works and grace because of a defectively optimistic anthropology, and opens the door to additional information about God or alleged special revelation from him to supplement what we already have.

Despite the fierceness of the Barthian attack and the negativity of much philosophy, however, natural theology is set to make something of a comeback. Many have dissented from Barth's strictures, especially on the ground that he left the gospel without the support that a genuine natural theology would give. Owen Barne, for example, is critical of the Barthianism he encountered early in his career. 'There is no point in confessing your sins to God or worshipping him if he almost certainly doesn't exist … but, alas, the systematic theology fashionable in the 1950s had no resources for dealing with such problems.'[10] The version of the gospel that Barth propounded seemed to have no grounding at all in human existence; it could not be tested, but only accepted or rejected. There is a sort of atheism about Barth's rejection of all human religion, a capitulation to Feuerbach that seeks to protect the gospel but does not succeed. Wolfhart Pannenberg, although indebted to Barth at some points, has taken his theology in quite a different direction, insisting that the Christian faith must stand before the bar of critical history, and that if it does so submit it will be justified. In his case, Christianity is related to universal history and culture in a way unimaginable in Barth. But there have been other developments as well, some of which are discussed below.

The Barthian dismissal of natural theology demanded a reading of the Bible and of Reformation theology that has not commended itself to others. Barth famously quarrelled with his friend Emil Brunner on this issue, and later seemed to agree that he had gone too far. James Barr, in his Gifford Lectures,[11] has submitted the positions adopted by Barth to a searching review. Leaving aside the unfortunate animus in Barr's tone, there is no doubt that his case against Barth's reading of Paul and Calvin has justice in it. Walter Brueggemann observed that Barr gives 'no clear or stable definition of natural theology'.[12] I would prefer to say that the vagueness to which Barr himself refers in his opening sentence enables him to include far more under the heading of natural theology than most people would allow. But in so doing he affirms the reality of the fourth condition I have propounded –

namely, that revelation comes in human dress – and he points out the real difficulties of separating natural theology and revelation: 'If one believes that God has revealed himself in his creation and continues to do so, why is that [phenomenon termed] "natural" theology and not "revealed"? ... Perhaps all theology is both "natural" and "revealed"?'[13] Thus the evidence Barr adduces from the Scriptures is in favour not so much of a natural theology as I have defined it, but of a general revelation. Neither the Bible nor Calvin offers any support for the practice of natural theology as an unaided human activity, but they both describe a general revelation, and this is something that Barth should have been quicker to acknowledge.

The that of a general revelation is scriptural, and is entailed by the gospel. The passages that speak of the knowledge of God through the heart, through the natural order and through history (e.g. Rom. 2:14–16; Ps. 19; Ezek. 32:15) do so on the explicit assumption that God intends so to reveal certain things. That there is such a revelation is inherent in both the second and the third boundary condition. In the second condition, human sin involves suppressing the truth that God has made generally known, and hence the universal guilt of those who turn their backs on him in favour of idolatry and immorality (Rom. 1:18–31). Thus the teaching of Scripture and the fact of human culpability lead us to affirm the existence of general revelation. Sin perverts our apprehension of general revelation, but in so doing is also defined and judged by that perversion. The general revelation of God provides the ground for general human condemnation. Barth misread the Bible (and especially Rom. 1) when he denied that the natural order spoke of God by God's appointment, and that men and women had no capacity to understand. It is true that general revelation does not lead to salvation, but this is because of human sinfulness, and the very text that tells us this (Rom. 1:18–21) is eloquent concerning the reality of such a revelation to human beings.

Likewise neither the third nor the fourth condition entails a Barthian conclusion. The finality and exclusivity of the gospel as a means of knowing God does not do so. In Barthian terms, as we have seen, the uniqueness of Christ as the only revelation is so pressed that there is no room for any other candidate; not even for Scripture itself, let alone for the experiences of other religions.

105

Thus the gospel is so isolated from human contact that the conditions of its entry into the world, and its transmission, are set at risk. The gospel confession of the finality of Christ as the revelation of God recognizes that the gospel takes the first place but not the only place. This is particularly clear as we observe the fourth condition, which arises from considering the incarnation, the verbal nature of the gospel and the way Christ lived it and the first preachers commended it. Human experience is not alien to the gospel, though the gospel has priority as the fundamental revelation of God.

Sorting out the issues

If, despite rejecting a narrowly defined natural theology, we are prepared to speak of a 'general revelation', in what terms should we do so? For example, is there anything to be gained from continuing to dialogue with those who regard themselves as exponents of natural theology, especially bearing in mind the renewed interest in this activity? A consideration of the second question suggests an answer to the first.

With some important caveats, and with a revolution in its approach, the business of natural theology retains some significance, largely because it overlaps with general revelation. In order to make the most of that significance, we need to adopt two strategies. First, we should treat the evidence in terms of experience rather than of mere reason; secondly, we should understand experience through the gospel, not the gospel through experience.

First, the theme of experience. A certain style of approach characterizes much natural theology. Traditionally, the discipline has been marked by an intellectualist strain. In the first instance, at least, nature is set against grace, and reason against faith. It encourages research, criticism, deduction, reflection and speculation. Thus the initial questions asked in natural theology concern the existence and the attributes of God rather than existential issues of salvation and the future, and the method employed is logical analysis. The danger lies in relying on mere deductive reason in choosing and assessing the evidence. Natural theology has often relied on a narrow view of rationality that demands definitive evidence rather than suggestive, deductive rather than inductive. The standards of proof have thus been set impossibly high given the nature of the subject under consideration, namely God and his ways. As a result, relevant evidence has been omitted.

Contemporary natural theologians have already tended to make this point, and have also been prepared to admit evidence that cannot yield deductive certainty but demands a different approach from that adopted at the high point of conventional natural theology. For example, there has been a move into the study – and hence the evidences – of history. But when Swinburne (to take one philosopher) seeks to rehabilitate the proofs for God's existence, he does so in what may be called an inductive rather than a deductive mode. He seeks to persuade by accumulating evidence rather than with foundationalist logic. The same could be said about Plantinga's restatement of the ontological proof, which is entered by way of presuppositions held in common rather than mere deduction.

We are seeing, in short, a more chastened natural theology, and one that fits in with the idea that there is in fact a general revelation. The business of natural theology under these circumstances is to trace what can be made of the general revelation, conscious that, in the words of H. R. Mackintosh, 'All religious knowledge of God, wherever existing, comes by revelation; otherwise we should be committed to the incredible position that man can know God without his willingness to be known.'[14] This is precisely the path taken by Dr Ian Markham in his recent 'essay in natural theology', where he seeks to demonstrate that critical realism is impossible without theism; he accepts that we may adopt an entirely relativistic notion of truth instead, but points out the consequences of so doing. He argues that 'The tradition of natural theology should not be viewed as an exercise in seeking arguments to persuade the non-existent "traditionless" person. Instead its role is to tease out the explanatory power of the Christian tradition.'[15] Significantly, he writes within the tradition of general revelation and with explicit appeal to it.[16] Although he calls his work a natural theology, however, it does not fit the definition I have given above, since it relies on both special and general revelation.

This introduces the second point, that experience should be interpreted through the gospel. The focus on experience is

107

theologically justified by Scripture's teaching about the nature of general revelation, by the fact of God's sovereignty over all aspects of our lives, and by the way the gospel commends itself to us and persuades us of its own truth. Despite the negation of natural theology and the limitations of general revelation, we may expect to find in them both intimations and confirmations of the gospel, provided that our apprehension of the grace of God, the sinfulness of men and women and the priority of Christ are not compromised. In short, when the gospel is preached it is appropriate to point to the ways in which, when accepted, it makes sense of our experience of the world. Experience intimates, the gospel enlightens; the gospel interprets, experience confirms. Neither the intimation nor the confirmation is foundational, since we may well misunderstand our experiences. In either case, the truth of the gospel still depends upon the word of God and the Holy Spirit; we are dealing here with intimation and confirmation, not with the essence of persuasion.

In the second half of this chapter, I shall pursue these matters by examining the theme of the gospel and human experience.

The gospel and human experience

Ralph Hood has offered the following elucidation of the concept of experience:

> ... to experience is to have a first-person subjective appreciation that is neither merely affect or cognition, but a more [sic] totalization of what it is that has happened or occurred. Not irrelevant is the linkage of experience to such terms as *expert* and *experiment*, both of which imply authoritative knowledge either by one who has been in the position to have known firsthand or in terms of the conditions under which firsthand knowledge can be acquired. The appeal to experience in this sense is absolute and fundamental. An appeal to experience is a claim that what is the case is what is actually found or encountered.[17]

This interesting description of experience does not discount the rational side of our knowing, but stresses that knowing has its

108

affective and holistic side too. In addition, it brings out clearly the aspect of experience that gives it its special flavour, namely its note of personal authority. 'I know, because this has happened, and it has happened to me.' There is, as Hood observes, an absolute side to experience. It often challenges the authority of the expert in the name of a different, immediate and personal form of authority. Conversely, the subjective nature of the authority of experience gives it an individualistic flavour as well. My experience may be pitted against your experience, or even your lack of experience. I cannot necessarily convince you of the truth of a proposition merely on the basis of my experience, no matter how strongly I feel. If my experience is open to duplication, however, my proposition becomes more persuasive.

Natural theology traditionally relies on reason. But knowledge gained by experience is arrived at, assimilated and assessed through reason, intuition, reflection, interpretation, imagination and creativity. Indeed, experience is frequently a given; often we do not seek it and cannot control it. Experience does not abandon rational thought, but calls for a wide exercise of thought and judgment. Despite the absoluteness of experience, with the authority that flows from that, our interpretation of experience may be challenged and overthrown. There is, admittedly, a tendency to favour one's own instant interpretation of experience. But sometimes it cannot easily be interpreted at once; sometimes further reflection leads to deeper appreciation of it, and sometimes our earlier interpretation is completely overthrown.

In my earlier discussion of the credibility of the gospel (chapter 1), I indicated that the gospel sought to persuade its hearers along three different lines. The first was its fulfilment of Old Testament promises. The second was a historical argument; the gospel presents the resurrection of Jesus as a historical event and seeks our acquiescence in its truth on the basis of testimony. The third was that the Jesus of the gospel makes sense of our experience of the world. It is obvious that none of these is a 'proof' in any deductive sense. Not even the appeal to prophecy is straightforward. On the contrary, they all appeal to our capacity for self-analysis, imagination, judgment, reflection and reason. As the parable of the sower reminds us, they tell us a great deal about ourselves; they sift us as they persuade us; they judge us as they inform us. In this, they suit the nature of the gospel itself and its intended function. The gospel brings us to a relational knowledge of God on the basis of his lordship and our obedience. This knowledge is based on the words of the gospel, which tell of the mighty deeds that God has done in Jesus, and it is brought home to our hearts through the work of the Holy Spirit. The gospel persuades by being that sort of gospel, not by being a metaphysical tract. These remarks apply particularly to the third of the conclusions given above: the argument that the gospel persuades by making sense of our experience of the world.

Human thought characteristically moves from what is known to what is unknown. When the gospel is preached, it invariably uses the language and concepts that refer to human experience in order to explicate itself. The gospel speaks of love, wrath, forgiveness, faith, repentance, sin and death. These are all common human experiences; in each case the gospel takes our inadequate understanding of the experience and gives us new and powerful wisdom about it. The reinterpretation is often so intense that it constitutes a revolution, a conversion of thought and practice. When we see the love of Jesus Christ, for example, a new and radical concept of love enters our culture and our persons. It is not that we had never before experienced love; rather, the love of Christ transcends and transforms our human loves: 'Greater love has no-one than this, that he lay down his life for his friends' (John 15:13). The same observation can be made about our concepts of justice, parenthood or death. In these and many other human experiences, we see the gospel first intersecting with the experience, and then challenging it with a new version of what that experience can and should mean.

When the apostles preached the gospel to Jews and God-fearers, they were able to start with an appeal to the authoritative Scriptures. But, as we can see from incidents such as the preaching of Paul at Lystra (Acts 14:8–20) and to the Athenians (Acts 17:16–34), and from the apostle's account of the gospel in his epistle to the Romans, a different approach was also adopted. The evidence from these sources is that Paul appealed to the felt contrast between (on the one hand) the common idolatry of the ancient world and (on the other) the implications of the created order and the deliverances of the human conscience. He knew that he could make these observations with considerable agree-

110

ment from all: everywhere there was an impetus to worship; that worship was unworthy of the ones who offered it, and was accompanied by immorality; and that immorality was condemned by the very people who engaged in it. The agreement Paul sought came from consciences touched by the Spirit of God to see the truth of the matter. Even in the wider culture, however, the truth of what he was saying was frequently acknowledged. A strong body of opinion among thinkers of the ancient world acknowledged the truth that God 'does not live in temples built by hands' (Acts 17:24), and that 'in him we live and move and have our being' (Acts 17:28).[18] For Paul, the facts of our experience with the world testified to the reality of God.

Paul would not be surprised that many people, now as then, disagree with his analysis of our situation. He was not offering a philosophical proof for the existence of God. He did not expect any rational person to come to the same conclusions as he did by necessary process through the function of the intellect. He thought of the knowledge of God, first, as something given by God, not as something arrived at by men and women. It was a general revelation. Secondly, he saw that the knowledge of God is a relational matter. We may, he suggests, have begun with the knowledge that God is Creator and should be worshipped, but that is definitely not the case with most people now. The knowledge of God is suppressed, and 'their thinking became futile and their foolish hearts were darkened' (Rom. 1:21). The experience of idolatry, in which human beings worship themselves or animals, is evidence of this darkened heart. Yet Paul was also capable of appealing to God's witness to himself in the natural world to enable his hearers to move from the known to the unknown (Acts 13:16–17).

The darkened heart; the created world; the wrath of God in history: these contain intimations of the truth. It is not surprising that the cosmological, teleological and moral arguments for the existence of God have been advanced and that, even when they do not convince, they touch something in the human mind. When the gospel of Jesus Christ comes, and the creative splendour of the one true God is revealed, the experience of being created makes sense, and the intimations of the truth are understood. Indeed, the contrast between our idolatry (whatever its modern versions may be) and the self-attestation of the God who 'has shown kindness by giving you rain from heaven and crops in their seasons ... [and] provides you with plenty of food and fills your hearts with joy' (Acts 14:17) will often be part of the process of communicating the gospel.

Does the gospel also assume a basic knowledge about God in its hearers? If so, from where would such knowledge come? It is notable that the Bible itself never argues for the existence of God. The possibility of atheism is acknowledged in Psalm 14:1, but only to observe that it is the fool who says such things. Atheism is treated as a spiritual rather than an intellectual problem. It seems that the concept of God is virtually universal in the world of the Bible, and the key question is not whether God or any god exists, but what the name and nature of God are. Even when Paul appeals to the revelation of God in the natural order, he is not arguing for the existence of God as such: 'what may be known about God is plain to them, because God has made it plain to them. For since the creation of the world God's invisible qualities – his eternal power and divine nature – have been clearly seen, being understood from what has been made, so that men are without excuse. For although they knew God, they neither glorified him as God nor gave thanks to him ...' (Rom. 1:19–21). It is God's nature, not his existence, that the world reveals (cf. Ps. 19:1–6). Humans are expected to know already that God exists. Our fault lies in the idolatry in which we engage.

These observations, together with the general religiousness of humanity, have led various theologians, including Augustine and Calvin, to the view that the knowledge of God is innate in the human mind, for God has ensured that we are born with it. 'There is within the human mind, and indeed by natural instinct, an awareness of divinity. This we take to be beyond controversy. To prevent anyone from taking refuge in the pretence of ignorance, God has himself implanted in all men a certain understanding of his divine majesty.'[19] There is much in this idea that attracts, but it is worth noting that it lacks specific biblical support. The closest passage is Romans 2:13–16, where the knowledge of the work of the law is implanted in people's hearts. Moo suggests that this refers to all Gentiles, and agrees that what is being referred to is 'an innate moral sense of "right and wrong"'.[20] If, as I would argue, the first obligation of the law is to serve the living God, and the conscience is already aware of the day of judgment (2:16), the point is incontrovertible.

112

The fact that sincere atheism exists is an obvious and powerful counter-argument. To claim that we have an innate knowledge of God seems to run counter to the experience of modern secular men and women. But two comments may be made. First, the Bible itself agrees that people deny the knowledge of God, and explains why this is so. To find that people have little knowledge of the truth and do not express it in true worship is consistent with Paul's analysis of the situation. Secondly, it is by no means clear that, because people have given up formal religion, they have abandoned the worship that Paul traces back to such a denial. Modern irreligion may be idolatry of a different order, but human bondage to things that are not God persists. Rather than being utterly godless, we may serve any of various ideological or personal gods.

Furthermore, to claim that people have an innate knowledge of God does not imply that all are aware of God in the same way from birth, or that it is impossible to make a sensible case for atheism. Our innate knowledge of God may mean only that we have a disposition to believe in God, of which we may remain unconscious until it is 'triggered' by some experience such as meditating on the natural world or being rendered guilty by conscience.[21]

Experience, the gospel and the theology of nature

In the final section of this chapter I shall illustrate some of its leading ideas by reference to recent attempts by scientists to create a natural theology. I suggest that while such efforts predictably come to little, they do provide data which, understood through the gospel, may intimate and confirm the truth of the gospel way of looking at the world.

After decades of an alleged war between science and religion, some scientists are prepared to raise again the big metaphysical questions with which religion also grapples. Physicists, in particular, are responsible for this new interest, and the names of Stephen Hawking and Paul Davies have become familiar to a very wide public through their books aimed at a popular audience. Davies especially has been explicitly raising the question of

113

God in books such as *God and the New Physics* (1984) and *The Mind of God* (1992). But there have been others as well. Frank Tipler of Tulane University has written on the subject of modern cosmology, God and the resurrection of the dead, claiming that theology is a branch of physics, that 'the central claims of Judeo-Christian theology are in fact true, that these claims are straightforward deductions from the laws of physics as we now understand them', and that he has 'been forced to these conclusions by the inexorable logic of my own special branch of physics'.[22] Robert Jastrow, Director of the Mount Wilson Institute, surveys modern cosmology for the lay audience and concludes: 'For the scientist who has lived by his faith in the power of reason, the story ends like a bad dream. He has scaled the mountains of ignorance; he is about to conquer the highest peak; as he pulls himself over the final rock, he is greeted by a band of theologians who have been sitting there for centuries.'[23]

It is hardly true that these contributions have changed the face of modern science. Tipler's book, for example, has been poorly reviewed. Furthermore, there seems to be little similar happening in other branches of science such as genetics. Nevertheless, it is right to ask what the theologian and the preacher may make of these works and whether they can be used to encourage a recrudescence of natural theology. Is it possible, for example, to argue for the existence of God in a secular society by pointing out that the chances that the universe developed just as it has done without a designing hand are infinitesimally tiny? This seems to be the point that has especially drawn the attention of thinkers such as Davies, Fred Hoyle and Swinburne.[24] Can we move from the nature of the world to the inevitability of the divine?

On the whole, there remain real difficulties with such an approach. The strictures of David Hume against the natural theology of his day are still relevant. The singularity of the evidence remains a haunting problem. How can we compare that which is designed with that which is chaotic, if God has designed everything? How can we interpose God into the order of cause and effect? Who is the God revealed by this process? Paul Davies suggests that the God of process theology is best suited to be the God who created the cosmos and is still creating; but there are other options.[25] Indeed, here lies a significant theological problem with the whole enterprise, and one that dogs all natural theology. The God revealed by the natural philosophers is not the God of the Bible. It has been suggested, for example, that the God of physics is credible where the God of the Bible is not, because the concerns of the latter with the human race seem puny compared with the concerns of the former in the cosmos that now stands revealed. Frank Tipler believes that he has proved God and the resurrection of the dead, 'the central claims of Judeo-Christian theology', but he denies the resurrection of Jesus and the doctrine of the Trinity.[26]

Indeed, in Tipler the basic theological objection to natural theology, which makes natural theology an unwelcome ally at best, is exemplified. Natural theology's theory of knowledge is not personal; it does not take into account the relationship of God and humanity revealed in the Bible; it assumes too much for the human intellect and is a form of the pride from which we need to be delivered. Despite the flourish with which Davies, Tipler and Jastrow announce their results, none of them has become a Christian, for there are parts of the biblical faith with which they cannot agree. Tipler writes as an atheist still,[27] and clearly prefers a version of deism as long as it favours an almost universal salvation. Jastrow began the 1992 edition of his book as he began the first (1978) edition: 'In my case it should be understood from the start that I am an agnostic in religious matters. My views on this question are close to those of Darwin, who wrote, "My theology is a simple muddle. I cannot look at the universe as the result of blind chance, yet I see no evidence of beneficent design in the details."'[28]

Jastrow's citation of Darwin brings us back to the issue of experience. For Darwin (according to this citation) and for Jastrow, the evidence raises questions it cannot answer. But it has forced Jastrow, Tipler and Davies to talk about God, and their discussion has created a huge popular audience of those who see the same puzzling point. Our experience of the world leads us to think of design and hence a designer, and yet we cannot move from this to a relationship with the designer, or even to full assurance that there is such a being, or to agreement about what the being must be like. Tipler insists that the true God must be a universally saving God, and that there can be no hell. But if he included in his data not merely the physical structure of the universe but the moral structure as well, and if he tried to draw from the natural and human history of the world a picture of the God who made it, hell would be very much on the agenda. Natural theology, when taken completely seriously, must incorporate evil, and hence tend to the conclusion that the God who rules the world has cruel, vindictive, brutish and careless elements in his character.

What we need, in fact, is not a natural theology, but a theology of nature. The sort of experience mentioned by Jastrow raises the question of God. But the human mind is not capable of drawing the right conclusions about God or the world from such experiences. Only the gospel will accomplish that. The gospel introduces us to the Lord who has made heaven and earth and indeed everything in the cosmos. It therefore speaks of the regularity of nature and its fundamental reliability. The Bible speaks of the goodness of the created order, existing as it does under the word of the God who declared it good. The Bible also presents us with the picture of a creation which is both separate from God and dependent upon him; it is not imbued with spirit, but may be studied in its own terms. Its regulating principle is the word of God. Through linking the creation unequivocally with Jesus Christ, the Word and Son of God, the Bible enables us to understand it as a place of purpose: it was created through him, by him and for him (John 1:1–3; 1 Cor. 8:6; Col. 1:15–16).

The gospel thus provides us with a framework within which to understand our experiences in and of the world. Through the teaching of Scripture, the world becomes a place of revelation, in which 'The heavens declare the glory of God; the skies proclaim the work of his hands' (Ps. 19:1). But the honouring of God and the learning about God that go on through these means depend at every point on the scriptural revelation. Likewise, when our experience of the world involves suffering, the framework of the gospel is what facilitates a true interpretation. Only the Scriptures reveal that 'the creation was subjected to frustration, not by its own choice, but by the will of the one who subjected it, in hope that the creation itself will be liberated from its bondage to decay and brought into the glorious freedom of the children of God' (Rom. 8:20–21). The eschatology of Scripture is essential for the emergence of a theology of nature. The biblical picture of the sovereign God who orders all things by his powerful word may lead to despair in our encounters with the world, unless it is interpreted through the gospel of the grace of God.

Finally, we should observe that if we give priority to a theology of nature that is taken from the Scriptures and centred on Christ, there is a fundamental gain for science. It is possible to overstate the role played by biblical Christianity in the rise of modern science, and yet it is also possible to miss an essential link. As Harold Nebelsick says, 'It is the Reformers' insistence on seeing the world through the "spectacles of Scripture", as Calvin put it, which was most important for opening the eyes and the minds of those who became responsible for science.'[29] By stressing the divine sovereignty, Christianity endorsed the ideas of order and regularity; by stressing the world's dependence on God, Christianity liberated it from being worshipped, by stressing its independence from spiritual forces other than God, Christianity encouraged the study of the world for its own sake; by stressing the goodness of the creation, Christianity made engagement with matter respectable; by stressing that openly speaking and sharing the truth is honourable, Christianity created a bond of personal trust between scientists; by stressing the value of work in God's creation, Christianity gave an impetus to the experimental labours that advanced our understanding of the world. In particular, in stressing the gospel of the grace of God, and hence the knowledge of God's fatherly care, Christianity enabled its adherents to shake off fear of lesser spirits, and so to relate to one God alone no matter what their circumstances of life. In these ways, the biblical faith helped to disenchant the world and create the scientific era.

Conclusion

The relation of Christianity and science vindicates the way in which we must think of natural theology and general revelation. There can be no doubt that a world ruled by the God revealed in the Bible speaks to us of his glory and power. But our original capacity to understand his revelation is limited by our rebelliousness. At most, the general revelation of God, touching us in various ways through human experience, serves to trigger a receptiveness to the gospel, which God may use to call us to himself. When we receive and understand the gospel, however, our relationship to the world is fundamentally altered. Now we understand it, and the experience of living in it, as we could never do before. Now we are in a position to worship God worthily, knowing that 'everything God created is good, and nothing is to be rejected if it is received with thanksgiving, because it is consecrated by the word of God and prayer' (1 Tim. 4:4–5). In the biblical revelation, centred on the gospel of Christ, we now have the canon by which all experience is to be understood. The Bible does not deliver science, but it yields the conditions under which science may be conducted, and herein lies a confirmation of the gospel's account of the world.

6

THE GOSPEL AND
RELIGIOUS EXPERIENCE

The erosion of the authority of the church and of the Bible, together with the collapse of natural theology, constituted a massive crisis for western Christianity. But some remained unmoved because they were convinced that the faith was built on the reality of an experience of God, and that this reality could be uncovered and used to rebuild true religion. The eighteenth century was not just the age of Voltaire and Hume; it was also the time of Wesley, Whitefield and von Zinzendorf, of pietism and evangelicalism. The Enlightenment was succeeded by the move to Romanticism. It is no accident that both the great philosopher Immanuel Kant and the great theologian Friedrich Schleiermacher were indebted to pietism, and no accident that the philosophy of the one and the theology of the other contained profound analyses of the experience of being human. Both were characterized by a turning inward. For Schleiermacher, if the revelation of God was not available without, perhaps the experience of absolute dependence could be pressed into service as a source and measure of religious doctrine.

The reality on which religion could be built was accessed through religious experience. Other possible means to the knowledge of God were unsatisfactory, even if they could be rehabilitated. Natural theology, scriptural authority, the church and its tradition – none of these did justice to the passionate response aroused by real religion. They would, of course, still have an important role. But such authorities suited a religion that was transmitted down through the years and that found expression in a social organism: they hardly fitted the immediacy of contact with God to which the Bible itself was witness. Indeed, although the Bible and the church spoke about the Holy Spirit, ordinary believers seemed like the disciples at Ephesus, who had to confess, 'No, we have not even heard that there is a Holy Spirit' (Acts 19:2). The reality of religious experience looked set to make up for the loss of authority suffered by the Christian faith, and to speak persuasively about God to the unbelieving world.

In short, there was a move from what George Lindbeck has called the 'cognitively propositional' in revelation, to what he calls the 'experiential-expressive'.[1] In his judgment, 'thinkers of this tradition all locate ultimately significant contact with whatever is finally important to religion in the pre-reflective experiential depths of the self and regard the public or outer features of religion as expressive and evocative objectifications (i.e., non-discursive symbols) of internal experience. For nearly two hundred years this tradition has provided intellectually brilliant and empirically impressive accounts of the religious life that have been compatible with – indeed, often at the heart of – the romantic, idealistic, and phenomenological-existentialist streams of thought that have dominated the humanistic side of Western culture ever since Kant's revolutionary "turn to the subject".'

William James devoted his 1901–02 Gifford lectures to the theme of religious experience, and in so doing produced a classic account, *The Varieties of Religious Experience*, which formed the starting-point for many discussions of its subject. Rather than focusing on a general consciousness of God, it analysed events of revelation and experience, such as conversion. In the early twentieth century Rudolph Otto's seminal study, *The Idea of the Holy* (1917), likewise exerted a great influence, with its description of the encounter with the divine that awed and yet fascinated. Likewise, since the nineteenth century popular evangelicalism has emphasized emotion, conversion and the 'second blessing' that tended to give experience a priority that it had lacked in Reformed theology.

It is true that after the First World War, the whole approach to revelation through experience was diminished by the neo-orthodox dismissal of religion on the one hand and the empiricism of much Anglo-Saxon theology on the other. But the times have changed. Barth's views are no longer dominant in theology, and the anti-foundationalist mood in philosophy has reduced the expectation that either rationalism or empiricism must rule in epistemology.[2] As a result, philosophy especially has seen a significant return to the study of religious experience and its inclusion in arguments for the existence of God and the truth of Christianity. Major recent works include those of Swinburne, Alston, Yandell and Davis.[3] On the whole, at the philosophical level, the contention is not that religious experience can validate belief in God, but that it is part of a cumulative argument that can justifiably do so.

Lindbeck has observed with some justice that the experiential and the cognitional accounts are different, and that from them arise diverse expectations of the nature and content of Christian doctrine. Indeed, the experiential account is often regarded as that which enables Christian faith to continue in its essence while dispensing with unfortunate relics such as the infallibility of Scripture. The approach I have adopted, through the gospel and the Scriptures, would fit better into the 'cognitional' tradition as he describes it. Yet both Scripture and the gospel support the view that human life yields much in the way of religious experience. Indeed, it is no accident that the evangelical movement of the eighteenth century, like its Puritan forerunner, had a famous interest in the whole matter.[4] These movements, while being 'cognitional' in that they appealed to Scripture as the source for the knowledge of God, insisted that formalism in religion was deadly and that genuine religious experience was vital for spiritual health. It seems that the relationship between an approach based on the gospel and one based on experience is not as simple as Lindbeck's taxonomy may suggest.

Religious experience may feed the soul, guide the mind or lift the spirit to ecstasy. It may also help answer the question whether there are revelations from God, and, if so, of what they consist. I have argued that the gospel is the proper starting-point for the

121

knowledge of God, and that this approach entails a recognition that the Scriptures are the word of God. I have also argued, however, that there are axioms or 'boundaries' to do with grace, sin, Christ's uniqueness and the human reception of revelation. The gospel has a key role to play in assessing claims to religious experience. It does not deny such claims automatically, as a secular thinker may do: it does not accept them automatically, as a religious thinker may do; indeed, it is itself the source of religious experience as well as a measure of their significance. This chapter examines the possibility and interpretation of religious experience in the light of the gospel.

The possibility of religious experience

The preceding chapter briefly described the nature of experience. The emphasis fell on a species of apprehension of an event that involved the whole person and gained a unique authority for the individual. It is possible, of course, to have a corporate experience, religious or otherwise, or to have an individual experience in a large crowd. In the end, an experience creates its own authority in the memories of those who have taken part in it. Religious experience differs only in being centred on matters of the spirit. Both descriptions are somewhat vague, since the words 'religion' and 'experience' are notoriously hard to pin down. It is commonly thought that religious experience may well include such events as prayer, guidance, visions, prophecy, glossolalia, meditation, mysticism, worship, conversion, miracles and a heightened consciousness of God, as well as an innate sense of the presence of God. But this is not an exhaustive list. In Islam it may also include political activity, since there is no distinction between sacred and secular.[5]

Four elements of religious experience indicate that those interested in revelation and the knowledge of God should investigate specific claims to such experience seriously.

The authority of experience

First, there is the personal authority that such claims engender. It is all very well for the philosopher to think about the existence of God and to come to a view, positive or negative, as a result of argument. The arguments may be sound or otherwise, but they are like those once employed to discuss whether a black swan was possible. The dispute was instantly put to rest, no matter how persuasively the opposing case had been argued, when the first black swan was observed. In short, the argument from experience, even in religion, has all the force of an empirical position.

Or, almost. The thing about God, of course, is that he is immaterial and therefore not open to experiment as swans are. Nevertheless, the personal authority evoked by such an experience cannot easily be gainsaid. It transmutes into a testimony, a witness to the truth. To deny what is said is to question the integrity of one who is often self-evidently sincere. In this connection Swinburne robustly calls on a 'principle of testimony' in the face of unwarranted scepticism.' There is a reality in experience that so often contrasts with the unreality of official religion and of having no religion at all. When experience speaks, church and even Scripture must be still: 'Come, see a man who told me everything I ever did' (John 4:29). Unlike formal religion and academic religion, it is by very nature relational, treating the knowledge of God as an entrance into friendship rather than as a puzzle. In this respect it is closer to the truth revealed by the gospel than is much official religion.

Furthermore, although God is immaterial and not open to empirical experiment, religious experience has an identifying mark that makes its recipients certain that they are in touch with the divine. The reason such experience is judged to come from God is that it is very strange. The 'God' aspect of an experience lies in its unexpected, non-human, non-natural force. It is otherwise inexplicable; when all other options are dismissed, the remaining one must be true, however disconcerting or unpalatable we may find it. The strangeness may lie in the timing, power, rightness, or numinous sensation that accompanies it. It is this 'godness' or 'divinity' of the experience that helps to constitute its revelatory power.

Dr W. R. Matthews, former Dean of St Paul's Cathedral, London, a philosopher of religion, and (to use his own term) a 'modernist' in theology, could hardly be accused of being either fey or fundamentalist. He recounts such an experience from his early life. He had been struggling with the intellectual side of the Christian faith and endeavouring to be more settled and clear in his beliefs. He writes:

I now come to an incident which I regard as a kind of divine guidance and which changed the course of my existence ... The experience, as it were, stands out from the normal and commonplace as though it had a timeless existence. I may add here that I am quite sure that it was not a dream, and when I come to tell it there seems almost nothing to tell. Though I do not know the date, I remember the day very well. It was a summer day when the sun flooded even Bishopsgate with glory. I had been in the London office of the Swiss Banking Corporation on some routine business and, as I came down the steps at the entrance into the full light of the sun, I suddenly felt that the sun was in me. That is how I describe the experience, but of course it is a most inadequate metaphor. I was taken hold of by a power, or Spirit, which filled me with joy and peace and courage. My doubts about God were transcended. When I read C. S. Lewis's book *Surprised by Joy*, I recognized the nature of the experience. There is, however, apparently a difference. His revelation was a supernatural assurance of the Incarnation of the Son of God, mine was a supernatural assurance of the reality of the Creator God who is love. Exultant happiness carried me away. I knew and felt that God was real and that I was a child of God.[7]

Matthews' account contains the note of authority that flows from such an encounter as far as the recipient is concerned. In his case it was a matter of assurance, both intellectual (concerning the reality of God), and affective (concerning his own standing before God). He knew and he felt; his feeling was part of his knowing, for this was indeed an experience. It enabled him to be both certain at the centre of his being and critical in his attitude to Scripture. It was of God, he is careful to tell us, for it was not to be explained by so ordinary a thing as a dream. His routine business at the bank contrasts with something that 'stands out from the normal and commonplace'; nothing is more ordinary than the sun, nothing more extraordinary than for the sun to be in you.

The accessibility of experience

The second feature of religious experience is that it is accessible. This seems very odd. If the essence of such experiences is their strangeness, they cannot by definition be commonplace. Furthermore, when religious experience of the highest grade is discussed it is clear that extraordinary spiritual attainments are granted to no ordinary souls. The mystic path is taken by few, and those who report the unitive experience that is the goal of so much mysticism are fewer still. The guru or holy man or woman is by definition a rare person. Yet the rarity of religious experience is not measured by the paucity of those who lay claim to them; it is also to be thought of as a relatively rare event in the life of many people or groups of people. Thus, although Olympian experiences may be the province of a few, simpler experiences may be accessible to the many. One result of the study of religious experiences conducted by the Hardy Institute in Oxford was to record a surprisingly high number of such events in people's lives, whether they were churchgoers or not.[8]

There are religious experiences that may be 'taught', or at least sought along well-established and relatively simple paths, and that are accessible to virtually any who will seek. The spiritual exercises of Ignatius Loyola take the seeker who is prepared for discipline into religious experience that affirms faith and changes lives. The baptism of the Spirit offered in Pentecostal assemblies introduces those who receive it to the strange world of glossolalia. These experiences do not need to become routine in order to be democratic. Their availability to all does not constitute proof that they cannot be from God. The fact that we may duplicate them in the lives of the many does not pass judgment on their power for the one. Nevertheless, it is fair to add that the experience that comes unsought, that occurs infrequently and that has significant intrinsic importance for a wide group of people is more likely to convince people other than the recipients that there is a divine order and that a genuine revelation has occurred. However, the sheer bulk of claims to religious experience is impressive. Many people in the Christian religion, and many others all over the world, claim to have had, and to continue to have, communion with the supernatural. What are we to make of revelation allegedly emanating from such sources?

Frequency in Scripture

The third reason we should take religious experiences seriously as a potential source of revelation is their relatively frequent appearance in the Bible. Those who wish to call the Bible the revelation of God cannot do so at the expense of the revelatory events contained in the experiences both recorded and promised in the Bible. One of the ways the Bible persuades us of the reality of God is by recording events in the lives of its heroes in which they encounter God. Dreams, prophecies, visions, miracles, answers to prayer, leadings of the Spirit, speaking in tongues – these and many more episodes are related. Furthermore, the early church may with some justice be regarded as a charismatic community, having the reality and the promise of the gifts of the Spirit in its midst. In his account of Christian prophecy Paul even speaks of the moment when a revelation may be given (1 Cor. 14:30).

The 'ecumenical' nature of religious experience

The fourth attractive and interesting feature about claims to religious experience is what may be called (for want of a better term) their 'ecumenical' nature. It is true that such experiences usually take on the hue of the tradition or the religion most familiar to the recipient. This applies to post-death experiences, speaking in tongues and having visions. But there is also a uniting factor at work, in which the experiences transcend the denominational and religious boundaries and bring participants together. (Sometimes, however, they sharply divide, as when the same experience is regarded as divine by some and as demonic by others.) It is often suggested that the experiences are diverse in their results but united in object, all being encounters with the one divinity. The fact of such experiences is an important bridge for the comparative study of religions and their mutual respect. The doctrinal affirmations that emerge may be contradictory, but the different participants all over the world may be in touch with the same reality.[9] As George Lindbeck notes, the 'experiential-expressive' dimension of religion 'interprets doctrines as non-informative and non-discursive symbols of inner feelings, attitudes, or existential orientations'.[10] In these circumstances it can be much easier to relate to others from different faith communities.

Indeed, at the popular level (as opposed to the sophisticated and intellectual constructs of religion) there is evidence that religious practices and basic beliefs have certain similarities the world over. There is a sort of 'folk religion' in which experience counts for much and doctrine for little. It is said that doctrine divides but experience unites. Yet much depends, of course, on the doctrinal understanding of the participants and on the importance given to such matters as doctrine and hierarchical power *vis-à-vis* the significant experience. In the history of the Irvingites, the same experiences were believed to be in part divine and in part satanic.[11]

Nevertheless, the popularizers of religious experience evangelise for that experience through anecdotes, testimonies and bearing witness. If others, even from different religions, bear the same witness, there is always the option of concluding that their story also is true. Since the reality of the divine and the revelation of the supernatural are being testified to, we have what may be thought of as firsthand evidence of a transcendent realm with which we may commune in some way; that God is real and that revelation exists. We do not have to demand that the revelation that comes in these circumstances be complete or even infallible. The fact that it is coloured by cultural factors suggests that it owes something to the human instrument through whom it comes. But the universal nature of such experiences, testified to in all parts of the world, in all the religions and denominations, makes a case for revelation that needs to be taken seriously.

Denying religious experience

The reports of the widespread incidence of religious experience in the western world have taken some secular observers by surprise. It had been assumed that the declining numbers of church attenders demonstrated the decline of religion at all levels. But this may not be the case at all.[12] The keen interest in eastern religious techniques and in New Age religion suggests that there is still a felt need for religion, even though the Christian religion in its formal setting may not meet that need. The problem is that the church is communal; it is also institutional and, in some areas of the world, part of the state; it frequently tends to be exclusive. Current social trends emphasize the individual and the personal;

and religions that do not demand group participation, but offer simple techniques with beneficial personal results, may well be more attractive. Nevertheless, the incidence of religious experience has not led to a wholesale return to belief in the supernatural (let alone Christianity). This is for several reasons.

Dismissing claims for religious experience

The initial response to anecdotal evidence about the supernatural among intellectual opinion leaders in the West is almost always one of suspicion. In the post-Enlightenment world, any such claim is regarded as untrue until proven true, and the standards of proof are set imposingly high. Claims for religious experience are regarded as tantamount to claims for miracles, and so the Humean cautions come into play. It is virtually basic to the intellectual culture to believe that reason has been pitted against faith, science against religion, to religion's very evident discomfiture. In the same way, the place of theology as such in universities has been severely questioned, especially when dogmatic theology is in view. 'Cognitive' theology has been refuted; 'expressive' theology is below reason. Theology is likened to astrology, as an outmoded system of belief. To refer to one highly influential example of those who have formed the mind of the modern world: when Sigmund Freud undertook his vastly influential study of the human mind, he did so, according to Edward Shafranske, in conscious opposition to religion. 'His motivation went beyond the heuristic to the political; he aimed at generating a paradigm shift ... in which science would usurp the authority of religion in the culture.'[13] Not surprisingly, he gave a thoroughly naturalistic account of religious experience.

There is a tendency, therefore, to dismiss all claims to religious experience *a priori*, in the same way that claims to have contact with extraterrestrial beings are dismissed. Virtually no evidence would be sufficient to support so inherently implausible an initial assertion. Furthermore, as with flying saucers, there is enough negative evidence and counter-explanation to make the denial an apparently sensible option. Claims to do with occult events, ghosts, spirits, healings, the paranormal, magic, ESP and the like have been accompanied by so many fraudulent and even deadly activities (e.g. the Jonestown disaster) that they cast doubt over all claims to do with the supernatural. Moreover, the converse of the certainty that attends personal experience is the propensity to self-deception. The tradition of religious experience is filled with tales as bizarre as they are ridiculous, as trivial as they are self-serving. Many of them bring no honour to the name of the god with whom they are associated. Finally, the claims based on experience are contradictory; they support mutually exclusive and antagonistic systems, and cannot be taken as evidence of the God of truth.

Even when the frequency of claims to religious experience, and the intelligence and integrity of some of those making the claims, are noted, therefore, the tendency is to offer an alternative, reductionist explanation. Most often, of course, a psychological explanation is given, suggesting hypnosis, or adolescent turmoil, or pathological states; but social and cultural expectation is an alternative rationalization that may be offered. Thus the fact that demonic possession is experienced in certain cultures but absent in others is held to make the phenomenon unlikely ever to be genuine. Or, to take another approach, the very strangeness that, in the mind of the recipient, has marked out the experience as supernatural, may be taken as evidence simply of ignorance or inexperience. Thus, for example, speaking in tongues, which is so significant to the person practising it, may be much less so to those who know that it is paralleled in other religions and among people who profess no religion at all. Likewise, it may be argued that some human experiences that are very rare but natural, such as pre-vision, have no supernatural connotations whatever.

A riposte to scepticism

Dr Caroline Franks Davis, in her book *The Evidential Force of Religious Experience*,[14] has subjected some of these suggestions, especially the psychological ones, to a searching critique. Without doubt there is evidence that experiences of a religious kind may follow the use of certain drugs. Without doubt, also, there is a correlation between certain sorts of experience and such factors as one's personality traits, stage in life and inner circumstances. Thus, it is not altogether surprising to find W. R. Matthews, as an intellectual and sensitive adolescent, having what amounted to a conversion experience, especially as he gives evidence of some preceding tension in his life at that time. But

there is important counter-evidence as well. There is no indica-
tion, for example, that many of those reporting such experiences
are mentally unbalanced or unstable. Indeed, they tend to be
psychologically healthy. There may be a statistical norm relating
to teenage conversions, but many do not fit this pattern at all. But
the main problem with the explanations is that they are reductionist; they do not in fact 'explain'. To trace the origin of an
experience is not to discredit it as a means of revelation to those
concerned. Likewise, to complain that the experiences are so rare
that it is better to accept a naturalistic explanation is to load the
dice; the very point of such experiences is their relative rareness.

In short, the secular critique of religious experience, true
though many of its observations are, still fails to account for this
kind of experience in such a way as to render impossible any
appeal to it as a revelation of God. In trying to prove a negative –
that there is no authentic instance of religious experience – it has
gone too far, and demonstrated an unfortunate prejudice in its
approach. Furthermore, it offers no help at all to those who claim
to have had a religious experience and need an interpretation of
what they have received. The secular mentality is thoroughly
irresponsible and doctrinaire, and one of its consequences is that
opportunity for the superstition it fears is in fact increased.

Indeed, it appears that a new intellectual climate is slowly
emerging in which claims to religious knowledge through experience will be accorded more respect. This is reflected both in
the philosophical works referred to above, and in the way that the
fierceness of the empirically driven attack on theology is being
moderated and a more tolerant mood is emerging. It can be seen
too in the historical study of the phenomenon of witchcraft, where
a dismissive rationalism has given way to a more thoughtful and
understanding approach emanating from social anthropology.[14]
But the mood of tolerance towards all entails a new intellectual
and social danger: not the unfounded rejection of all religious
experience, but the undiscriminating acceptance of it all. The
gospel, as the revelation of God, addresses both these problems: it
does not endorse all experience, but certainly endorses the concept that religious experience represents. The gospel remains of
pivotal importance.

It is therefore to the scriptural presentation of the gospel that
we now turn. Once again we note the four parameters that guide

130

the discussion: the grace of God, the sinfulness of humankind, the uniqueness of Christ and the 'humanity' of revelation. These principles emerge from the gospel itself; to deny them is to return beyond the point at which the truth of the gospel was accepted. Using them enables us to bring the biblical gospel into fruitful contact with religious experience.

The gospel and religious experience

The interpretative primacy of the gospel

The Bible describes many religious experiences; it even encourages religious experience. There is evidence that it assumes an innate knowledge of God (see chapter 5 above). But, in the Bible, experience is secondary to the word of God. Only so can the grace of the gospel be established. Experience is shaped and tested by the word, not the reverse. This is the key point: the priority of God's word must be maintained. The word enables us to discriminate between experiences, and to encourage those that are for our good and the glory of God, since not all experience is good or comes from a good source.

This is one of the great lessons of the Old Testament. The religion of Israel contained much powerful ritual, given by God himself. And yet he warned his people through the prophets about the danger of confusing the experience of God in such religion with the truth: 'For I desire mercy, not sacrifice, and acknowledgment of God rather than burnt offerings' (Hos. 6:6). Even the prophet who could do signs and wonders was to be eschewed if he then taught contrary to the word of God: 'you must not listen to words of that prophet or dreamer' (Deut. 13:1–3). In the same way, Jesus spoke directly to those whose ministry included signs of power and might that may have been regarded as authenticating them in the sight of God and humankind: 'Not everyone who says to me, "Lord, Lord," will enter the kingdom of heaven, but only he who does the will of my Father who is in heaven. Many will say to me on that day, "Lord, Lord, did we not prophesy in your name, and in your name drive out demons and perform many miracles?" Then I will tell them plainly, "I never knew you. Away from me, you evildoers!"' (Matt. 7:21–23). It is noteworthy that the guilty parties are not simply those who have received spiritual experiences, but those who have administered them, lest there be any doubt about the relative significance of experiences as such.

We find exactly the same priority in two important passages in Luke's Gospel. In the first, there is no doubt that the disciples' great experiences are approved: "'Lord, even the demons are subject to us in your name!' He replied, "I saw Satan fall like lightning from heaven. I have given you authority to trample on snakes and scorpions and to overcome all the power of the enemy; nothing will harm you. However, do not rejoice that the spirits submit to you, but rejoice that your names are written in heaven"' (Luke 10:17–20).

In this saying, Jesus puts his emphasis not on the mighty works but upon the salvation of the disciples. Their focus is to be fixed on the heavenly book, not on the earthly experience, presumably because the experience can be so misleading. We have already noted that one of the key features of experience is its authority in the life of the individual. It is notoriously difficult to gainsay a person's own experience as understood by that person. Jesus challenges experience in the name of reality.

The same point is at issue in the parable of the rich man and Lazarus (Luke 16:19–31). The passionate request of the rich man for the miracle of a resurrection, which he suggests will warn his brothers of what lay in store for them, is denied in favour of the word of God: 'If they do not listen to Moses and the prophets, neither will they be convinced even if someone rises from the dead' (16:31).

The priority of word over experience is evident in Pauline theology. It was, after all, his direct experience that those to whom he preached the gospel wanted wisdom on the one side and signs on the other. He was not unfamiliar with the power of God in miracles (Gal. 3:5), or with the wisdom of the Greeks (Acts 17:28), but he memorably contrasted such things (and even baptism) with the gospel. 'Jews demand miraculous signs and Greeks look for wisdom, but we preach Christ crucified: a stumbling-block to Jews and foolishness to Gentiles' (1 Cor. 1:22–23). The gospel of grace was to be the measure of all experience, spiritual or intellectual; not experience the measure of the gospel (1 Cor. 12:1–2; cf. Gal. 1:8). The same point is integral to another part of 1 Corinthians, where once again Paul was dealing at close quarters with religious experience in the form of gifts such as glossolalia and prophecy. Although it is clear that he himself was involved in the exercise of the gifts, and could thus speak with great authority to those who were also involved, and although he identified the exercise of prophecy as being based on revelation (14:30), he put all these manifestations very firmly under the control of the existing, 'public' word of God: 'If anybody thinks he is a prophet or spiritually gifted, let him acknowledge that what I am writing to you is the Lord's command. If he ignores this, he himself will be ignored' (14:37–38).

It is worth emphasizing that Paul was no stranger to spiritual exaltation. His strictures did not arise from ignorance or jealousy. In a remarkable passage in 2 Corinthians, he reveals that he had been the subject of a spiritual experience that involved being in paradise and hearing 'inexpressible things, things that man is not permitted to tell' (12:4). It is manifest, however, that he mentions this experience only with great reluctance and in a way that draws attention to Christ rather than to himself (12:9). He is also aware that there are religious experiences, in the form of miracles, that are inspired by demonic forces and have the power to deceive (2 Thess. 1:9–10). In fact, Paul did not attribute to the religions of his day the power to bring people to a saving knowledge of God; to him idolatry was the worship of demons (1 Cor. 10:20). Thus, in common with Jesus and the Old Testament, Paul firmly subordinated religious experiences, and indeed all religion, to the word of God that centred on Christ.

Given the role assigned to Scripture by the Reformers in the sixteenth century, it is not surprising that a clash of priorities should have been evident at the time. The medieval church placed no theological barrier in the way of miracles done in the name of Christ and the saints, at least as a possibility. There was also an awareness of false claims and demonic activity. However, Reformation thinkers such as Calvin did not meet fire with fire. They accepted the possibility of demonic signs and wonders, but repudiated the idea that God was active in the miraculous in the contemporary world. There was, of course, no doubt about the biblical miracles, or about the capacity of God to work miracles now, should he choose to do so. But, through observing the revelatory function of the miracles of the Bible, and especially of the New Testament, the Reformed theologians came to the view that miracles had ceased.[15]

In so doing, they did not banish God from his world. Their doctrine of God's sovereignty was too powerful for that. Calvin and his followers were aware of God's active power in the world. God answered prayer; God arranged even the details of everyday life; God brought healing from sickness; God superintended extraordinary events. But all this fell short of the miraculous, and it is better to characterize this activity as 'providential' rather than supernatural. They did not completely deny the possibility of supernatural interference in the world; but such interventions, even if apparently directed to a good end in human eyes, were demonic. The believer was encouraged not to seek the miraculous interventions of God or of the saints, but to live under God's providential hand. Certainly no spiritual relationships were to be entered into except the fundamental relationship with God himself. In this way, the creation came very clearly into one sphere of influence, and any other apparent wonders belonged to evil. The doctrine may be reminiscent of Stoicism, as some have thought; although it is well to remember that Stoicism was essentially pantheistic. But what made the decisive difference was the gospel. The experiences of life, for good or for ill, were all to be interpreted through the gospel, which taught with great power that God was not merely sovereign but also Father. In other words, the Reformation teaching potently asserted the priority of the gospel over experience. But, unlike secularism, it did not deny the reality of experience. Instead, it reinterpreted it in a highly significant way. The decline of magical explanations of reality owes a great deal to this application of biblical teaching in the theology of nature. But two items from the seventeenth century warn us that such a theology of nature may develop in a less satisfactory way.

First, Oliver Cromwell's schoolmaster, Thomas Beard, wrote a popular religious book called *The Theatre of God's Judgements* (1597), in which he brought together anecdote after anecdote to illustrate the workings of God's providence in the world. He had a sharp eye for stories that revealed how God had blessed the good and cursed those who disobeyed him by committing such crimes as Sabbath-breaking and Catholicism. But what may have begun as an attempt to interpret history through the eyes of the gospel soon came to see history as an independent expression of the mind of God. In short, history as interpreted by Beard became the locus of revelation, a view also found in his pupil. For Cromwell was given to interpreting events and to drawing from them conclusions about the mind of God in such a way as to set another source of revelation along-side Scripture.

The second illustration appears to come from the other end of the religious spectrum, but it arrives at a similar result as far as the Bible is concerned. John Locke took the Protestant refusal to allow for miracles to what many would regard as its logical conclusion. In criticizing the standard Protestant position, he declared that the special illuminating work of the Spirit in conversion amounted to a miracle, and therefore the account of it in Protestant thinking could not be correct. He reduced the matter of becoming a Christian to an entirely natural phenomenon, a view that fitted well with Pelagianism and, of course, with deism. In this way the Protestant emphasis on the sovereignty of God was made to fit the Newtonian mechanistic universe that was becoming the standard account. This took place at the expense of the Bible's teaching about the grace of God and the work of the Spirit. Both developments will receive closer review in due course (see chapters 10 and 11 below).[16]

Scepticism unwisely denies the significance and even the possibility of all religious experience. But likewise there is a widespread religious credulity or superstition that reinforces scepticism. I have noted already the discrimination exercised by the Reformers on biblical grounds. They neither denied nor endorsed all religious experience, and their wisdom in this area contributed to the fruitful new attitude to the theology of nature referred to at the end of the last chapter. As well as emphasizing the priority of God's word, they proclaimed the sovereignty of God, which we now explore.

God's sovereignty and religious experience

It has already been observed that the Bible is replete with material that counts as religious experience. Some of its stories have, of course, achieved the status of classics: Moses at the burning bush, Elijah at Mount Carmel, Isaiah in the temple, the disciples at the transfiguration come instantly to mind. But there are many other instances of miracles, answers to prayer, dreams and visions, prophecy and encounters with heavenly beings and with God. The life of God and the life of the people of the Bible seem to have intersected at many points, and there is no doubt that Scripture depicts a God who is near at hand, powerful and interventionist. At the same time, however, it is worth observing that the Bible contains much else besides stories of religious experiences. Indeed, it is not a handbook of such events, written to introduce us to the concept and the techniques, but a book that tells the story of salvation, with the people of God as its human focus. The miracles of the Bible are not spread indiscriminately throughout its pages, but cluster around certain important events.

Moreover, its instances of religious experience tend to be intentionally revelatory in nature. Certainly they produce other effects as well; the enemies of the people are defeated, the sickness is cured, the prayer is answered; but in case after case, even when healings are involved, the chief end in view is that people will be drawn to God, his ways and his word. This is true, for example, of Moses, Elijah, Isaiah and the disciples, mentioned already. It is true of the healing ministry of Jesus, which certainly involved compassion, but was intended above all to show that he was the one who fulfilled the hope of Israel.

The Bible also shows us that sceptical interpretations of religious experience are beside the point. Reductionist critics often seem to assume that the Christian view of God and the world is deistic; that God allows the world to run on mechanically, interrupting only when he sees the need to do so. The biblical view is of a sovereign Lord, who is 'sustaining all things by his powerful word' (Heb. 1:3). Nothing, no matter how small, occurs without him. When we speak of the strangeness of a miracle or of a religious experience, then, the strangeness is not because God has involved himself where he has not done so before. Nor is it necessarily the case that God has used a new and unknown method. Some of the works of God may for ever be beyond our comprehension at any level; but just as in the ordinary course of events he uses the creation to accomplish his ends, sending rain from the clouds and warmth from the sun, so, even in the events we call religious experiences, we may often be able to trace his ways and see what it is he has used to accomplish his ends. The surprising element may be its timing, or the fact that something happened at

136

all. An experience of this nature cannot be 'reduced' to its constituent parts and then dismissed.

These points may be illustrated, for example, in conversion. Those who have been converted will certainly regard it as a religious experience and attribute its final agency to God. A deeper theological understanding may attribute it all to God's grace, exercised through his choice and his call. In no way, however, does this mean that we cannot see the human elements in this transaction and understand how they have operated to achieve the result. Do most conversions occur in adolescence? God has arranged it so, given the openness of the adolescent, and given that it is an appropriate time for large decisions about marriage, jobs and other commitments to be made. Since God has appointed the preaching of the gospel as the chief means of conversion, and has committed this work to human beings, we must see that using the full efforts of his servants, and the response mechanisms of those who hear and respond, is not at all inconsistent with his rule over the world. The moment of conversion is open to the analysis of the psychologist, and will yield interesting observations. But neither the psychologist nor the convert will ever be able to discover a specific 'God element' in the occurrence, since it is the whole person and the whole experience that come under God's controlling hand.

Consideration of God's sovereignty enables us to adopt a discriminating account of religious experience in general. On the one hand, we do not have to follow those who, because of their naturalistic philosophy, dismiss all claims to such experiences as either fraudulent or misinterpreted. On the contrary, the Bible shows us that the world is filled with spiritual powers and that there is a real chance that human beings may be in touch with them. On the other hand, our theology of nature reveals that God habitually uses the created order itself in accordance with its own nature to accomplish his ends. There is an economy of method about God's work. Thus we may regard a particular occurrence as extraordinary, but it is not even necessarily the case that God has acted in an unusual way. It may simply be the timing that is extraordinary; or it may be the interpretation put on the event by the context in which it occurs that determines whether it is significant or not.

Recognizing these truths offers freedom in two directions.

First, we can be free from doubting the sincerity of those who tell us about their religious experiences. While fraud and self-deception remain common, they do not fully explain all that happens. The secularist position is required to prove a negative, which is impossible; and to dismiss widespread and serious human testimony, which is implausible. Secondly, however, we can be free from credulously accepting all strange events as miraculous. There are more strange events than the cynics will allow; but these events are more 'natural' than the believers will accept. There is no need, for example, to regard pre-vision as impossible. God can certainly grant a dream predicting some future event if he should so wish. But we do not have to conclude that every case of pre-vision is a special revelation of God simply because it is so unusual an event. There is some evidence to suggest that such phenomena occur in both religious and non-religious contexts. The important point is not that such an experience may occur; in one sense it is 'natural', not 'supernatural' (to use an unhelpful term). The question is whether the event has any significance in God's scheme of things. To answer that, we must again turn to the Bible and the gospel.

The significance of experience

If we give religious experience the priority the gospel gives it, we neither deny its reality nor accept it without discrimination. What more can be said about it, however? Three points may be made.

Experience of God is indispensable

First, in the gospel way of thinking, experience is indispensable. To say that the gospel has priority is one thing; to say that we do not need experience is another. For the gospel itself brings experience of peace with God. From the gospel we learn about repentance and faith; we learn to love God and to serve him; we learn about prayer and trust in his promises. The book of Psalms, for example, is a priceless store of the experiences of the people of God, and invites us to share those experiences at first hand. It is the lack of the firsthand experience of God that is so deadening and damning in our churches. Unconverted 'Christians' constitute one of the biggest barriers to the work of God. Unconverted pastors drive the true knowledge of God from the church. When

138

the people of God cannot bear witness to God's help in their lives, there is cause to question the reality of their grasp of the gospel. All Christian people can tell of the faithfulness and nearness of God, unless they lack perceptiveness trained by the Scriptures, and memory of what God has done.

One illustration of this point comes from the Christian experience of assurance. To be sure of God's forgiveness and acceptance is one of the great blessings of the gospel. Its fundamental ground is always necessarily the work God did for us in reconciling the world to himself in Christ Jesus, which was promised to us in the gospel and sealed in our hearts by the Holy Spirit. In times of doubt and anxiety it is to the gospel that we turn; when we rightly doubt our own righteousness there is nowhere else to go. But that is not the whole picture. According to 1 John, for example, we can and should examine our own lives and experience to see if they confirm the work of God within us, and hence to be reassured that his work for us is not in vain. 'We know that we have passed from death to life, because we love our brothers' (1 John 3:14). 1 John was written to address the decay of true teaching, and the result of such decay is moral turpitude as well as doctrinal error.

Experience is a necessary concomitant of the gospel, but it comes in different ways. To say that all need to be converted is to affirm no more than that repentance and faith are necessary to apprehending Christ. But the manner and timing of conversion may well differ widely from person to person, and we ought not to lay down any rules as to the circumstances in which faith and repentance become a reality for people. For some, conversion may be connected with the sacraments of the gospel; others may have no memory of not being repentant towards God; others who have resisted the gospel for many years experience a deathbed conversion; others may have served other gods. All these patterns and more are possible, since human experience is so variable. Indeed, that is why we cannot use experience itself as the source and measure of the truth. The truth must determine experience, though experience may illumine and support the truth. (There is a further discussion of these matters in chapter 11 below.)

General revelation includes experiences of God

Secondly, however, we do not have to conclude that the only

genuine experience of God is linked to the explicit gospel. If we accept the view outlined in the previous chapter, that there is a general revelation of God from which certain truths ought to be drawn, there is no need to limit the revelation to the natural world as such. Saul was able to raise Samuel through the medium at Endor (1 Sam. 16); Balaam was confronted with an angel on his way to curse Israel (Num. 22:21ff.); Caiaphas prophesied without knowing that he had a revelation (John 11:49–53); Cornelius had a vision that led to the preaching of the gospel and to his salvation (Acts 10:1–8). God is sovereign, and he providentially gives what and where he wills. In a real sense, he is his own evangelist, and testimonies abound of men and women coming to Christian faith triggered by unsought-for experiences, although delivered by the gospel. We need to add, of course, that according to the New Testament there are religious experiences that are not of God, in which human beings encounter the demonic world. This, too, is always a possibility in the realm of experience, and reminds us that we need the interpretation of the gospel in order to discriminate.

It ought not to surprise us, therefore, that there are so many reported instances of religious experience from all around the world. Nor should it surprise us that they so often contradict one another (for the sources of such experiences and the capacity of human beings to understand and to record them differs immensely), or that the details of these experiences often conform to the prevailing religious culture. We do not need to regard all such experiences as useless and wrong. However, the same conditions as those explained in the previous chapter apply: the gospel reveals human sinfulness. Just as the revelation of God through nature is distorted and twisted by those of us who receive it, so, too, is experience. The axioms of grace and of human sin continue to apply. On its own, experience may perhaps function as a 'signal of transcendence', to use the phrase of sociologist Peter Berger; but in that case we are certain to distort it so that it will not lead to salvation.

Two of the leading figures of artistic culture in the latter twentieth century, the art historian Sir Kenneth Clark and the novelist and Nobel Prize winner Patrick White, both report moments of such powerful religious experience that they could no longer doubt the existence of God.[17] But neither was finally a believer in the Christian sense, Clark frankly admitting that the moral cost would be too great. Likewise, a significant number of people have reported on their experience 'after' death; they have been conscious of having died and have been brought back to life again, perhaps in the operating theatre. From some of this group has come the reassuring message that there is nothing to fear in death or the afterlife; it has been the gateway to something like heaven.[18] If we assumed that genuine 'death' was involved in such an experience, Christians would be most unwise to abandon the priority of the gospel and claim that this experience proved the reality of heaven and the afterlife. The testimonies of those involved do not conform to the gospel, but offer spurious hope. Either the testimonies are true or the gospel is true; we cannot have both. This brings us to the third and final point of this discussion, namely the significance of Christ.

The uniqueness of Christ

I have already mentioned the 'ecumenical' nature of religious experience. Without doubt, if we concentrate on experience as the key source of our knowledge of God, it will lead to a position in which the religions of the world will be asked to contribute their riches to our understanding of revelation on almost equal terms. But I have argued instead that priority must be given to the gospel as the interpretative grid for all experience. Although such a remark applies as much to claims made by Christians as to those made by others, it nevertheless places the gospel in an entirely privileged position. This is the axiom of uniqueness. There can be no doubt, furthermore, that this privileged position depends in the final analysis on our Christology. Christians have had different views of the value of general revelation in whatever form, and hence of the religions of the world; but they have with virtually one accord given Christianity a unique status based on their commitment to Jesus Christ as the one and only Son of God, and hence the bearer of a singular revelation.

It is true that this privileged position has been eroded in recent years, especially in the post-Barthian era. There has been a revolution in the thinking of the Roman Catholic Church since Vatican II, where positive and authoritative remarks about other religions began to be made. Considerable thought has been given to the relationship between the church and the salvation of the world, and the meaning of the phrase 'No salvation outside the church' has been reassessed. In both Protestant and Catholic theology there is a far readier acceptance of the view that the peoples of the world will be saved through the religions of the world, and that each of the major religions partially reveals the truth about God. John Hick represents this position with great boldness within the Protestant tradition.[19] It is worth noting, however, that In doing so he has had to repudiate important elements of the New Testament teaching about Christ.

It is possible, of course, to undertake a detailed analysis of the teaching of the religions based on their revelations. Keith Ward has done so for the major religions.[20] But determining what is the foundational point for discrimination remains the problem. The determination to make Christ that foundational point has three features to commend it.

First, it fits in with the Bible's own account of human religion (other than the one based on the covenant), which is uniformly negative as a means of salvation. What is lacking in more recent Christian responses is the frank recognition that the foundation documents of the Christian faith, forged in the heat of evangelistic mission, give no ground at all for compromise with other religions or for the belief that salvation may be found in any name other than that of Jesus Christ (Acts 4:12). On the contrary, the religions of the world are regarded as emerging from the inventiveness of the sinful human heart. In response to the protest that the biblical writers were unable to contrast their gospel with the great classic religions of the world, it is enough to say that the New Testament emerged from the conflict with just such a religion, namely Judaism, for which the writers had the highest regard as God-given, but which they now regarded as a way of condemnation rather than of life (2 Cor. 3:6; Heb. 8:13).

Secondly, it is important to note that the nature of Christianity, in which the appeal to the historical Christ plays so central a part, invites an assessment of the truth about him. The gospel may be accepted or rejected. Indeed, the western culture has been making that assessment in a particularly negative way in the last three centuries. Many people have deliberately chosen not to be Christian. In other words, it is perfectly clear that the largest of the world's religions may be judged for its truth or error, and that it is possible for its basic tenets to be proved wrong. Only from an unstable and untenable midway position can we accept the gospel but not its implications, or hold religion to be a matter of faith but not of truth. We must conclude from this that the sentimental view that all major religions are *a priori* valid is nonsense, and known to be nonsense by millions of people. We are not exempt from applying the test of truth to religious claims, whether based on experience or on revelation.

Thirdly, therefore, we are cast back on the need to assess the gospel in its own terms. We have to ask how it fits with the revelation of God in the Old Testament; how it fits with our experience, which the gospel corrects and of which it makes sense; and whether the witness to the resurrection is true. In all this, the vital question remains, what do we make of Christ? The answer to that must be the starting-point. Its implications must be accepted and acted upon. The huge and costly Christian missionary exercise can be justified only by the confession that Jesus Christ is Lord of all. The power of experience is such that it can change a life dramatically. It can rightly be persuasive and transforming. But its power must not then be turned on the gospel so as to change the gospel and the terms on which we come to know God. The gospel, and the experience that flows from the gospel, retain their priority, or we have nothing with which we may assess the validity of the experience.

Conclusion

My discussion of religious experience began with the observation that, since the Enlightenment, experiential Christianity has been widely favoured over cognitional Christianity. Must we really choose between them in this stark form? The answer arising from the nature of God's revelation must be no. It is the gospel of Jesus Christ that Christians have to offer an unbelieving world, and it is the gospel that is the power of God for salvation. But in accepting the gospel of Christ's lordship, we accept a revelation that in itself is both personal and propositional, that authenticates itself as it both captures the heart and informs the mind, and that sees in human experience the actuality of God's general revelation. It entails, too, an acceptance of the Bible as the word of God, and hence the Bible's assessment of general revelation and natural theology.

God does reveal himself in human experience, but it is only through his word that we may truly apprehend his revelation. The proper Christian strategy in the world therefore remains the proclamation of Jesus Christ as Lord. But this proclamation should be accompanied by its interpretation of the experience of being human in the world, including religious experience, in such a way as to enable those who hear it to see that God is sovereignly at work in their experience, summoning them to faith in Christ, and empowering them to live for God's glory in the world once they have come to faith in him. But this, when it happens, is a gift of God's grace through his word and Spirit.

7

THE AUTHORITY OF SCRIPTURE

With some reason, scepticism about authority is deeply ingrained in western culture. The authorities of church, state and the intellect have let us down badly enough. Some genuine progress has been made by overturning authority, by an irreverent attitude to convention, and by questioning whether what we are told is true. This interrogatory spirit is especially encouraged in western education. Those who have taught students from different cultures will quickly appreciate the truth of this. There are other major cultures that instil in the student such respect for authority that anything taught by the teacher is automatically believed. In family and business life, the elderly are accorded special honour, and their opinion is followed even if the younger person knows it to be wrong. In such cultures, the idea of questioning or being critical of teacher or textbook is rarely contemplated. While this attitude may be of great assistance in the good ordering of the classroom, most educators in the West judge it to be deleterious to real education.

Liberal western education aims to produce independence in the student. Individuals' maturity is assessed by their capacity to fulfil themselves independently of others and to take responsibility for themselves. Its ethical ideal may be summed up by the 'one very simple principle' at the heart of John Stuart Mill's conception of social liberty: 'that the sole end for which mankind are warranted, individually or collectively, in interfering with the liberty of action of any of their number, is self-protection. The only purpose for which power can be rightfully exercised over any member of a civilized community, against his will, is to prevent harm to others. His own good, either physical or moral, is not a sufficient warrant.'[1] Mill regarded this principle as 'entitled to govern absolutely the dealings of society with the individual', and concluded that 'Over himself, over his own body and mind, the individual is sovereign.'[2]

The attitudes that are valued are love of freedom, tolerance, questioning, experimentation and pragmatism. Some educators would argue that these are the very values needed in a democracy. We are aiming to produce not subjects but citizens, able to govern themselves and to resist the incursions of those, whether priests or politicians, who try to usurp power. Liberal education demands the free exchange of ideas, and is therefore antipathetic to any form of censorship. Furthermore, such a liberal education is especially appropriate for the scientific culture that is foundational to the prosperity of the western world. The boast of science is that it does not bow to authority or reputation. It was born in escaping from a culture in which it was thought that the past was always right, that the fathers had all the votes and that there was no need to disturb established opinions by experiment.

Its educational system is but one way in which our society reveals the value that it sets on freedom from outside constraint. Mill's principle has been taken to heart, and has found applications that would have astonished him. In particular, Mill's quest for truth has been overtaken by the widespread contemporary view that there is no attainable truth. Gertrude Himmelfarb has traced the progress of the seductive 'one very simple principle' into the paradoxes and contradictions of contemporary liberalism, observing that 'this particular principle is all the more appealing because it conforms to the image of the modern, liberated, autonomous, "authentic" individual'.[3] Likewise, the critical thinking of the educational system has important positive effects. But it has developed in a society where individualism is prized, and where there is a tendency to make the subjective life of the

146

individual the master and measure of truth. Two of the most influential thinkers of modern times, Marx and Freud, explicitly followed Feuerbach in his judgment that the idea of God was the creation of the human heart, that God is Man writ large. One of the slogans that has accompanied modern literary theory, 'the reader is the author', gives the individual the same privileged position with regard to 'the text'. (See chapter 9 for a further discussion of this point.)

It is not surprising, therefore, that the authority of the Bible is so severely challenged. It is the major 'text' in western history to speak of 'God'. Both concepts, God and the text, are prey to radical subjectivism. The text is now the servant of the autonomous reader; God is the result of our own projection. The charge is not merely that there are historical difficulties and inconsistencies in the Bible in the form in which it has come to us; as Gunton has pointed out, there is nothing new here. The problem is not merely the ethical criticisms that have been launched at it, for once again there is nothing new in this. Nor is it the clash between Darwin and Moses, for even conservative scholars of the standing of B. B. Warfield quickly saw that respect for the genre of each writer could alleviate the tensions.[4] None of these problems should be lightly set aside. But we need to recognize the far more profound cultural, theological and spiritual problem: that we are living in a culture that deliberately and pervasively exalts human autonomy and dismisses God, as demonstrated in the privatization of religion and conventional morality. It is not surprising that Mill exalted human freedom, given his rejection of the Bible's view of sin. Himmelfarb observes that his paean to individuality 'reflects an extraordinary optimism about human nature'.[5] Mill's philosophy involved rejecting what he called the Calvinist idea that our passions, desires, impulses, feelings and susceptibilities are more likely to be corrupt than good, and also 'a barely concealed animus in On Liberty against religion, against a morality sanctioned by religion, and against a people still respectful of orthodox religion'.[6]

We discuss the authority of the Bible, then, in a society shaped by the thoughts of Mill and other libertarians. Not surprisingly, this way of thought affects the church as well as the world. We need to go back to the nature of Christian authority, and this means returning once again to the fundamental level of the gospel itself. From the gospel of the kingdom of God, understood in terms of the lordship of Jesus Christ, we may learn something of the nature of the authority of Scripture over us. This will help us to grapple with the wider issue of the authority of Scripture in the church and its relationship with other claimants to authority.

The authority of Jesus Christ

The gospel tells us that this is a hierarchical world. The Creator is not dead and gone, a forgotten notion from long ago. He is alive and active in our world and he will be the author of a new heaven and a new earth at the end of our world. Many of the characteristic names given to him in Scripture – king, Lord, shepherd, redeemer, almighty, lord of hosts, husband, father – speak of his ongoing power. But it is not of brute strength that they speak. They portray not so much power as authority, the right to rule over us and to take responsibility for us. Indeed, such a relationship is described in the opening chapters of the Bible, where human beings owe all to God and live freely within the boundaries he set out. His absolute power is directed towards us constantly. Without it we could not exist for a moment. It provides the very groundwork of our whole being. But his authority is not exerted in precisely the same way. This is a relational matter. Instead of confronting us with his essence, his 'face', so to speak, we are related to him mediately, through his word. Thus Israel was spoken to through Moses the prophet, and in these last days God has spoken to us all through his Son. The word has God's authority, although it is not identical with him. The word creates the true freedom of relationship. It binds by its limiting, public and fixed character; it frees because it requires faith and response, interpretation and application to the moment.

The fall is the race's rebellion against its maker; the gospel is the maker's command to resume our proper relationship with him. This is the significance of Jesus' preaching, concentrating as he did on the kingdom of God. It is the significance, too, of the apostles' preaching when they 'proclaimed Christ', or, to use Paul's phrase, preached 'Jesus Christ as Lord'. The interim period in which we now live, as we await the coming of the kingdom of God in all its fullness, is rightly called the kingdom of Christ. He is consistently portrayed in the New Testament as ruling even now, seated at the right hand of the Father. The giving of the Holy Spirit demonstrates his ruling power. The Spirit brings the gospel word home to the hearts and minds of those whom the Lord is calling to himself. The proper response of all humankind, Jew or Greek, is to 'turn to God in repentance and have faith in our Lord Jesus' (Acts 20:21).

It is hardly necessary to say how greatly this contrasts with modern versions of the good life, based as they are on a vision of autonomy and the apparently limitless expansion of free choice. From the Christian point of view, the drive to autonomy and away from God is an extreme expression of the sin of rebellious pride stemming from Adam. As with all sin, it distorts something good, namely the freedom God gives his human creation. In the same way, the bondage so typical of societies that do not value human autonomy is also sinful, distorting the interdependence that is part of God's will for humanity. But the starting-point for the gospel in our society lies exactly where its greatest quarrel with God is, namely in the area of authority. The gospel promises its blessings by seeking our submission to the Lord.

What is the nature of this authority, and how does it relate to human freedom? We can instantly dismiss one possibility. The Lord's authority does not ask us to negate the self. We are not called to become so self-forgetful as to lose ourselves in him. Nor is there any suggestion that our relationship with him is that of a robot, or indeed anything mechanical, to its owner. It is not a question of sheer power bending another to its will without consent. We remain personal beings, and the relationship of which we speak is personal. But this reminds us, too, of the nature of freedom. It is not, as so many think, the capacity for complete self-determination. Human beings are never free from other powers that determine their lives. The problem of freedom is not the choice between having a master and being masterless; it is the problem of which master we have. Christian freedom is liberty from the false powers of sin and death, with their ways of thought and their evil consequences, and submission to the true Lord, who made us for himself and loves us. It is by exploring the nature of this relationship that we discover what freedom means. In fact, it is a relationship of authority and submission, involving command and obedience, and it is this that human beings find so hard to accept.

149

The nature of Christ's lordship shows us the meaning of true freedom. He is called 'Lord', a title of honour and rank. At the end of the age, every knee will bow to him and every tongue will own that he is the Lord (Phil. 2:9–11). His title, however, has been granted him on the basis of his saving work, when he did not exploit his position in heaven but took the form of a servant so that he could lay down his life for his people. He has now been appointed as the judge of the living and the dead. His return will be public and glorious. He is able to promise even now that he will be present with every Christian person, no matter how long this age may last. He promises, furthermore, that no power in heaven or earth – political, physical, spiritual, or even death itself – will be able to separate him from those who belong to him. He will be their Lord throughout, until they share his final victory. Our version of human freedom must take all these realities into account.

Consider the appropriate way to relate to such a Lord. The New Testament teaches that it is through repentance and faith. Repentance is submission to him, with sorrow for offences committed against him and a determination to live in accordance with his will. It is not an outward and forced submission, as when a conquered prince unwillingly yields to his conqueror; it is the submission of the heart, both total and permanent. Faith means entrusting oneself to him for salvation and for direction, and hence abandoning all other lords and gods we may have served, and entering into an exclusive relationship with this one Lord. It is important to notice that these categories are not new. They constitute the worship the people of Israel were called upon to give their covenant Lord. There is a fundamental continuity between the piety of the Old Testament and that of the New, despite the revelation of the triune nature of God in the New. The truth that 'I desire mercy, not sacrifice, and acknowledgment of God rather than burnt offerings', like so much else, belongs to both Testaments (Hos. 6:6; cf. Matt. 9:13).

The New Testament identifies Jesus Christ as the Lord to whom covenant fealty is due. In doing so it uses a number of images. The Christian person is to stand in relation to Jesus as a servant, one who says, 'I make it my aim in all things to please him' (cf. 2 Cor. 5:9), and one who endeavours to bring every thought captive to Christ (cf. 2 Cor. 10:5). Indeed, the New

Testament is not embarrassed at times to describe Christians as slaves of Christ. We are his soldiers, working to his orders; we are his sheep, who obey his voice; we are his disciples, who do all that he commands us to do. The church is depicted as the bride of Christ and as his body, both of them images intended to bring out, among other things, the heartfelt service we owe him. The piety of the New Testament (like that of the Old) is absolutist, in the sense that it demands not the negation of self, but the surrender of self: the believer is to 'deny himself and take up his cross daily and follow' Christ (Luke 9:23).

But the Lord is also the brother (Heb. 2:11) and God is also the Father. Indeed, Galatians draws a specific contrast between slave and son. The Christian's period of slavery has finished and the freedom of the adopted heir has begun. At the most fundamental level, the triune nature of God himself teaches us about the nature of relationship and of freedom. The Persons are eternal and indivisible; they are equal in power, majesty and glory; they are bound together in mutual love. However, neither the nature of the relationships within the Trinity, nor such images as friendship, contradict the basic pattern established by the gospel, namely Christ's lordship. They show what sort of Lord he is: one who admits his servants into his confidence, and who treats them with the intimacy of family. But sons, too, obey fathers, just as the Son obeys the Father. The image of sonship is one of freedom from things that are not God (the law as justifying agent, the elements of the universe), and freedom to obey the one who is God. The use of these images and others establishes that the language of our freedom is the personal language of trust, hope and love. Christian freedom is found in union with Christ, not in autonomy.

The Lord who has set us free in order to bind us to himself is the Lord of love. It was by accepting the limiting condition of servanthood that he achieved salvation for his servants. In doing his work he was bound by promises already given, by a covenant already made. His own faithful character bound him to give himself, not only in becoming a servant but in the most telling unfreedom of all: incarceration, the tying of his hands and crucifixion. And yet this unfreedom was the perfect example of his freedom to do what needed to be done for the ones he loved and for his own glory. We have seen that John Stuart Mill's version of freedom is based on a high estimate of human goodness; he

151

does not admit to the moral and spiritual bondage of the human race. Correspondingly, his version of freedom feeds the idea of self-determination. The virtue of the autonomous person is tolerance; the virtue of the Lord's person is love.

The children of modernity and postmodernity understand the difference and act accordingly. Love is slavery to the other; tolerance 'lets be'. Tolerance calls upon us to give others space, to let them make their own mistakes, to let them grow through experiment. Tolerance promotes the individualist ethos, and distrusts commitment. It is no accident that the New Testament thinks of the relationship between Christ and the church as analogous to that between husband and wife; or that there is a widespread modern unwillingness to enter into the marriage covenant at all. In New Testament terms, the bride finds her freedom in obedience to her husband, just as he is free in the gift of his love even if it were to involve his own death. Just so, in the original Genesis story, freedom meant acting by faith in the words of the Lord; bondage meant choosing to believe that the word of the Lord was false.

Acceptance of the gospel, then, is the beginning of true freedom for us. Absolute freedom is a chimera; it ignores all the relationships in which we stand and ought to stand. Christ's lordship frees us from bondage to what harms us, and frees us to be the people we have been created to be. The rebellion against hierarchical forms of social life is futile; it creates misery because it cuts across reality. When it has to do with our relationship with God, it brings condemnation in its train. Genuine and fulfilling human relations, at all levels, can exist only because of promises and faithfulness to promises. These curtail freedom in order to create freedom – the liberty of trust, hope and love. Freedom from death, sin and judgment is not bondage, but liberty. Having a Lord is not a fretful and unpleasant state of affairs, but one for which we have been created.

Two great truths stand out from this, confronting not only the world but the church, for the power of the world's longing for autonomy has affected the church and has weakened its hold on the authority of Christ. The first truth is the absolute nature of this authority. If Christ is indeed the Lord, it is incumbent upon all who own his lordship to serve him, to endeavour in all things to please him, to bring every thought captive to him. 'Come to me,'

Jesus said; '… learn from me' (Matt. 11:28–29). That is the business of being Christian, even when obeying Christ puts us at odds with our culture. There is evidence enough that the church wishes to serve both Baal and Yahweh, to limp between two positions. In the final analysis, much of the rejection of the authority of God's written word arises not from problems with the form of the Bible but from a desire to maintain at least some human autonomy understood in a liberal sense.

The second truth is that it is integral both to our bond-service to Christ and to our freedom that his authority is mediated by his word. The gospel by which his authority is established is a set of words. When we receive Christ by repentance and faith, we receive the truth about him as the Word of God. There can be no authentic version of Christianity without a linguistic entity known as the word of God. It can be spoken in different ways and translated into different languages. Like other words, it may be trusted, obeyed, rejected, repeated and recorded. When we receive Christ Jesus as Lord, furthermore, we are receiving the old covenant as the word of God, because the old covenant and the gospel vindicate, interpret and fulfil each other. To do otherwise is to believe in a Jesus other than the one who is given to us in the gospel. The gospel knows only a Jesus who regarded the Old Testament as the word of God and treated it as such. To accept him as Lord and yet not to accept his word on this subject is absurd. Furthermore, to receive the gospel is to make the words of Jesus and his apostles the word of God: 'teaching them to obey everything I have commanded you' (Matt. 28:20). There are not two canons of Scripture, but one. The question is merely whether the Gospels and epistles should be added to the existing and authoritative word of God. Since our commitment to Christ as Lord entails the belief that the new fulfils the old, it would be strange not to join the two together as one.

The authority of Scripture: covenant

The key consequence of accepting the gospel is, therefore, that Jesus Christ becomes our Lord, exercising the authority of his kingdom in our lives. From the gospel, we can see both what the nature of his authority must be and also the means by which he exerts it. The instrument of his authority is the word, and the word must therefore reflect the style of his authority. In chapter 3 I indicated how this is already the case, as we see from the closeness of the link between kingdom and covenant. The fall was a rebellion against the kingdom of God; the covenant restores that kingdom, as the Lord, through his word of promise, enters into a kingly relationship with his people. God's covenant arrangements differed from time to time, depending on the developing state of his people. The covenant with Abraham bound a family to the Lord; the covenant through Moses bound a nation to him; the covenant with David bound a kingdom to him; the covenant through Jesus binds his people to him. Through words of promise given and received, the parties limit their freedom of action by committing themselves to each other.

I have already noted (in chapter 3) that in the account of the giving of the Sinaitic covenant we read of the 'Book of the Covenant'. The phrase 'Book of the Covenant' or 'of the Law' occurs several times then (e.g. Exod. 24:7) and later (e.g. 2 Chr. 34:15) to refer to the public recording of the covenant and its stipulations. This transfer of the word 'covenant' or 'law' to the writings that record these things contains a true insight. The Scriptures of the Old and New Testaments are 'covenantal'. Their origin is in the Lord's covenant with his people (for in the end the new covenant 'encapsulates the key promises made throughout the Old Testament era ... while at the same time transcending them',[7] and in the business of recording it, declaring it, expounding it, applying it and illuminating it. The covenantal people of God have the Book of the Covenant, which is coterminous with the Scriptures. The covenant origin of Scripture then reveals both the authority and the nature of Scripture. We can continue to honour its authority, while at the same time recognizing the special features that help to determine the sort of authority it possesses. Thus, on the one hand, the covenantal approach challenges the view that the Bible is merely a textbook for finding out about God. On the other hand, it challenges the view that it is merely a witness to the word of God. Neither adequately describes the book through which God rules his covenant people.

The authority of Scripture is the personal authority of the Lord over the people whom he has saved. It is not a book about God, in the same way that *The Compleat Angler* is a book about fishing. Just as the knowledge of God is relational, so the

154

Scripture functions to give that knowledge, and to lead its recipients in the truth of what it means to be ruled by God. That is not to say that the truths about God are not communicated in Scripture; on the contrary, it is there above all that we are taught about God. Scripture serves a definite didactic function, and is the foundation of doctrine. But its didactic function is exercised in the context of relationship with God; it is shaped by the knowledge of the God who says, 'This is the one I esteem: he who is humble and contrite in spirit, and trembles at my word' (Is. 66:2). The authority of Scripture is the authority of the Lord, who exercises that authority first by redeeming his people and then by placing them in covenant loyalty to himself: 'Then he [Moses] took the Book of the Covenant and read it to the people. They responded, "We will do everything the LORD has said; we will obey"' (Exod. 24:7). In short, the chief issue of authority is a spiritual one. It is a question of obedience.

When we think of the Bible as the ultimate form of the Book of the Covenant, we are saying that its origin lies with God, and that it is fitting to call it the word of God. Its authority stems from its origin in the mind of God; he is its ultimate author. But the word 'origin' also refers to the human origin, the way God arranged for such a book to come into existence. The original Book of the Covenant is described as emerging in this way: 'When Moses went and told the people all the LORD's words and laws, they responded with one voice, "Everything the LORD has said we will do." Moses then wrote down everything the LORD had said' (Exod. 24:3–4). Chronicles describes the Book of the Covenant found in Josiah's day as 'the Book of the Law of the LORD that had been given through Moses' (2 Chr. 34:14). The Bible represents God as speaking, and on occasion speaking directly to his prophets; but here, as so often elsewhere, it portrays the next stage, namely the recording and passing on of the word in sermons or in written form or both.

In so doing the Bible makes two points that help to reveal its authority and nature. First, the origin, the authorship and hence the authority of the words belong to God. Secondly, it is the Lord's custom to use the gifts and skills of his chosen prophets to pass on his message. In this, Moses stands as the exemplar. He is presented to us not as a religious genius, able to discern the truth about God in a way not given to others, but as a servant whose task it is to transmit and apply the word that comes to him from beyond himself. He is the first of a long line of servants of the covenant who address Israel in the name of God, and seek to transmit his word to this people. One of the characteristic features of the Bible is the prophets' phrase, 'Thus says the LORD ...' They are certainly not embarrassed to see their words as his.

This is a particular example of the way the Bible treats the relationship of God to the world, and especially to the human world. God's initiative and power are not exercised at the expense of either his own or human power. When he wins the battle for Gideon, he reduces the army to vanishing-point, but he still uses the swords of the men of Gideon and a stratagem designed to put the Midianites to flight (Judg. 7). When he uses Paul the apostle to do great things, he does so by incorporating the energies and intellect of a truly remarkable man. The incarnation is the supreme instance in which the human is incorporated faultlessly in the divine for the divine purpose. The crucifixion was no mock event, Christ's suffering no illusion. So, likewise, the joint effort of God and human beings in the production of the word of God is typical of God's pattern of dealing with us, and contains within itself no necessary suggestion that the human contribution vitiates or compromises the divine.[8]

The origin of Scripture: inspiration

I have used the category of the covenant to speak of both the authority and the origin of Scripture. It is more customary to speak of the manner of the divine authorship of God's word as 'inspiration'. In one sense there is no need to invoke this category. To say that the Bible is covenantal establishes the authorship of God and hence the authority and nature of the Scriptures. However, since the expression arises from the Bible's own account of how the word of God came, it is useful to explore the matter further. It has the benefit of introducing the work of the Spirit into a consideration of the Scriptures. The link between the Spirit and the one who brings the word is frequently made, as in the description of Jesus himself in John's Gospel: 'For the one whom God has sent speaks the words of God, for God gives the Spirit without limit' (3:34). It was the business of the inspired prophet not to offer philosophical observations, but to communicate divine truths. The authority of the message arose not from the prophet but from the divine source. When Peter wishes to emphasize the authority of the prophetic writings, he says, 'And we have the word of the prophets made more certain, and you will do well to pay attention to it, as to a light shining in a dark place, until the day dawns and the morning star rises in your hearts. Above all, you must understand that no prophecy of Scripture came about by the prophet's own interpretation. For prophecy never had its origin in the will of man, but men spoke from God as they were carried along by the Holy Spirit' (2 Pet. 1:19–21). In short, God is the author of Scripture; we must therefore pay close attention to it.

Through studying the Bible itself we can see that, in fact, revelation is communicated in a number of ways. 'Inspiration' is the appropriate category as long as the work of the Spirit is involved. That is, although the idea of inspiration may have arisen from something like divine possession, it can equally be used of other modes of revelation, as long as the result can be attributed to the Spirit of God. This we have seen in Peter's description. The prophets saw visions (e.g. Ezek. 10) and the word of the Lord (e.g. Amos 1:1); they heard the voice of the Lord in his temple (e.g. Is. 6:8); they studied and commented on the writings of the other prophets (e.g. Jer. 31:3–6); they used sources in non-biblical literature to write books of history and wisdom (e.g. 2 Kgs. 18:19–25); they wrote letters addressing specific situations (e.g. Jer. 29). The different personalities, historical situations, linguistic skills and styles of the authors are plain to anyone who investigates the matter. The Lord's hand is not shortened that he cannot use these and many other ways of communicating what he wishes to reveal. His providential ordering of events even includes his ordering of the words of individuals who were entirely unconscious of the experience of inspiration as they uttered or wrote their inspired words. Caiaphas, for example, was completely unaware of speaking at the Lord's command; for him the ordinary processes of reason dictated what he was going to say. So he unwittingly spoke the word of God: 'He did not say this on his own, but as high priest that year he prophesied that Jesus would die for the Jewish nation, and not only for that nation but also for the scattered children of God, to bring them together and make them one' (John 11:51–52).

The method of inspiration

Two problems need to be addressed in talking about inspiration. The first is to do with its method. Hardly a reference to inspiration in the last hundred years has failed to exploit the confusion between 'dictation' and 'inspiration'. Whatever the author's view about the category of inspiration, we are assured that dictation is not intended. It is clear that, despite fervent protestations to the contrary, evangelicals are suspected of holding the view that God dictated the Bible word for word to its human authors, and that the human contribution was therefore minimal. The truth is that evangelicals have been careful to indicate that 'inspiration' entails no particular manner of human contribution, only the need to assert the ultimate divine authorship of the text and therefore its authority. However, the evangelical response may have been too defensive. The vehemence with which 'dictation' is dismissed, and the almost inveterate desire to attribute it to evangelicals (or 'fundamentalists'), is suggestive of a problem being concealed. After all, while it is true to say that the Bible exhibits a number of ways in which human utterances are also thought to be divine, it gives us, in the case of Moses and the Book of the Covenant at least, one example very close to 'dictation' (Exod. 19:6–7; 24:4; 34:27). Indeed, the Ten Commandments were originally written by God directly (Exod. 32:15–16); and if the prophets claim to be speaking the word of God by quoting him as they so often do, 'dictation' may not be an entirely inappropriate description of such an event.

The idea of dictation is easier to attribute to the pre-Enlightenment writers than to more modern ones. They were prepared to use such phrases as 'the divine pen-men'. Such words are now rarely heard from evangelicals, let alone from their critics. But the theories of inspiration that have emerged over the years to displace the earlier beliefs, and that emphasize genius rather than providence, reflect much less accurately the Bible's own account of how divine words enter human language. It may well be that the pre-Enlightenment authors understood a truth that we ignore for cultural reasons. How do we see Moses at work in Exodus 24:4, if not as the divine amanuensis? Evangelicals need to ask their critics what it is that constitutes the problem. If indeed Moses and others display instances of divine 'dictation', we most

158

assuredly have the word of God, with little room for human creativity to shape it. Is it the baldness of the claim, the brute fact of
so fearful a thing as the actual word of God, that is the underlying
problem? For if there is indeed a dictated word of the Lord, may
there not be any others of equally immediate authority? Furthermore, if (for example) such a carefully wrought literary production
as John's Gospel is also the 'word of God', why should we be
troubled by the idea of dictation as such, since the authority of the
resulting entity is the same? Is it possible that what we are seeing
here is the manifestation, within the theological thinking of the
church itself, of the quest for autonomy characteristic of western
culture as a whole?

There are two ostensible reasons why the idea of dictation is
dismissed. The first is theological: God typically acts in the world
in and through his servants. Here a caveat needs to be entered. As
indicated already through the illustration of Gideon, there is no
doubt that this is indeed the usual way in which the Lord works.
But the Bible does not suggest that it is the only way. 'The LORD
will fight for you; you need only to be still,' was the word of
Moses to the Israelites at the sea (Exod. 14:14). God's providential ordering in the world is regular and habitually employs
secondary causes; but this is not an absolute restriction. His
powers are also evident in ways that demonstrate that he does not
need us to perform his work in the world. His work is usually
providential; sometimes, it is better to say that it is miraculous. If
God is God, we must be careful not to reject the latter interpretation because of a prejudice against miracles.

The second reason dictation is so readily dismissed is hermeneutical. Since the nineteenth century there has been a massive
shift in the method of understanding the Bible. The humanity of
Scripture has become a key element in reading. Even the suggestion that the Bible was to be read 'like any other book' was once
capable of causing controversy and consternation.[9] However, the
advances made in the reading of Scripture by taking explicit
notice of its human context and authorship have vindicated this
new emphasis. More will be said about this in the next chapter.
Suffice it to say that, despite these advances, the positive fruit of
this method cannot of itself justify overlooking the real nature of
the book under discussion. Its origin is both human and divine.
To affirm that the Bible is to be read like any other book is not to

say that the Bible is to be read *just* like any other book. There are profound differences as well as similarities, and the idea of dictation may well stand as a witness to something vitally significant that has been neglected. In any case, dictation is not the only mode of divine inspiration recorded in Scripture or even the most prominent one; but it is one of them.

The event of inspiration

The second problem to be addressed in discussing inspiration is the link between the parts of the Bible that are said to be inspired and the whole. It may be argued that the Bible contains words from God but that it is not right to call the whole of it the word of God. After all, parts of it are definitely the word of human beings about God, and even to God, which we cannot endorse as words from God. Scripture even records words said by Satan; in what sense can they be said to be the word of God? A similar question that is sometimes raised concerns what may be called the less 'inspiring' parts of Scripture, such as the lengthy genealogies of Chronicles.

There are two lines of comment on these questions. The first is the observation that, despite this apparent difficulty, that is exactly how the New Testament treats the Old Testament. The Scripture, or the holy Scriptures as they are also called (Rom. 1:2), form a special corpus of writings that may be known as 'the very words of God' (Rom. 3:2). There is no suggestion anywhere that we may affirm only those parts that are attributed directly to the Lord. When Jesus quoted the editorial comment in Genesis 2, that 'the two will become one flesh', he did so under the rubric, 'the Creator ... said' (Matt. 19:4–6). When Paul quoted words specifically attributed to God in the Old Testament, he introduced them with the striking phrase, 'For the Scripture says to Pharaoh' (Rom. 9:17). When the epistle to the Hebrews referred to words of David about God, the author attributed the words to both David and God: 'Therefore God again set a certain day, calling it Today, when a long time later he spoke through David, as it was said before: "Today, if you hear his voice, do not harden your hearts"' (Heb. 4:7). In short, the practice of the New Testament was to treat the whole of the Old Testament as the word of God, acknowledging both the human authors and the divine author, and recognizing that God could be the author of words about

160

himself or to himself as well as formally speaking words from himself.

The second observation concerns the nature of communication in general. No communications between persons stand on their own. All have a context. The context may have a far less significant role to play in the process of communication than the content. It may merely be the boundary or frame of a work of art. Yet, without the boundary, without the context, the central part cannot speak accurately and effectively. Sometimes it is what the communication does *not* say that makes sense of what it does say. So it is in Scripture. To delineate between the parts of Scripture that are inspired and those that are not, whether on the ground that some parts are more powerful than others, or on the ground that only some parts even claim to speak directly from God, is to remove the background that makes sense of the foreground. It is to fall into the same intellectualist trap as those who wish to treat Scripture merely as a doctrinal handbook. Only by having Ecclesiastes and the Gospel of John in the same volume can we know what God is saying to us. Furthermore, to say that some parts are more 'inspired' than others is to treat inspiration as a response by the reader rather than as a characteristic of the text.

The singularity of Scripture

On this account, the authority of the Lord and the authority of Scripture are obviously bound together. The covenantal Scripture is the instrument by which the Lord Jesus rules over his covenant people. This has both a corporate and an individual reference. Christ's lordship is exercised over the individual; but at an even more fundamental level his rule is exercised over a gathered people, and our interest must be in the authority of Christ over his church and in how that is exercised. But what of the relative position of Scripture compared to other authorities that claim the allegiance of God's people? We turn, in the rest of this chapter, to consider what we may call the singularity or uniqueness of Scripture. Strangely, we must begin by staking the claim of the Scriptures over against God himself, so to speak, for there are those who wish to displace the Scriptures in the name of God. Thus the proper relationship between God and Scripture will occupy our attention before we turn to two other authorities:

tradition and reason. The relationship betwen Scripture and the Holy Spirit will be the subject of the last section of this book.

Scripture and God

All Christians accept the authority of God. But those who emphasize the authority of Scripture are often explicitly challenged about their attitude to God. It is said that in giving so prominent a place to Scripture they obscure the authority of the God in whom they profess to believe. This accusation takes two forms.

It is reductionist

First, it is argued that the mystery of God means that our communication with him can never be satisfactorily reduced to the verbal. The verbal is too prosaic, too academic, too merely human: 'No particular statement can be affirmed unequivocally to be the revelation of God. It both is and is not revelation.'[10] If God is God, our awareness of him ought to contain much that cannot be spoken. Thus our appreciation of God may be much more sacramental rather than verbal, numinous rather than plain. The emphasis on the word, typical of evangelical Protestantism, does no justice to the hiddenness of God, and reduces him to an object to be studied rather than regarding him as a person whose numinous presence is to be adored. Indeed, it constitutes one more attempt by the human race to control God, to bring him down to our size, to comprehend the incomprehensible. The contrast between Catholic and Protestant worship tells the story: the one full of mystery, appealing to all the senses, sacramental, divine; the other plain, simple, unsymbolic, appealing mainly to the ear.

Edwyn Bevan's classic work recounts an incident that makes the point neatly: 'I remember once hearing a man describe in conversation an experience of his when he was visiting an English cathedral. Service had not yet begun, but the organ, if I remember right, was already playing. He described how the ancient building around him, the half-light, the waves of music, as he wandered about, gave him a rich sense of the numinous; and then he described the fearful fall into bathos, into dreary tedium, when the music ceased and he suddenly heard a voice proclaiming through the aisles, "To the Lord our God belong mercies and forgivenesses, though we have rebelled against

Him."'[11] Bevan makes some critical remarks about this attitude, but it usefully illustrates what many people think: that the realm of religion is best left to experience, uninterrupted by the verbal. In terms of revelation we are better off with the symbolic, the sensuous, and, at best, the 'still small voice', which is what the prophet Elijah heard in his eerie confrontation with God. That sort of experience is truer to the nature of God than the mundane belief that we hear him or read him in sermon or book.

There are several points to be made by way of reply. It might be as well to begin with Elijah's experience (1 Kgs. 19) because of its constant abuse in the service of the numinous. The prophet was returning to the location of one of the greatest of all verbal revelations, Mount Horeb, or Mount Sinai as it was also known. He was travelling back to where God was known to speak. There were mighty manifestations of the Lord's power in earthquake, wind and storm. But the text says specifically that the Lord was in none of these things. Indeed, the 'gentle whisper' that followed (verse 12; almost certainly a mistranslation; the NRSV has 'a sound of sheer silence'), was a reminder that the Lord is a speaking God. And so he was for Elijah, for the story climaxes with the Lord addressing his prophet in what constituted the real revelation.

The whole Elijah episode is a testimony to the observation that, great and overwhelming as the Lord is, mysterious to us as his person may be and far above us in all majesty and power, he nevertheless addresses us by word. The word is the gracious approach of this great God to us; it is not given so that we may despise it or pass it by in the interest of higher religious sensibilities. The voice in the cathedral may not have had the numinous or aesthetic quality of the music, but it was the word of the living God that was being spoken, the glad and joyous tidings of the gospel. It is not those who value the word who are treating God as an object, but those who declare that the word is not sufficient for them. God has made himself vulnerable in the word; his life is given in the word as he binds himself to us. When Israel encountered the living God, as Moses reminded them, 'You saw no form of any kind the day the LORD spoke to you at Horeb out of the fire. Therefore watch yourselves very carefully, so that you do not become corrupt and make for yourselves an idol, an image of any shape ...' (Deut. 4:15–16).

As his great speech nears its conclusion, Moses specifically puts the word of God within their reach. They do not need to ascend to heaven to find it, or cross the sea to obtain it. 'No, the word is very near you; it is in your mouth and in your heart so that you may obey it' (Deut. 30:14; cf. Rom. 10:5ff.). It is God who has decreed that his word is the appointed trysting-place between him and his people. This arrangement was symbolized by the Ark of the Covenant, by the Tent of Meeting, and later by the temple in Zion. It is fulfilled in his Son, who is his Word made flesh, and in the gospel that is near us. Attempts made in the name of religious experience to say how God should communicate with us typify the very problems with natural theology that confronted Paul when he met demands for wisdom and miracles with the word of the cross (1 Cor. 1:18–25).

It is idolatrous

The second accusation levelled at the evangelical attitude to Scripture is that such a position entails bibliolatry, or the worship of the Bible instead of God.[12] After all, it is said, God, not words about God, is God; our relationship is with him, not with words about him. If we honour the Bible in the way evangelicals do, we are inevitably prone to intellectualize our faith, and to put the Bible (or really our interpretation of the Bible) above God himself in importance. The result is pharisaism of the sort that confronted Jesus. It also means that, instead of looking for the new lessons that God has to teach us, we are always stuck in a book, conserving our version of the past.

The difference between Muslims and Christians in their understanding of their respective Scriptures is of interest here. The Muslim view of inspiration really is dictation, for it is understood that the Prophet received the Qur'an directly from God. 'There is no human partnership in the Qur'an; it is all of God.'[13] Strictly speaking, there is no call for a translation or comment on the Qur'an. The physical book itself must be treated with the greatest reverence. It is unthinkable that it should be placed on the floor and moved with the foot, for example. But Christians, on the whole, even evangelical Christians, have no such inhibitions about the Bible. We would say that we revere the contents as coming from God, and that this book is the word of God. But we do not confuse the outward form of the word with the word itself, as bibliolators would.

164

There is indeed an instinctive and proper distinction between God and the Bible. The one is not the other, and anyone who worshipped the Bible would be guilty of bibliolatry. Is it fair, however, to accuse evangelicals of bibliolatry? (It may be worth observing that if evangelicals have been guilty of this sin, it has been an inveterate offence of Christians of all types throughout history.) The charge is more flashy than true. We return once more to the gospel that first brings us the knowledge of God. Much has already been made of the fact that the gospel and the knowledge of God are relational, not merely intellectual. That is the nature of the knowledge of God that the gospel brings. But the gospel is inescapably verbal; it is the word of God. We are asked to believe and obey it. In doing so, we are believing and obeying God himself, who by this means brings us into relationship with himself. If this is wrong, so too is our treatment of the Bible, for our attitude to Scripture flows out of our attitude to the gospel.

Consider a further point. This is exactly our human experience of the connection between ourselves and the language we use. If one person communicates with another, say through a letter, the recipient neither confuses the instrument with the sender nor separates the inseparable. It would be intolerable for the recipient to say, for example, that he did not keep to arrangements for a meeting, set out in the letter, because they were only words and not the person. One can never plausibly say, 'I did not believe your words, because they were not you.' Even in human affairs we stand by our words. As you treat my words, so you treat me. I am rightly offended, in a personal way, if you slight, disregard, disobey or contradict my words. I think you have done these things to me. Likewise, if you trust my word, you are trusting me; if you obey my word, you are obeying me; if you honour my word, you are honouring me. That is the nature of language and persons in everyday experience.

So it is in the case of the Bible. Indeed, it is more so in Scripture, because the God who speaks is intangible to us. He cannot rely on body language. Or, if it is said that he relies on 'body language' in the incarnation, such language is accessible to us now only in the language of Scripture. In any case, again and again, in both Testaments the word of God is treated as God himself is to be treated. As Jesus said, 'The words I have spoken to you are spirit and they are life' (John 6:63). Joshua urged the people in his day: 'be very careful to keep the commandment and the law that Moses the servant of the LORD gave you: to love the LORD your God, to walk in all his ways, to obey his commands, to hold fast to him and serve him with all your heart and all your soul' (Josh. 22:5). Likewise Moses promised the Lord's blessing 'when you and your children return to the LORD your God and obey him with all your heart and with all your soul according to everything I command you today' (Deut. 30:2) In Hebrews, the word of God is given the function of God: 'Sharper than any double-edged sword, it penetrates even to dividing soul and spirit, joints and marrow; it judges the thoughts and attitudes of the heart' (4:12). Jesus said, 'If anyone is ashamed of me and my words in this adulterous and sinful generation, the Son of Man will be ashamed of him ...' (Mark 8:38). If the evangelical doctrine of Scripture is bibliolatry, so is the attitude of the Bible writers themselves and of Jesus.

To sum up: there is no way in which Scripture and God are in opposition to or rivalry with each other. God is the author of Scripture and has provided it as a covenantal appointment by which he rules his people. Our misuse of Scripture is an offence against God. It is always possible, however, that our use of Scripture may put us at odds with God. We need to remember Israel in this regard. Israel was the nation of the book, and set great store by the Scriptures. Yet Jesus told them, 'You diligently study the Scriptures because you think that by them you possess eternal life. These are the Scriptures that testify about me, yet you refuse to come to me to have life' (John 5:39–40). Their study of the Scriptures was profound, but unbelieving (6:47). (The question of reading Scripture will be taken up in chapter 9, and the issue of the voice of the Spirit as a supplementary revelation from God in chapters 10 and 11.)

Scripture and tradition

Tradition is that which is passed on or passed over, just as a prisoner may be 'traditioned' or passed over to a new captor. In terms of a culture, it is prior experience encapsulated and transmitted to the present; tradition is the vote of history. It has authority as being at least the findings of experience; but it may have the authority of a highly respected source as well. Just as experience contains within itself the idea of authority, so does tradition. It allows the authority of the past (even the recent past) to have a voice in the present. It allows authorities of the present to appeal to the authority of the past in order to establish a point. When tradition is encapsulated in actions or in patterns of behaviour, it enables us to act habitually and therefore without constant interrogation.

Scripture is set over tradition

Scripture has a threefold relation to tradition. First, it is set over tradition in so far as the tradition is man-made. This was precisely Jesus' point in his controversy with the Pharisees as recounted in Mark. 'You have let go of the commands of God and are holding on to the traditions of men' (7:8). The pharisaic traditions were not intended to counter the existing word of God. Instead, they explained and elaborated that word in a legal tradition that had gained in power over the years. Jesus' criticism was that the tradition of interpretation had secured such authority that the Pharisees failed to acknowledge that it was contradicting the intention of the command of God. It was absolutely necessary that the priority and authority of the word of God itself be allowed free play, no matter how venerable the tradition may have been. This remains the fundamental theological point in discussions of tradition.

This fits exactly with the route of revelation that, as we have seen, is taken by the gospel. It is sometimes argued that the Bible is the church's book, for the church produced the Bible, determined its inspired contents, guarded its existence and interpreted its message. In the words of Lawrence S. Cunningham, 'Catholics believe that when the Scriptures are proclaimed in church, that is not only the correct place to hear the Scriptures but in that proclamation we are listening to the word of God.'[14] But this priority of church over Bible misstates the fundamental truth, found in the Bible itself, that it is by the word of God that faith arises (Gal. 3:1–5), that the church owes its existence to the word of God (Eph. 2:20), that God's word is the powerful force that accomplishes his purposes (Heb. 4:12–13), and that the gospel is God's word that saves us (Rom. 1:16). The church owes its life to the word. The Bible cannot be separated from this word, and the church cannot rule the Bible, not even by claiming to be its sole licensed interpreter.

167

Scripture contains tradition

Secondly, the New Testament contains elements that the writers themselves identify as traditions, and that are identified with the word of God itself. Thus the gospel had been 'traditioned' to Paul, and he uses this fact to demonstrate its authenticity, since the sources from which he received it (namely the Lord and his apostles) were unimpeachable (1 Cor. 15:3–7). Likewise, of the Last Supper he writes, 'I received from the Lord what I also passed on to you' (1 Cor. 11:23). It is clear that here and in other places we are dealing with material thought of as the word of God; indeed, it is possible that all our material about Jesus was initially 'traditioned' verbally. It is evident that 'tradition' is being used in a different sense here. The concept is related to such words as 'witness' and 'apostle'; it helps to explain the coming into being of the New Testament as we now have it. The tradition in such a case, as we can see from the two examples mentioned already, had the authority of Scripture itself, in an early stage of its development. The point about the authority of tradition is not so much its history as its source, and its source may be judged, as was the New Testament itself, by its conformity to the existing word of God.

Among the early generations of Christians, elements of the tradition about Jesus other than what we have in the written tradition may have survived and been used in preaching and teaching. Certainly a 'rule of faith' developed (perhaps the forerunner of the creeds), which was used to distinguish truth from error. But to what extent can we see these traditions as having an independent life apart from Scripture? To what extent are we privy to extrabiblical traditions that have the authority of Scripture? The Council of Trent appeared to endorse the view that, in Scripture and tradition, we have two sources of revelation, speaking of 'the written books and unwritten traditions which, received by the Apostles from the mouth of Christ himself, or from the Apostles themselves, the Holy Ghost dictating, have come down even unto us, transmitted as it were from hand to hand'. To both Scripture and tradition it accords 'equal affection of piety, and reverence' (Session 4). Professor R. P. C. Hanson points out, however, that as far as independent tradition is concerned, 'authentic oral tradition had virtually died out by about 250', and that all the fathers agreed that the content of the rule of faith 'is identical with that of Scripture'. He concludes, 'As a source of original information independent of Scripture, tradition is useless.'[15]

A slightly different way of putting the matter has emerged in Roman Catholic theology since Vatican II. The Council itself was more circumspect regarding the claim that tradition constitutes a second source of revelation apart from Scripture. Instead, 'both of them, flowing from the same divine well-spring, in a certain way merge into a unity and tend towards the same end'.[16] Nevertheless, 'both sacred tradition and sacred Scripture are to be accepted and venerated with the same sense of devotion and reverence'.[17] Tradition is linked indissolubly with the episcopal office, regarded as being in the succession of the apostles. It encompasses 'everything which contributes to the holiness of life, and the increase of faith of the people of God; and so the Church, in her teaching, life, and worship, perpetuates and hands on to all generations all that she herself is, all that she believes'.[18] The Council made it explicit that tradition, Scripture and the teaching office of the church are bound together here: 'It is clear, therefore, that sacred tradition, sacred Scripture and the teaching authority of the Church, in accord with God's most wise design, are so linked and joined together that one cannot stand without the other, and that all together and each in his own way under the action of the one Holy Spirit contribute effectively to the salvation of souls.'[19]

In this theology, extrabiblical tradition and Scripture are seen as constituting a partnership – no doubt with Scripture as the senior partner – for the transmission and interpretation of revelation. This does not correspond to the tradition of which we read positively in Scripture, for that was part of the formation of the canon itself. The function of tradition and of the teaching office lies chiefly in the interpretation of Scripture, but so authoritative is the teaching office ('The task of authentically interpreting the word of God, whether written or handed on, has been entrusted exclusively to the living teaching office of the Church, whose authority is exercised in the name of Jesus Christ'),[20] and so pervasive the tradition ('Sacred tradition and Sacred Scripture form one sacred deposit of the word of God, which is committed to the Church'),[21] that the authoritative singularity of the Bible itself is inevitably compromised.

The words of the Council allow Scripture insufficient room to challenge the tradition, especially when both are beholden to a teaching office that itself lays claim to infallibility. The positive things Scripture says about tradition do not apply in this case, for the traditions of Scripture concern the very making of Scripture in the first and unique generation of apostles and witnesses. The crucial point is that the Bible itself gives no ground for saying that the apostles handed on a magisterial interpretative role to bishops, or that such persons were to be their successors. The whole intricate arrangement for the passing on of such authority to bishops is lacking in the crucial documents. There is no appeal in them to an established and authoritative interpreter of the text; rather, Christians are called upon to read, understand and apply them for themselves. Despite the suggestion that Vatican II represents a significant step forward in the Catholic understanding of tradition, it seems to lock up the Bible even more securely than before in the keeping of the church, rather than in the keeping of the Lord of the church, who uses it to rule his people.

Tradition safeguards the interpretation of Scripture

There is, however, a third element of the relationship between the church and Scripture, which acknowledges the trajectory of Scripture through time. Although all Christians are expected to learn the Scriptures for themselves through reading or hearing them read, the Scriptures also provide for a teaching ministry. Wherever the gospel has gone it has been accompanied by the development of a teaching pastorate. The teacher's authority is significant, but not absolute. The Christian and the church are still bound to judge for themselves whether what is taught is true. There is, therefore, a genuine use of tradition that allows God-appointed teachers to speak beyond their own generation as they teach and apply Scripture. This may include such expressions as liturgy and architecture. It is always fair to ask, especially when some great change is mooted, whether it is of a piece with the tradition of the understanding of God's word. For this reason, innovations such as the ordination of women need to be examined with great care. In this case, to innovate is to say that generations of Christians from the very beginning, including all the great teachers of the Bible, have misunderstood the mind of God on this point. Such a conclusion may be true; the Reformation is a standing reminder that the teachers of the church may be

170

seriously in the wrong, perhaps for cultural reasons. But it is also worth noting that the Protestant Reformers went to considerable lengths to trace their theological ancestry to the opening centuries of the church, despite the distance of space and time.

There are, of course, equal and opposite errors to avoid. One is the belief that the tradition should determine the interpretation of Scripture; the other that tradition should have no say at all. We characteristically acquire our traditions from denominations, and may accord them a longer history and a deeper inherent authority than they deserve. A most disturbing recent development is the constant use of the word 'tradition' as an excuse for ill-founded ecclesiological beliefs and practices by ourselves and others. In cross-denominational discussions, it has become customary to handle all sorts of disagreements by saying that it is 'part of the tradition'. By the use of this handy stratagem we isolate our own and others' ideas and practices from the sharp scrutiny of the word of God. Conversely, much contemporary church life seems to suggest that we are the first Christians, and that we begin with the Bible and nothing else. On the contrary, every Christian is heir to the interpretation of the Bible that issued in the great Christological and trinitarian dogmas. These shape the very nature of our Christianity, whether we know it or not. They constitute authorized, traditional ways of reading the Bible. The Bible stands over them and independent of them in principle, but every generation that passes simply confirms that they are, in essence, the true reading of Scripture and so unrepealable.

However respectful we may rightly be of tradition, which gives a vote to the past, we need to recognize that it is at its most useful in helping us to interpret Scripture. But it can achieve this role satisfactorily only if we recognize that the word of God (even a traditioned word of God) must take sovereign priority over tradition, no matter how venerable the latter may be or how suitable it was for a bygone age. The sharpness of the gospel must not be compromised.

Scripture and reason

It is customary among some theologians – especially Anglicans – to laud a threefold pattern in theological method, namely the use of Scripture, tradition and reason in various combinations. Indeed,

it has become one of the clichés of history that this is *the* distinctive
Anglican theological method; the point is made as though others
are not privy to the secret, or are unable to share the cool detach-
ment of the Anglicans.[22] Sometimes this is accompanied by
negative remarks about theologians such as Tertullian, Luther,
Kierkegaard or Barth, who are alleged to have dismissed the use of
reason in theology. And here lies the puzzle. These are among the
intellectual giants of the history of Christian thought. None of
them eschewed the mind, for the mind is not eschewed in
Scripture. 'Be transformed by the renewing of your mind' is one
of the best-known of Paul's injunctions (Rom. 12:2). 'Stop thinking like children,' he told the Corinthians. 'In regard to evil be
infants, but in your thinking be adults' (1 Cor. 14:20). It is not the
fact that reason is used in Christian theology that is in question, but
the use made of reason. The apostle's ideal stemmed from the
gospel of the lordship of Christ: 'We demolish arguments and
every pretension that sets itself up against the knowledge of God,
and we take captive every thought to make it obedient to Christ'
(2 Cor. 10:5). The doubts expressed about the capacity of the
human mind in regard to the things of God stemmed from a
strong conviction about what sin does to the intellect: 'the sinful
mind is hostile to God. It does not submit to God's law, nor can
it do so' (Rom. 8:7). When Paul preached his gospel he commended it not on the ground that it was a 'reasonable belief', but
as 'a stumbling-block to the Jews and foolishness to Gentiles' (1
Cor. 1:23).

Luther's angry reactions to the use of reason in theology did
not defend the irrational.[23] He stood for the principle, however,
that the gospel must be judged on its own terms, and that the
human intellect is not a neutral and calm umpire, well able to
deliver a dispassionate verdict. If we think of reason as the
faculty for making logical judgments in accordance with the
facts, it is easy to assume that something very much like common
sense constitutes what is reasonable. It follows that the claims of
the Christian religion, especially the Bible's claims, merely need
to be subjected to the deliberations of common sense before
being let loose on the world. This has the advantage of reducing
potential conflict with the opinions of others. It fits in well with
those movements in theology since the seventeenth century that
have valued moderation and reason. They have produced

172

versions of Christianity that showed first that it was the most reasonable religion and then that the deliverances of reason formed a most acceptable religion. Of course, in the scepticism of Spinoza, Voltaire and Hume, reason was pitted against Christianity. It was then necessary for the Christian apologist, having submitted to the terms of the encounter, to modify the claims of the Bible, to make it conform with what reason had to say. The criticisms of the morality of the God of the Old Testament were felt to be most telling, for instance; and many abandoned any attempt to defend the Bible, other than by suggesting that it dealt with various stages of the evolution of the race, an idea that was ultimately at odds with belief in the inspiration of Scripture.

And, indeed, common sense is in that guide in many aspects of life. We are committed to the view that there is one truth as there is one God. We are hardly likely to be satisfied with a view of the truth that simply judges the Bible for its inner coherence. Most versions of the Christian faith assume that the Bible actually corresponds in some way with the world, and that its teachings and historical roots in our space and time are genuine. That being the case, we want our understanding of the Bible to incorporate the insights of research and criticism. When the Bible and contemporary science appear to conflict seriously, as do Moses and Darwin, we rightly look to our interpretations both of the world and of the Bible to see whether either is fundamentally at fault. We prefer to be logical rather than illogical. We may therefore be forced to modify one or other of our interpretations, or even, in an extreme case, to abandon one altogether. Yet it is also common sense not to panic at contradictions, but to suspend judgment while giving further thought to the matter.

The Bible reminds us, however, that when we value reason or common sense, we need to ask, 'Whose common sense? Whose reason?' We may believe that the form of the reasoning mind is the same in every human being, but reason is no more divorced from experience, culture and personality than is the will. We are far less inclined to believe in neutral reason now than in the eighteenth century. In philosophy it seems likely that the stranglehold of empirical thinking on epistemological theory has at last been broken. We should no longer adopt the model of the physical sciences, or at least an earlier version of how the physical sciences work, to understand how all genuine knowledge arrives.

173

We can see ever more clearly that science is not value-free, and that systems of thought such Marxism and Freudianism, which had a massive impact in the twentieth century in determining for many people what is 'rational', are definitely not examples of value-free science or even of science in any sense. On the contrary, both systems are premised on the rejection of Christianity as the invention of human minds. We have begun to realize that all human reason betrays personal and spiritual commitment, which affects the pronouncements of 'common sense'.

The failure to relativize common sense when faced with the Bible has had malign effects in theology and hence in church life and in evangelism. It has contributed to a cultural enslavement of the Bible, in which its message is sanitized for public consumption in the present world. It will always be the case, of course, that readers of the Bible will bring the presuppositions of their own experience to the text. Sometimes, these presuppositions yield fruitful results, as new questions are asked and as nuances missed in a previous generation are recovered. But the reverse is often the case, and the word of the Bible is suppressed or ignored. Indeed, we have experienced massive attacks on the Bible in the name of Christ. The Old Testament in particular has suffered, with the result that it has become commonplace even in the church to believe that the God of the Old Testament and the God of the New are different. Some sections of the church are incorporating into their life elements that they admit are at odds with the teaching of parts of the Bible, but that have arisen from the demands of the culture in which we live. Indeed, very serious issues are now being raised about the translation of the Bible and the need to conform the ancient text to the susceptibilities of the common sense of contemporary culture. All translation is affected by culture; some translations are consciously conforming themselves to its ideologies.

I am not, however, advocating the subjectivism that would follow the complete relativization of thought. On the contrary, if we start from the Bible itself, a commitment to objectivity is called forth.[24] Reason must be related to the Bible understood as the word of God, and conformed to this foundational truth. According to the doctrine of creation, we are made in the image of God to rule the world he has given us. The world itself is no emanation of God, but a contingent order, separate from him and yet relying on him, and bearing the marks of his rational mind. The gospel frees us from false views of spiritual connections with the world, and enables us to study it with confidence. Reason aims to conform us to the truth, and the truth is there to be known. It involves false starts and false assumptions; it requires trial and error; it makes us bump up against reality and hurt ourselves on its sharp edges. But truth is not merely a social construct; it does not merely impose the mind upon the stuff of the world around us. It recognizes reality, and approximates ever more closely to that reality. In all things it requires love, sympathy, insight, intuition and humility if it is to reach its goal. That conclusion frankly recognizes the nature of human beings: that we are not merely thinking machines, but do our thinking out of a certain heart and in a set of relationships. There is no call for a sceptical philosophy or a solipsism of the spirit.

That is why we need the gospel in order to be able to think. In matters to do with God, our minds are especially darkened. We cannot think straight. 'How can you believe if you accept praise from one another, yet make no effort to obtain the praise that comes from the only God?' (John 5:44). As with the will, so with the mind. The gospel leads to the transformation of the mind, the capacity to see the truth about the world, denied to us when we were unbelievers. It does not lead to anything like complete knowledge ('Now we see but a poor reflection as in a mirror', 1 Cor. 13:12); nor does it make us more able mathematicians (for example) than unbelievers, though it may improve our reasoning capacity as such. But in the matter of how the world really runs, for what purpose, according to what standards and to what conclusion, the little child shall lead them. Once we have accepted the gospel way of knowing God and the scriptural authority to which it leads, to turn round and deny the teaching of Scripture is to engage in self-contradiction, in true irrationality. By accepting the gospel we are confessing that God has miraculously entered the world in the person of his Son, that he has spoken by his Spirit and that his word is present in the world. It seems strange to have made so unfashionable a confession and then to draw back in disbelief of the Bible.

That is not to say that the Bible is all sweetness and light. On the contrary, it contains stories and aphorisms enough to offend almost all canons of common sense and morality. The Bible's speech is never as crude as the pornography around us. Remarks that the Bible is bawdy or crude reveal more about the speaker's ignorance of the Bible than about the book itself. The Bible certainly recounts crude and horrible events, and does not cover the horror with conventional discretion. But neither does it titillate or delight in violence or in perversion. The real problems lie elsewhere: in the creation of the world in six days, or in extravagant miraculous events such as the sun's standing still, all the animals being saved in an ark, a speaking ass or a resurrection from the dead. Such accounts not only smack of folk tales; they seem to presuppose a view of reality utterly at odds with the scientific one at the base of our culture, which has overwhelmingly proved itself reliable. Furthermore, what are we to make of a book in which God is portrayed as endorsing the killing of populations, and which speaks so clearly of horrendous judgment for all and everlasting punishment?

It is entirely right to use these questions to re-examine our understanding of the Bible. It may be that commonly held and long-established opinions about its interpretation need to be revised. The current re-examination of what the Bible says about women has been provoked largely by cultural forces outside of Christianity, but it has been a healthy and salutary exercise. Likewise, Darwinism created a hermeneutical crisis that led to advances in the way biblical texts were read. The presence of symbolic or aetiological stories is now more readily apprehended, and this has led to exegetically fruitful results, as the Bible is freed from the burden of answering inappropriate questions. If, in the end, however, it could be shown that the early chapters of Genesis were intended to be read as a 'scientific' account of origins, then we should read it in that way, aware that it would lead to a major confrontation with the ruling ideas of our society, but confident that the problem must lie with Darwinian evolution. After all, no scientific theory is immutable, but can certainly be used idolatrously.

The fundamental question is not so much the separate elements that cause us to question the Bible, though each one needs to be examined closely. The real question is whether we can believe in a God like that. The habit of choosing to incorporate some parts of the Bible into one's theology and to neglect or reject other bits is dishonest. It is not true to the way the Lord of Christianity himself treated the Bible; indeed, it is his teaching on judgment and hell that is frequently emasculated. There are few sterner words about divine punishment than those of Jesus himself: 'And you, Capernaum ... I tell you, it will be more bearable for Sodom on the day of judgment than for you' (Matt. 11:23–24). It is worth observing that he not only threatened Capernaum, he also assumed that the judgment on Sodom was fitting. In this (and in other cases) he seems to have shown less sensitivity than many modern moralists. The God of Jesus was the God of the Bible, the God who raised the dead and did works of judgment.

We ought not to neglect the value of the Bible's plain speech. We are swimming (some would say drowning) in the world of postmodern culture. The Bible is one of the few accessible genres that speaks with a different accent. Its vitality, roughness, harshness and determination that we realize that there is a God and that there will be a day of reckoning offend modern sensitivities. But they need to do so. Indeed, the very strangeness of the Bible is one of its chief advantages. It seems to come from an older and less sophisticated time, to speak in powerful tones, to remove the coverings of human existence. If it connects God with the destruction of nations, it also portrays him as the avenger of the innocents and the protector of the widows; it gives us the raw materials for a profound meditation on the horrors of our own genocidal age. It says to us that even here, God is involved, that things are not out of his control. The cruel death of the Bible's central person, in the malice of human beings and the judgment of God, shows us that God takes the suffering of this world with absolute seriousness. The destruction of Sodom illumines the cross and is illuminated by it, just as the resurrection of the dead illumines the powers of the one who can make the sun stand still, should he be pleased to do so. They all show that our human understanding of the world, scientific as it may be, is reductionist. A great eschatological act is not beyond the bounds of possibility.

In the end, the Bible is the most reasonable of all books, for it conforms with reality. It is our culture that is irrational, our minds that are darkened. Just as the gospel commends itself to us by making sense of our experience, so too does the Bible. It insists on bringing moral judgment to bear on our existence, and revealing the truth about the human heart. It brings before us a standard of morality and godliness that would absolutely transform the world were we to live in accordance with its precepts. It provides a pattern of the relationship between the sexes that endorses the difference while affirming the equality. It majors on forgiveness of the wounded conscience. It gives hope for the future. Undoubtedly it cuts across many of the ideas held most dear in the culture. It is all the more important, therefore, that Christians should not capitulate to the contemporary mores. It is the difference of Christianity that will make the biggest impact, and, if indeed the Bible is the word of God, we may be sure that it will prove to be centred on the 'the power of God and the wisdom of God' (1 Cor. 1:24).

In short, human reason in all its variety is a most useful servant of the gospel. But where reason or tradition becomes the master of the gospel, dictating how the word of God may come to us, it serves only that evil from which God aims to free us.

Conclusion

The authority of Scripture is set within the whole issue of human freedom. We cannot understand the nature of that authority except by seeing how it flows from the preaching of the kingdom of God. By his kingdom God frees us from our spiritual enemies and brings us into the service of his Son. In God's kingdom Jesus becomes the covenant Lord of God's people, ruling over us through the Scriptures, which are his 'Book of the Covenant'. This ruling function determines the nature of the Scriptures, and in particular the singularity of their authority. We have further things to learn from their covenantal nature, and so the next chapter deals more directly with the study of the covenantal Scriptures.

8

THE NATURE
OF SCRIPTURE

I have been arguing that we must retain an exalted view of the authority of Scripture in order to be consistent with the Christian gospel. When we are brought into a saving relationship with the one we call 'Lord', we expect to be ruled by his covenantal word, and in the final analysis that word is the Scripture. In the conventional language, Scripture is the uniquely inspired revelation of God. Because of this origin in God and the covenantal function it has been given, we rightly expect Scripture to exhibit two features that reflect God's character: unity, because God is completely consistent, and truthfulness, because God cannot lie. The alleged failure to exhibit these characteristics has played a part in the loss of the authority the Bible once had. Even more significantly, it has a vital bearing on the subject of how to read the Bible (a topic examined in the next chapter). The present chapter explores the nature of the unity and truthfulness of the Bible to see what is and is not being claimed on its behalf. In order to accomplish this purpose, I shall enlist the help of biblical criticism properly understood.

Criticism and Scripture

The Bible is a book, intended to be read, and read as God's word. The art of reading is inevitably critical; it concerns itself with evaluating the reality of what it is encountering, and it seeks to enable others to read and understand effectively. As long as texts and readers exist, criticism will be a by-product in the service of both. But there is an ambiguity that affects and afflicts the exercise of criticism. One dictionary definition renders the business as 'The art of estimating the qualities and character of literary or artistic work; [specifically] the critical science which deals with the text, character, composition, and origin of literary documents'; but it also gives 'fault-finding' as a nuance.[1] Is criticism constructive or destructive? We need only think of the various battles that break out in the never-ending war between the artistic and the critical communities to be aware of the tension caused by the ambiguity. What is the critical task? Is fault-finding integral to it?

Fault-finding is indeed integral to the critical task of whatever level, as long as the task is committed to the search for truth and is itself guided by the highest standards of integrity. It is through finding fault with certain readings, for example, that the textual critic is able to proceed. But the critic himself would be at fault if the fault-finding were done from a spirit of prejudice or the misguided view that finding errors was the goal of the critical procedure. Even the important task of exposing a fraudulent document is not complete until the critic has determined what it is (as opposed to what it is not). Why a document was forged and by whom remain vital historical questions, sometimes of greater importance than the original enquiry. To say that a document was forged does not prejudge its significance or value.

It ought to be a principle of criticism of whatever type, however, that the critic is the servant of the artefact, not the reverse. The fundamental task of the critic is not demolition, but understanding and transmitting that understanding. It is to stand beside other viewers or readers, helping them to understand what it is that they are observing. The human critic can never offer a comprehensive understanding, but there may still be genuine critical insights not understood even by the artist herself or himself. The evaluation of a text may be negative; by certain canons of literary or historical judgment the text may be defective, trivial or unworthy. Such judgments are necessary, but they need to be based on the truth of what is being observed. That is, attention must be given to such matters as genre and style, which provide a fitting context for evaluation. But, although the judgment may be negative, it should also be respectful. Criticism that fails to be humble will fail to be criticism.

Can there be a theory of biblical criticism as such? If it is fundamental to the critical task that an artefact be assessed for what it is, how much more so the Bible! In the first place, this means recognizing that the Bible has come to us in the form of texts written and assembled by human hands. The Bible has to be read, it is fitting, therefore, that the art of criticism should be applied to it; and it is not surprising that a deeper understanding will ensue, and, indeed, that God will use the art of human criticism to protect, explain and establish the text itself. Given the nature of the Bible, textual, literary and historical criticism has been applied fruitfully in the service of the reader. We now know more about the history and geography of biblical times than at any stage since the passing of the ancient world. There have also been notable advances in our understanding of how language works. Likewise, the recent development of narrative criticism has given an understanding of historical narrative that has served to enrich our reading while at the same time challenging the prematurely negative judgments of historical critics on features of the text they found puzzling.[2]

But the divine origin of the Bible is also an indispensable part of its reality. The besetting sin of modern biblical criticism is the failure to be humble, to respect the true nature of the object of its art. Virtually since the inception of modern biblical criticism, many of its practitioners have proceeded on the operative assumption that the Bible is merely a human production. They have reversed the order of authority of God's word and of human reason (as discussed in chapter 7), and have given culture the opportunity to dominate Scripture. In the words of German theologian Michael Welker, 'It is no secret that biblical criticism has totally destroyed all attempts to divinize Scripture or to attribute any form of "supernaturalness" to it.'[3] Taking their cue from the physical sciences in deciding to study the world as though God did not exist, literary critics have proceeded as though the Bible were only the work of human hands. But the methodology is flawed. Since it is in fact the work of human hands, their work has not been in vain; since it is not only the work of human hands, their work has failed to be truly critical. The consequence has been an inability to enlighten. It can hardly be disputed that the vast outpouring of critical commentaries on the text has done little to make the Bible better read or preached. It is not surprising that even among the guild of biblical critics it has come to be recognized that some of the procedures of earlier critical studies contributed little to our understanding of the Bible.[4]

The gospel confronts the biblical critic with an inescapable prior question: do you believe that God raised Jesus Christ from the dead? If God raised Jesus, then a naturalistic account of the world is impossible, for we have been shown that the world is run by a sovereign God, responsible for the causal processes and able to vary them as he pleases. A positive answer reveals a willingness to allow for the category of miracle; that in itself, given that the Bible contains many accounts of miracles, will make an immense difference to the way the text is treated. But we need to go further. The same gospel leads to an inspired Bible. Inspiration itself falls into the category of miracle. At this point, hesitations arise even among professed theists, because this seems more than an ordinary miracle. They may be willing to accept what may be called 'miracles of intervention', like those recorded in the Bible. But such occurrences are birds in the bush; the inspired Bible is a bird in the hand.

Naturalism has been decisively refuted by the bodily resurrection of Jesus from the dead. If such an event has taken place, it is clear that naturalism is far too narrow a creed; it is the ultimate reductionism. But there is a constant temptation for theists to compromise with naturalism. In the case of the resurrection itself, compromise takes the form of denying the resurrection of the body. In fact, it is the resurrection of Jesus' body and his continued bodily life that constitute the supreme 'standing miracle', the demonstration that God does run the world. It changes our whole perception of reality. The flight from the bodily nature of the resurrection among some Christians shows an unwillingness to acknowledge that God is at work in the arena of physicality. It is, not surprisingly, accompanied by a denial of the inspiration of Scripture, for to confess inspiration is to confess that, contrary to

182

naturalism, there is an order of divine acts that affect the world and continue to do so.

The theory of biblical criticism, then, involves the singular art of doing justice to a text that is uniquely divine, yet pluralistically human, in its origin, content and function. The search for the understanding of any text must be founded on the basic truths about the text. God's inspiration determines that unity and truthfulness characterize it; but what sort of unity and truthfulness characterize this inspired but human text? A critical method based on the truth of the nature of the object of the criticism will display a capacity for reading it in profoundly satisfactory ways. The challenge is to develop an appropriate pattern of reading, a matter that will be further addressed in the next chapter.

The unity of Scripture

Despite the manifest differences in the origin, style, date and content of the books in the Bible, it has been traditional to treat the whole as one book, the word of God. This arises, of course, from the belief that the God who never lies speaks self-consistently and without contradiction, and that he is in a direct sense the author of Scripture. Unity has been, then, a key interpretative principle. Bible-reading presupposes one divine mind behind the text, and the basic strategy is to compare one part with another. In recent times, however, it has become customary to stress the diversity of the Bible. It has been suggested, virtually as a matter of theological principle, that we ought to notice the many voices of Scripture, and to allow each its say, even if they are interpreted in a contradictory way.[5] The voices of John and of Paul concerning Christology, for example, can be allowed to utter irreconcilable 'truths'; there is therefore no one Christian faith, even in Scripture. Consequently, I shall discuss the unity of Scripture under two headings. First, the canon of Scripture: on what grounds is it right to treat this collection as a unity? Secondly, the nature of unity: what sort of unity do these books possess?

The canon of Scripture: the fact of unity

Most people, when they first encounter the Bible, assume that like other books it forms a self-evident and authentic unity. Even our printed editions of the Bible may, however, raise questions. One of my own earliest encounters with the Bible left me puzzled: when the teacher asked my class to turn to a New Testament book, I found that the Bible I shared with the boy next to me did not contain it. My friend was Jewish, and it was then that I discovered that Jews and Christians share many of the Scriptures, but not all. Later, I found that my father's Roman Catholic Knox version contained more books than I was accustomed to. The problem of the canon had begun to impinge on me. What is the Bible? On what grounds were its constituent books chosen?

Further theological and historical study revealed the extent of the historical difficulty. Neither Jews nor Christians can point to a particular moment, council or person as the authority that determined the extent of the biblical literature once for all. The present disagreement reflects the more general uncertainties of an earlier time. With regard to the Old Testament, the diaspora Jews acknowledged a wider range of books, in the Septuagint translation, than did the Palestinian Jews at the time of Jesus. However, more recent investigations have shown that the Old Testament canon was settled and fixed as early as the second century BC. Evidence that had been thought to indicate disagreement over the range of books to be acknowledged as Scripture witnesses only to the varieties of books read and used within Judaism and the early church. The Old Testament canon was universally accepted by all branches of Judaism, as well as by the non-Marcionite early Christians, and is the same as the Jewish Bible and Protestant Old Testament of today. With regard to the New Testament, the authenticity of books such as Revelation and 2 Peter was doubted in some regions of the early church. These were accepted only with difficulty. Other books, such as the *Gospel of Peter*, were accepted in some parts of the church but rejected in others. They were finally excluded. The key issues for the acceptance or rejection of a book seem to have been authorship, consensus among the churches, and theological consistency.[6]

The problem of the canon has become particularly acute in our own day in the academic study of Scripture. The difficulty is even more fundamental than the question of the range of Scripture: the issue now is whether we should have a canon at all. Indeed, abandoning the canon is implied in the abandonment of inspiration. The doctrine of inspiration results in identifying a set of writings as possessing a unique authority. But if there is no inspiration, strictly speaking there can be no Bible. Admittedly, by force of custom and the tenacious grasp of the churches on the Bible, it has continued to be treated as a unity even for purposes of academic study. But there are signs that we are witnessing the last days of a tradition of biblical study that presupposed the canonical status of sixty-six books.

Without inspiration, it would be better to have two looser categories, 'literature of Israel' and 'literature of the early church'. This would reflect the actual history of the times, and recover the voices of those who have been excluded from authorized literature because they were judged to be heterodox. Furthermore, there is a discernible trend to insist on the independent value of the Old Testament by giving it the title 'Older Testament' or similar, and by providing for each Testament to be studied in a different department. Of course, the Testaments have for many years tended to be divided, even in Christian theological colleges and seminaries, but now universities are tending to make it a precondition for the study of the biblical literature. The idea that there is a single canon, or even a canon at all, except in an attenuated sense, is waning. This result should have been long foreseen.

There are two key issues here, and they must be approached in the right order, recognizing their relative importance. First, and of chief importance, we need to know whether there is in fact a canon of authoritative literature. Only secondly do we need to consider the problem of the extent of the canon. The first is the question of God's activity: has God spoken? The second is the question of human recognition: where has God spoken? The main question is thus not the limit of the canon, but its existence. If the category 'word of God' is accepted, all that remains is to establish its limits, which is done through the human recognition of the truth. My argument is that the unity of Scripture is bound up both in the fact that there is a word of God and in the human activity of recognizing it.

The fact of the word
First, therefore, is there a 'word of God'? The answer has been given in earlier sections of this book. Once again, in terms of method, we return to the gospel and what may be called the

185

elements of the gospel way of knowing God. In the gospel we have the word of God, which is validated by its connection with an existing word of God, namely the Old Testament. Coming to know God through the gospel is the result of the impact of the Holy Spirit. The Spirit inspires the word and illumines the mind. The Spirit does not bypass the human mind but enables it to recognize the word of God for what it is (see chapters 10 and 11). The gospel invites us to look at certain facts. Central to the verification of the gospel is its connection to the Old Testament. Those who confess that Christ fulfils the Old Testament necessarily trust both those gospel words that they consider to be 'the word of God', and also the word of God that is the Old Testament.

The existence of a lengthy, authentic, canonical word of God is thus presupposed by Christian faith. As Paul says about Israel, 'They have been entrusted with the very words of God' (Rom. 3:2), 'written to teach us' (15:4). When Christian scholars doubt the existence of the inspired canon, they doubt the very foundation of their own faith. The present agitation about the disunity of the canon arises more from disbelief in inspiration than from a true assessment of any disharmony in the books themselves. The most basic 'conflict' has to be the one between the gospel and the Old Testament. When that is resolved, as it must be when a person becomes a Christian, the canon exists, and the books are read in a unified way.

The recognition of the word
But is this unity artificial? How do we acknowledge the reality that constitutes the Bible, both the divine authorship and the human production? Paradoxically, those who are very keen to press the disunity of Scripture do so in the face of the human history of the books themselves. There are already distinct limits to the disharmony they find. Even if we assume that there is no inspired word of God, these books have still been brought together by people who thought they saw in them an underlying unity. From the beginning it was believed that one of the marks of a true prophet was consistency with God's previously existing revelation (Deut. 13:1–5). As we know from the study of Israel's history, there were many prophets whose words were not regarded as worthy of inclusion in the holy writings. The collection did not come together by accident; there was always some sense of coherence and of choice.

186

Furthermore, those who made the choice always looked for a sense of the consistency of God in the writings.

Nowhere is this clearer than in the case of the New Testament. Its various books were deliberately chosen out of a number of candidates, and an explicit criterion was consistency. Even more importantly, the very existence of the New Testament itself depends precisely on a major exercise of this criterion. The great quarrel between the Jews who believed in Jesus and those who did not was over this point: does the New Testament fulfil the Old? The confession of Jesus as Lord is a resoundingly positive affirmation that it does.

The unity of the Scriptures is not, therefore, at any level, incidental. Even at a human level, it was planned. Indeed, another feature of the human production of the Scriptures tends to the same conclusion. When the biblical books were being written, they stood, for the most part, self-consciously in a great tradition. The later writers were often aware of the prophecies and books that made up the tradition before them, and played their own exegetical role in elucidating, quoting, challenging, explaining and applying it. From the very beginning there was the feel of a unity, in the sense that the word of God was recognized as having created the people of God. The covenant was basic to the people's life; it was the original canon and the wellspring of the scriptural teaching.

But we need to go further than this. The processes of human recognition are not mere chance, or superior insight. They certainly reflect human thought and decision-making, but, in accordance with the gospel-way of knowing God, they are also the result of the illumination and providence of the Holy Spirit, who uses human minds and wills to accomplish his purposes. The two are no more opposed than the divine and human authors of Scripture. As far as recognizing the canon is concerned, the most crucial question (as I have already noted) is the original gospel question. The Jewish Scriptures are indeed the word of God, so a canon exists; have we the right to add to it? Christians have always regarded the Jewish canon as true but incomplete. It must be added to by the gospel, and ultimately, therefore, by the New Testament.

The decision about the actual extent of both Testaments is marked by two basic features. First, once it was decided to add material to the first canon, no real dispute remained over the vast majority of books. The foundation was quite secure. Secondly, some differences of judgment about the limits of the canon remain, but they cannot be resolved except by the work of the Spirit along the same lines as his prior inspiring and illuming the gospel. In other words, no appeal to human authority as such can resolve the matter; we are properly committed to God's way of proceeding. We still need to examine such matters as doctrinal consistency, authorship and provenance as we consider what in fact speaks to us God's word. In theory, at least, it may be possible even now for a forgery to be discovered (say among the Pauline letters) and discarded from the canon. The likelihood (given the testimony of Christians about these writings as the word of God) is remote. In fact, with good reason we trust the decisions of those who were closer to the events than we are, and God's providential care for his own word.

The canon of Scripture: the nature of unity

The critical assessment of any artefact moves from the whole to the part and then back to the whole. We take in a whole canvas, for example, then focus on individual features, and then stand back once more to see the whole in the light of the parts. To take in the whole without the study of the part is to miss the depth and variety that contribute to the significance of the whole; to concentrate only on the parts is to lapse into incoherence and final meaningless. An earlier generation tended to bring the four Gospels together in a sort of *diatessaron* dedicated to the life of Jesus. But this made it virtually impossible to appreciate the contribution of each evangelist as such. One of the great gains of modern critical approaches to Scripture is the recognition of the individuality of the various authors or bodies of material, and the consequent freedom to study the parts for their own sake.

There is much to be said for this newer perspective. Indeed, its contribution is essential. It pays due regard to the unique contributions of the individual authors and corpora to the totality of Scripture, and enables us to understand better what each is saying. It rightly hesitates to move to alleged parallel passages. Rather, it is prepared to stay with the voice of the text being studied, as is essential to any proper listening process. It allows the individual to speak for himself without insisting on a too immediate conformity. It seeks to avoid the temptation of flattening the Bible out and treating it as one-dimensional. Too

188

little recognition of the particularity of the texts leads to proof-texting, plucking verses and aphorisms from all over, with little or no regard to their immediate context in the biblical story. In the end the whole suffers, because it depends upon giving each part its due.

But is there a whole, of which the individual books and writers form part? Our commitment to the Bible as the word of God already answers this question. There is a limit to the investigation of the parts; indeed, even at the human level there are limits. To write on 'the theology of Paul', for instance, really means to write on the surviving Pauline letters; Paul himself is not available to us, and his theory is not normative – only his canonical letters are. To restrict ourselves to writing on each of the evangelists rather than on a *diatessaron* is to forget that all four describe one life, one Jesus, not four. If it is irresponsible not to examine the parts, it is equally irresponsible not to bring the parts into connection with the whole.

The difficulty of the particularistic method of pursuing the critical enterprise is that the Bible becomes fragmentary and so meaningless. It may yield satisfying radical results, but it is poor criticism, since it does not reflect the essential truth about its object. It neither reflects the reality of how the Bible came to be Scripture in the first place, nor helps the church to be ruled by God. If the early church had adopted such a view of Scripture, the trinitarian dogma could not have emerged, for it was assumed at every point that the Scriptures were a unity and did not contradict themselves. As F. W. Norris points out, 'Within his *Theological Orations* Gregory [Nazianzen] uses over seven hundred and fifty scriptural citations and allusions to establish his points. What he argues is that the Trinitarian position he holds makes better sense of more Scripture than the subordinationist position given to the Son and the Spirit which his opponents hold.'[7] Of course, some would prefer a church in which Arians and trinitarians could co-exist. Yet one of the great crises of contemporary Christianity is that the internal pluralism affecting both the doctrine of God and Christology threatens to lead to its demise.

A further unifying factor sums all this up. The Bible is a book of promise and fulfilment. When Jesus met his disciples after the resurrection, he told them that 'Everything must be fulfilled that is written about me in the Law of Moses, the Prophets and the

Psalms' (Luke 24:44). These three categories summarized the entire Old Testament as we now have it. Jesus drew all three into a unity of testimony to himself, giving them the same central motif as the New Testament. In other words, the Bible is the story of Jesus Christ; he is its unity, since 'no matter how many promises God has made, they are "Yes" in Christ' (2 Cor. 1:20). The unity of which we speak is a personal unity, the unity of a painting that, containing many different elements, is yet a portrait of one person. It is not simply a matter of discovering Jesus in every Old Testament text, but of relating the whole of the Old Testament to the drama of the kingdom of God that Jesus preached, and thus illuminating the truth about him. Likewise, it is sound to assume that, although the New Testament writers may have had differing understandings of Jesus at various points, these are not contradictions. Where an author does not mention one of the chief points of Christology, it does not necessarily mean that he was ignorant of it; but whether he was or not, we are interested in the picture of Jesus built up by the New Testament as a whole rather than in speculating about the knowledge of various writers. The unity of Scripture commits us to a holistic account.

To call Scripture the word of God does commit us, therefore, to what may be called the critical practice of unity. But what kind of unity? At this point the idea of the covenant is again helpful. The covenantal word is God's means of relating to his people, teaching them, guiding them, succouring them, identifying them and giving them the words to say to him. In other words, given the multifaceted nature of the relationship set up by the covenant, it seems proper that the Lord of the covenant should provide his people with his word in the different forms needed to sustain the relationship itself. To give as Scripture a book belonging to a single genre would be to squeeze the relationship into a narrow cast. It would, furthermore, presuppose a human situation unrelated to time and space, in which the eternal word of God could meet us in the same way wherever and whenever we may be. It has been the custom in the church to treat the Ten Commandments, for example, in such a way, as though they were a species of natural law. But the Decalogue is embedded in a certain historical section of Scripture and bears the marks of particularity. Hermeneutics involves discerning the universal word in the

190

particular word and recognizing that the universal does not exist apart from the particular. As Moses says, 'the word is very near you; it is in your mouth and in your heart so that you may obey it' (Deut. 30:14).

The different facets of the relationship set up by covenant are revealed by the names and titles of God. He is the Lord, who calls forth our trust in and loyalty to him; he is the Saviour, whose mighty deeds in rescuing a people are to be constantly recalled; he is the Father, who promises that his children will inherit all things with Christ; he is the Holy One, whose words of wisdom guide and instruct the lowly; he is the Spirit, who inspires the prophets to apply the covenantal provisions; he is the Judge, who tests all things by the standard of his word, he is the Shepherd King, whose voice leads the flock. As each of these names reveals, the Scriptures with all their various facets feed and sustain the relationship between God and his people. The law tells us how to walk in the ways of the Lord. The books of wisdom show us how to fear him in the concrete situations of life. The Psalms give us the words to celebrate the events of salvation and so to praise him; they also show us how to question God, and how to speak boldly to him as we pour out our hearts before him. The prophets show us how the word of the Lord is to be applied, and hold out the promises of God. The commandments teach us what the Judge is seeking. The promises of the Father sustain faith against the contradictions of the world. The complexities of life and the variety in our relationship with God are met in the Scriptures.

Let me illustrate further the reference to the narratives of Scripture. If we were to take the view that the narratives are merely particular, their significance would be very limited. One reads them, waiting for the moment when the author draws the doctrinal or ethical conclusion. But, although there is undoubtedly a didactic element in the narratives of Scripture (see e.g. 1 Cor. 10:11), they work at other levels as well.[8] Most importantly, in the Scriptures we have the outworking of the covenantal promises in the life of the people; their history is known as prophecy for that very reason. The promises provide the interpretative grid for events; the unfolding story creates for the community that common stock of ideas and truths that is necessary if it is to flourish. A prominent example is Stephen's speech as recorded in

Acts 7. Someone has quipped that Stephen's listeners murdered him because he bored them by recounting their history. But the recounting of that history was so dangerous precisely because of the interpretation Stephen put upon it. It claimed the people's history for a novel interpretation; the community's history was the source of self-understanding, the language of their conversations and the ground for intense debate.

In fact, the bookthing of Scripture is narrative, and although many different hands contributed to the different stories, by the time the New Testament had told its tale a consecutive story from the first Adam to the last, from the first garden to the final city, had unfolded. But the narrative of Scripture itself rests on the fact that the characteristic word of God is a promise, and the promises create interest in their fulfilment. The promises and their fulfilments make the Scriptures covenantal; they make revelation historical in its form; they foster the prophetic mode; they encourage the piety of Israel in psalm and wisdom and story. Tracing the outworking of the promises creates the necessity of history; it also creates the necessity for biblical theology, the placing into context of the texts of Scripture along the line of the revelation of God. Furthermore, it turns history into eschatology as the people see their history to be pregnant with meaning awaiting fulfilment. A covenantal book is a thoroughly eschatological book.

There is truth in the contention, therefore, that, as the word of God, the Bible does not contradict itself but is a unity. But if the Bible is to do its job of presenting Jesus Christ as Lord in all his fullness, it needs the complex unity that emerges from the co-existence of many parts and many different types of literature. Sometimes, indeed, there will be tension between the elements of Scripture and sometimes superficial contradiction. Jesus tells us that 'He who is not with me is against me', and conversely, 'whoever is not against you is for you' (Matt. 12:30; Luke 9:50); the book of Proverbs carries direct contradictions in adjoining verses: 'Do not answer a fool according to his folly ... Answer a fool according to his folly ...' (Prov. 26:4–5); and whereas Exodus lays down the principle, 'I will not acquit the guilty' (23:7), Romans tells us that God 'justifies the wicked' (4:5). No doubt the list could be extended many times over. But to ask for an absence of such contradictions is to miss the point that God prepared the Bible to fit the real lives of real people. At times the fool must be answered and at times he must not; both statements are required if the whole truth is to be known. Between Exodus and Romans came the death of Jesus, which shows how God can be both 'just and the one who justifies' (Rom. 3:26). Human life is complex, and the life of God is mostly hidden from us. In order to be both one and true, the Bible must contain such apparent anomalies. The way we read such a Scripture is pursued further in the next chapter.

The truthfulness of Scripture

The crisis of the Scripture principle was born out of the clash between the confession that the Bible is infallible and the perception that it contains errors of fact, morality and theology. My argument that the Bible is the Book of the Covenant has led to the conclusion that it has a special authority over the church and the individual, and that it has the nature of a gift to us, something with which we are not in a position to quarrel. As the Lord's provision for his covenantal people, it governs us, and is beyond repeal and beyond cavil. It has, so to speak, a functional truth that necessarily reflects the truthfulness of God. Nevertheless, Scripture was given through the mediation of human beings and in human language. Is it possible – indeed, is it desirable – to apply words such as 'infallible' and 'inerrant' to Scripture? To appreciate the answer to this question, we must think further about the function of Scripture as the means by which God rules us. In particular, we shall best see how this works if we understand the requirements of faith, for faith rests on the truthfulness of God.

The nature of faith

In his prayer to the Father as recorded by John, Jesus says, 'your word is truth' (17:17). This simple statement sums up the thought of the whole Bible. It constantly celebrates the power of God's word. He is the God who can and does bring to pass whatever he promises. His word is the truth not merely in that it is completely honest, but also in the concrete sense that he accomplishes exactly what he says he will do. It is a human characteristic to lie, and to promise sincerely but to be unable to fulfil the promise. In these matters, God is utterly different. His word is never failing.

193

Take the language we find in the prophet Micah. He makes the bold prediction that in the last days the Lord's house will become what it should be. To this house the nations will come, and from it the Lord 'will teach us his ways ... The law will go out from Zion, the word of the LORD from Jerusalem'. The result will be eschatological peace and bliss, where 'Every man will sit under his own vine'. The word of the Lord will bring liberation; but it also guarantees liberation. Why is the prophet confident in this ideal future? 'For the LORD Almighty has spoken' (4.1–4). The ground of all his hope is the utterly trustworthy character of the God who has spoken; it is the word of this Lord. He confesses, like Jesus, that 'your word is truth'. The prophetic material here is absolutely typical of the whole Bible. If God has spoken, the matter is settled. His word cannot be gainsaid or broken. It is infallible.

This is true even in passages where the prophetic prediction seems to fail. Light is thrown on such occurrences by the story of Jonah. The Lord declares through his prophet, 'Forty more days and Nineveh will be overturned' (3:4). In the terms of the book, there is no doubt that this prophecy emanates from the Lord. But, although it is unconditional, it is unfulfilled, as the prophet feared. Of course, the Ninevites' repentance has interposed, and so too has God's 'repentance' in the sense of turning away from what he was going to do. But God's changed course of action here is based on the unchanging nature of his character; Jonah knew what would happen because he 'knew that you are a gracious and compassionate God, slow to anger and abounding in love, a God who relents from sending calamity' (4:2). Jonah's knowledge of God was based on Exodus 34:6, which portrays the Lord as 'the compassionate and gracious God, slow to anger, abounding in love and faithfulness'. In other words, it is the character of God, made known through the word of God, that determines the non-fulfilment of this prophecy. Indeed, the prophecy created its own non-fulfilment. If God had acted otherwise in the situation created by the repentance of the king and his people, the word of God would have failed. It failed, in fact, in order not to fail.

We are being introduced here to the inner working of the infallibility that we ascribe to the word of God. God's word is truth by very definition. That is why some contemporary versions of

Christianity eschew the clear identification of the Scriptures with the word of God. We do not want the alleged inadequacies of the Bible to reflect adversely on God. But the problem in making this division is not only that the gospel itself leads us to call the Bible the word of God in the full sense, but that the nature of faith requires the infallible word of God. When we declare the Bible to be other than God's word, or doubt whether anything bearing his name is available to us, we destroy the faith that relates us to God. That is what is at stake in modern discussions of revelation.

Let us begin once more with the gospel. It comes to us claiming to be the word of God. It invites our repentance and faith, and promises us a relationship with the living God based upon the work of Christ. To receive the gospel is to receive a word of promise and to believe that the word is what it claims to be, the word of God. Faith is indispensable in all relationships, especially when we relate to one another on the basis of promises. Faith in itself is weak and vacuous; it draws its strength from its object. We are saved not by faith *per se*, but by faith in Jesus Christ. 'Faith' is not hard to achieve or to exercise. It is one of the commonest human experiences. But it carries no significance unless it is properly grounded in the truth. Faith that is placed in the counterfeit or the spurious is superstition. It has its own ill effects and may even produce its own false comfort, as when the citizens of Jerusalem trusted in their possession of the temple of the Lord in the days of Jeremiah (Jer. 7:4). Subjectively, there is nothing to distinguish faith and superstition. Both are the exercise of the same faculty. But they are completely different in their results, because one is based on the truth and the other on error.

In much modern Christianity, this distinction is hardly understood. The subjective possession of religious faith is regarded as sufficient, as long as it is accompanied by some sort of regularity in Christian worship or identification with the church. The religious experience of conversion is sufficient to guarantee entry into some circles. But no matter how fervent the religion, how loyal the worshipper, how spectacular the conversion, all is worse than useless if the faith so exercised is not directed to its true object, namely the Lord Jesus Christ as he comes to us in the word of God. If we are to have a relationship with God it must be based on the truth: 'your word is truth'. Furthermore, the inability to trust the words of another corrupts a relationship. It becomes difficult to sustain a relationship with someone who is an inveterate liar, or even merely unreliable. What we say and who we are are intimately connected. Conversely, the trust that grows from the experience of finding a person and his or her words reliable liberates us to enjoy the flowering of friendship. Such trust is the indispensable basis of friendships that are rich, deep and satisfying. To tell another, 'Your word is truth', is to say that he or she is absolutely reliable.

Since the Christian gospel holds out to us the possibility of friendship with God and calls forth our faith in him, it is not at all surprising that it is based on words. Nor is it surprising that it requires words that are absolutely true, for that is the nature of friendship, especially of a friendship involving the complete surrender of one's life to the will of another. There is a necessary absoluteness about the obedience of Christian worship that is unparalleled in any other relationship – even marriage, which is its closest human analogue. The absoluteness corresponds to the object of our faith, namely God himself. It requires us to say, 'Your word is truth.' If we doubt the veracity of God's word, we cannot experience the full flowering of Christian faith; our faith may be mere credulity or superstition. Indeed, much Christian practice is superstition, since it makes no effort to conform itself to God's word. Because much Christian theology is premised on the conviction that we have no reliable word from the Lord, the consequences for Christian faith are calamitous.

Much of what I have said is disputed in the name of faith itself. Some point out the insecurity and riskiness of faith, quoting Paul's statement that we 'live by faith, not by sight' (2 Cor. 5:7). Surely the very point of faith is that it is not certain. It is said that faith based on certainty loses its character, and becomes knowledge; we erroneously attempt to bring forward the eschaton, in which we know 'as we are known'.

This reasoning is more plausible than cogent. It completely misunderstands faith. To illustrate from human relationships, my faith in an utterly reliable person is strengthened and enhanced by the certainty of its object. If that person promises to meet me at a particular time, but I doubt the reliability of the promise, my shaky faith is not better or more heroic than certain faith. It simply hinders the relationship. 'If any of you lacks wisdom, he should ask God, who gives generously to all without finding

196

fault, and it will be given to him. But when he asks, he must believe and not doubt, because he who doubts is like a wave of the sea, blown and tossed by the wind' (Jas. 1:5–6). The opposite of faith is not certainty, but doubt.

In any case, we should not confuse the inner with the outer. Depending on my personality, experience or sinfulness, my subjective faith may be wavering and uncertain. But the quality of my faith makes no difference at all to the quality of its object. It neither redeems the unreliable nor destabilizes the trustworthy. My poor faith will grow stronger, as experience shows me that I can trust the one in whom I have confided. It is all the more important, then, that the object of faith should be secure; this is the secret of friendship, obedience and freedom. The words of God are characteristically forward-looking; they come to us as promises. We have the promise, for example, that 'I am with you always, to the very end of the age' (Matt. 28:20). In casting doubt upon Scripture as the word of God, we destroy faith in such promises. The tension of faith is between the word spoken by the Lord and the word spoken by the serpent, or by the world, which tells us that the word of the Lord is not true. Faith is willingness to live by promises, to regard them as infallible, because 'your word is truth'. If we are to have real faith, we must have infallible words; that is, words whose truth we can rely upon absolutely and from which we do not dissent; words we can study, learn from, assimilate, use, obey and trust. These are the infallible words of God.

The infallibility and inerrancy of Scripture

It may be granted that the words of God must be infallible for the purpose for which they have been given, namely to advance his kingdom in our lives. This would mean that we fully accept the counsel of Scripture, its authority in our lives and our thoughts. But should we also speak of its inerrancy, that is, its freedom from error of any type, scientific, historical and geographical as well as theological? At first glance this would certainly seem to be the unassailable consequence of identifying the Bible with God's word, which we have argued to this point. If God never lies and his word is truth, there seems little reason to doubt that his written word must have exactly those characteristics. Indeed, the argument of the previous section seems to hinge on that point, and it is accepted as true by those who, for that very reason, deny the inspiration of Scripture.

But that is not quite the case. The argument with which we have begun, namely the requirements of faith, and indeed the more basic argument about the nature of a covenantal book, are functional. We describe the characteristics of the Bible from the function it performs in the economy of God's salvation. It is possible to argue, therefore, that, in accordance with the function for which the Bible has been designed, the Scriptures are infallible; they will not fail as the agent of God's rule over us. But the same reasoning does not demand inerrancy. It could be said that the very willingness of God to approach us in human speech betokens a condescension on his part, a godly willingness to accept the limitations of that speech and to accommodate himself to the ordinary ways of communication, which involve errors of fact that do not vitiate the main message being passed on. The biblical writers were not modern scientists, and God did not provide them with the language or insight of science as we understand it. Likewise the canons of ancient history-writing and those of our own era are not identical, and God did not suggest to the writers of Scripture that they incorporate footnotes into their method of operation. Indeed, we may say that purity of speech is only one relevant aspect of the character of God. As we have already noted in the case of Jonah, such attributes as his changelessness are also relevant. Thus, for Malachi, God's willingness to return to his people was premised on the fact that he does not change (Mal. 3:6–7). The tension between God's changelessness and his return requires a flexible use of language, and even the presence of formal contradiction if the truth is to emerge.

Likewise, it can be argued, God's desire to allow for human freedom leads to a moderate version of infallibility. He superintends the production of Scripture, ensuring that it is of a character that will fulfil his purposes for it, but not interfering beyond that with the ordinary process of creating literary works. This view is entirely consistent with a conservative view of the historical accuracy of the Bible on theological grounds. Given the significance of history for the revelation of God, it is inconceivable that the Bible should contain major historical flaws, although there may be minor errors of fact. The presence of major historical flaws would be inconsistent with the function of Scripture, and so may be discounted. After all, it matters not at all for salvation whether Jesus was entering (Luke 18:35) or leaving Jericho (Mark 10:46) when he healed a blind man, or whether he told his disciples to take (Mark 6:8) or not to take (Matt. 10:10) a staff on their journey. Scripture is not deceptive in what it has set out to achieve.

The early critics of the Bible and its defenders were well aware of apparent discrepancies and contradictions. The apologists answered critics with such explanations as they thought appropriate, assuming infallibility and the theistic conviction that God can and does act miraculously. A different strategy is called for if the bodily resurrection of Jesus is declared to be not only a non-event but an impossible event. It is one of the axioms of modern historical criticism that history must be written in the same way that science is claimed to be done, without recourse to God or the supernatural. Thus when the story of Jesus is told in contemporary history, the historian is bound to stop at the sepulchre. She or he may declare the grave to have been empty, but cannot, as a historian, say that Jesus was raised from the dead. This by no means proves that Jesus did not rise from the dead in history or that it is irrational to think that he did. It merely shows the limitations of naturalism, and that the modern practice of history cannot always know or tell the truth.

Modern approaches to Scripture built on historical criticism frequently adopt very radical reconstructions of the histories of Israel, Jesus and Paul, giving a picture entirely at odds with the biblical one. But the underlying problem here is philosophical rather than historical. The Bible contains theistic history, and the secular historian can hardly pass judgment on it. Thus biblical criticism must declare its hand from the start: is it to be based on theistic or on naturalistic premises? If the latter, it may have interesting, important, even enlightening things to say about the Bible, but in the end it cannot do justice to the reality of the text, because it proceeds on a supposition directly opposite to that of the Bible itself.

The acceptance of infallibility without inerrancy has something to commend it. Those who wish to confess inerrancy as well, however (as I do), regard infallibility alone as insufficient to guard all that belief in inspiration properly commits us to. They use the word 'inerrant' to signify 'the quality of being free from all falsehood or mistake', and hence assert that 'Holy Scripture is entirely true and trustworthy in all its assertions'.[9] This includes all matters historical and scientific in its scope. They would argue that the 'limited' infallibilist position is inconsistent with what we know about God's speech. He is the one who never lies, and is all-knowing. It is inconceivable that his word should contain error. Furthermore, it is difficult to maintain the infallibilist position consistently. Admittedly, there is a vast gap between the alleged minor errors, such as those involving Jericho, and the historicity of the resurrection. A great deal of historical truth may be jettisoned before the infallibilist is prepared to say that an unacceptable point has been reached. But jettisoning the mass of details will lead to the very situation that must be avoided, namely creating a 'historical' Jesus who is able to stand in judgment over the Jesus of the Gospels. The details themselves are part of the history, and the New Testament calls upon historical details of the Old Testament in order to make important theological points. The idea that we may limit infallibility to Scripture's teaching about faith and behaviour is impossible to sustain: in fact, it is strange to stop short at infallibility.

Is there any way of reconciling these two viewpoints? Actually, they are not as far apart as may at first appear. Indeed, it is tragic that evangelicals have polarized on these matters. Of course, there are those who accept the infallibilist position because it enables them to retain the name 'evangelical' although they do not in fact accept the authority of Scripture. There are also 'inerrantists' who go to absurd lengths to 'explain' discrepancies in Scripture without considering what their views properly entail. Five points of overlap between the two positions should be noted.

First, responsible members from both groups speak of the autographs, rather than copies or translations, as being inspired. While it is true that the providence of God may be relied upon to ensure that we may trust our Bibles to be the word of God, it is not possible to say that an inerrant Bible exists in the world today. The alleged errors and discrepancies of Scripture may sometimes be nothing more than copyists' mistakes, as we know to have been the case with the textual transmission of the documents. The idea of the autograph, however remains basic in our search for the original. The problem constitutes no more of a threat to the purity of God's word than does the parallel textual difficulty.

Secondly, both groups accept the proposition that we must interpret each Scripture in the light of its literary genre. Thus we should not assume that the inerrantist position necessarily entails a so-called 'creationist' view of Genesis 1. It is perfectly possible for inerrantists to hold that there are figurative elements in the early chapters of Genesis. There remains considerable flexibility of interpretation of the biblical corpus along these lines. However, biblical interpreters should also have the integrity not to appeal to genre merely in order to lessen the tension between the culture in which we live and the biblical witness.

Thirdly, both groups agree that scriptural writers often use approximation, hyperbole, metaphor and the other ordinary features of language, and that interpretation must take account of this. Many of the alleged errors of Scripture are detailed by critics every bit as wooden-headed as the radical 'defenders' of inerrancy. It is clear, for example, that in some cases Jesus' meaning, rather than his exact words, has been recorded. Furthermore, both groups agree that many descriptive passages or phrases are 'phenomenological' rather than 'scientific'; that is, they use the common observations, categories and expressions of ordinary speech (such as speaking of the sun rising) without involving either the divine or the human author in error.

Fourthly, both groups agree that in the process of writing the historical sections of Scripture, selection has been used, and not necessarily the whole story is told. This, of course, is a feature of all historical writing, but it should be acknowledged that ancient and modern historical methods are not identical. Truth and fraud are the acknowledged canons of both, but whether either is involved in a particular work depends upon a number of factors, including the expectations of the reader. Such devices as the topical arrangement of material do not necessarily involve error. Indeed, it may be better to distinguish the biblical histories from others even in the ancient world, noting that the Old Testament histories were classed with the prophets. What they give us is God's view on the historical process. This does not make the history any less authentic; on the contrary, the biblical documents themselves gave an impetus to the writing of history. But it determines the distinctive interests of the historians and allows them

201

to write God into the narrative in a way not open to the secular historian.

Fifthly, neither group claims to be able to explain all the problems posed by Scripture. While infallibilists may leave some of them aside without anxiety, as not being inconsistent with their view of Scripture, inerrantists do not need to claim that they can reconcile all discrepancies or explain all difficulties. They claim only that in principle all may be explained. In order to maintain their viewpoint they can point to quite a number of alleged difficulties from the past which have now been resolved in the light of increased knowledge, and can offer possible or probable explanations for a number of the remaining difficulties. Such explanations cannot, by their nature, completely demonstrate that the Bible is not in error at the point under discussion. But they function to remind us that plausible (or implausible though true) explanations may in fact be found, and that many of our problems arise simply from ignorance of the ancient world and of the background to the problematical passages.

When the views of the two groups are compared, then, the differences are relatively slight. The infallibilist has the advantage of being somewhat untroubled by the problems that are raised, and can draw attention to the function of Scripture, which, after all, remains the chief concern of the entire discussion. Yet a commitment to the inspiration of Scripture entails a commitment to its uniqueness, which flows not from natural reason but from the gospel. It is much sounder, and more in conformity with the gospel and the covenant, to refuse to attribute any ultimate error to Scripture. Scripture is God's gift through human authors and, although it bears the marks of its humanity, it is also the covenant document. It is not for us to put it aside or to pass judgment on it. Our own ignorance and lack of discernment should constantly remind us of the limits of our reason. There is a tendency among biblical scholars to over-emphasize the security of their own positions, and to assume far too readily that they are detecting error rather than exposing their own lack of knowledge. In this respect it is sometimes the ancient historians who are better guides to what we may expect from the Bible than the specialists.

We may make another observation about the merits of these two approaches. Difficulties in the text inspire different responses. Infallibilists can ignore a discrepancy such as the one about Jesus and Jericho as a matter of no significance. Inerrantists do not have to see the matter as being of great importance, but neither can they simply ignore it. It provokes thought and study. At all times such study must be done in the knowledge that no satisfactory answer may be found, and inerrantists do not feel committed to answer every problem that is raised. Furthermore, they realize that the suggested answer may not be the true one. But the effect of the inerrantist position is to stimulate continued and often very fruitful exegetical and theological reflection in order to see whether some explanation can be found.

Conclusion

The Bible is a strange book, and with every decade that passes, its strangeness becomes more apparent. It is virtually the sole survivor, in the western world at least, of the books of antiquity. Caesar, Plato and Augustine are still in print and read by many. But they have no audience even remotely comparable with the Bible. Its sayings and stories have entered the culture as no other book has. But biblical illiteracy is apparent, and where the Bible is read its message is not always understood. It is as if we have been asked to host a visitor from another culture, where the possibilities for misunderstanding are high. Such a visitor poses a threat to our own way of doing things by showing us alternatives we may never have thought of. Equally, we may judge the stranger by the mores of our own society and find him lacking for all the wrong reasons.

The human disciplines in whose name we question the integrity of the Bible do not have the last word. In many ways the Bible has always been an outsider, challenging its own contemporary culture as it challenges ours. The opening chapters of Genesis fitted no more comfortably with ancient cosmogonies than with our own; the Bible's willingness to provide the human narrative from its origin to its destiny and to judge the meaning of it all in terms of good and evil always threatens the evaluation of those who do not have such a lofty viewpoint. But strange though the Bible is, it is also perennial and profoundly human. The ancient wisdom of the Proverbs, the cries of the Psalms and the stories of the 'former prophets' speak recognizably to human experience to this day. Much of the church's present-day unease with the Bible is for all the wrong reasons, a tragic capitulation to worldliness. Like the cross, the Scripture is a paradox of God's self-revelation – foolish to the cultured, but wise beyond all measure to those who are being saved.

9

ON READING
SCRIPTURE

Nicholas Wolterstorff distinguishes between two uses of Scripture: on the one hand, 'reading the Bible to discern what God said or is saying by way of the text', and, on the other, 'reading it to discern the literary qualities of the text'.[1] Despite his warning that the academy feels 'distinctly uncomfortable' with the first option, I have argued that the gospel itself requires a properly critical reading of the Bible as God's word. Authentic biblical criticism will respect the Bible's reality as the word of God delivered to us through 'apostles and prophets'. For this reason readers can lay aside neither the theological nor the literary qualities of Scripture. God's gift to us is a literary revelation in which he speaks. If we wish to read the Bible well, therefore, we must engage in the appropriate strategies, both literary and theological. Is it possible to develop an approach to reading the Bible that is critical but also aims to discover 'what God said or is saying'? I maintain that it is, and, furthermore, that such an approach makes sense of the Bible and restores our capacity to read it well.

This chapter does not aim to offer an introduction to methods of interpretation, or to hermeneutics. Rather, I am concerned with the more fundamental issue suggested by Wolterstorff's use of the word 'reading'. Our interpretation of Scripture must arise from an analysis both of the reality of the Bible and of the activity of reading. Our techniques cannot be worked out independently of that reality and that activity. Whatever hermeneutical principles may need to be evolved, they should reflect the actuality of the work with which they deal: the Bible is God's book and needs to be read appropriately.

The whole subject of reading has been the focus of intense critical interest in the last decades. The ideas of scholars such as Roland Barthes, Jacques Derrida, Stanley Fish, E. D. Hirsch and Paul Ricoeur have penetrated literate society and have had an obvious impact on biblical criticism. Able discussions of these movements from an evangelical viewpoint may be found in Anthony Thiselton's *New Horizons in Hermeneutics: The Theory and Practice of Transforming Biblical Reading*,[2] and Kevin J. Vanhoozer's *Is There a Meaning in this Text?*[3] As Vanhoozer points out, contemporary theories of reading often reflect secular and anti-theistic philosophies.[4] A Christian response will begin with the God who speaks, and will have positive implications for reading all texts in a culture where the word itself is under deep suspicion. To enhance Bible reading, we need to understand three things: the purpose of criticism, the nature of the Bible and the process of Bible-reading. Furthermore, we must explore these issues with this question in mind: what happens when our understanding of all three is shaped by the gospel, to which we have given our prior commitment?

The purpose of criticism

In itself, the business of reading requires no special justification, training or analysis by the reader. We learn to respond to the written word through our experience of the spoken word. We do not need to engage in analytical reflection in order to speak and listen well. Likewise, most reading and writing is done without the slightest analytical thought about the processes involved, but is perfectly satisfactory to those who use these means of expression and communication. As with all things human, however, language has, from ancient times, engendered considerable and helpful reflection, leading to a critical appreciation of texts. Criticism may thus be described as the activity of 'defining, classifying, analyzing, interpreting, and evaluating works of literature'.[5] In other words, it functions to help us read well.

In the previous chapter, I maintained that authentic criticism involves respect for the true nature of the object of its art. Not all would agree with this general principle. It is a moral principle rather than a self-evident observation on a state of affairs. How can it be justified? The answer arises from the covenantal nature of the text with which we are most concerned, and which has in fact been the prime reading material for most language groups in the world. It has two stages.

First, the promises of God are at the heart of the Christian gospel. The very nature of promises, and especially promises in the form of covenants, require them to originate with an author, and to be capable of being read in the same way by both author and recipient. Any recipient therefore has a vital interest in the author and in the meaning of the promise itself, especially when the author is God.

Secondly, it is in the very nature of this covenantal gospel to challenge the critic to act in the service of the neighbour, and thus to purpose, in his or her work, to aid the writer and to illumine the reader by involving them in this reflection, and by enabling them to see what may be seen. When we approach criticism from the point of view of the gospel, we must conclude that there is both an objectivity and a moral obligation in criticism: true criticism arises from the service of the word of promise on behalf of readers and writers. Such criticism seeks to appreciate its object for what it is, and to reveal the truth about it. Its general tasks are to explain the processes of expression and reception, to engender delight in the word, and to enhance the power of language to affect the world by using and interpreting it appropriately. It evaluates the text for the sake of the reader and of the writer. Its basic purpose is to help us to read the covenant.

But biblical criticism has far wider implications than those. All critics need to be servants of what they read. It would be well to remember the words of Samuel Johnson, no mean critic himself: 'Criticism is a study by which men grow important and formidable at very small expense.'[6] We need to return to that attitude that sees service as the key to the whole endeavour, in which the critic may be thought of as the representative reader, who reads and reports on the text in the name of all readers and for their benefit. Such an attitude is particularly apposite for reading the Bible, but it has something to say to criticism in general, and offers a challenge to that variety of literary (or artistic or musical) criticism that sets itself up as a discipline in its own right.

Not all would agree that criticism exists to be of service. Many critics do not see their role in that light. It cannot be said that they are trying to serve the writer, the text or the reader. There are those who would regard the question of truth as misplaced, or endlessly deferrable. Some would regard themselves as the servants of the reader only in the sense that they are enabling the reader to be liberated from the dominance of the text. For others, the text is open and malleable; it can be rearranged and reread; it can be communicated in many different ways. The critic can become the foster-parent of the text without accepting the responsibility of parenthood. Others would not regard their work as being of service in any sense at all. Criticism is a discipline in its own right, having broken free from adherence to its object and its consumers, and is an intellectual debate carried on in and around texts with no immediate thought that it may be of any use to others. In this case it becomes a derivative, even parasitical, art, living off but not contributing to its host.

But the art of criticism cannot so easily escape the obligations imposed by love for the neighbour, and this is recognized in the standards observed by most critics. It may be that excessive interest in fictional texts has blurred the sense of moral responsibility in some critics. But the reader and the writer (even the deceased writer) are persons, not abstractions. To them, as fellow human beings, we owe the duty of truth and, indeed, of neighbourly love. I am not saying that criticism has to be uniformly (or even at all) positive towards its object, or monochrome in its approach. In fact, morally responsible criticism, Christian or not, will validly commit itself to adverse judgment on vicious or poor writing. It will not be ashamed of discriminating on moral as well as on literary or historical grounds. But, at a more fundamental level, the most liberated critic is formally committed to telling the truth, to not being a knowing party to deception. That is a feature of the responsibility of any 'conversation', not least of commentaries on the written works of others. The practice of deception is condemned by all, meaning that moral responsibility is seen to be the critic's lot, whatever his or her ideological framework. If this is so, in order to be true to itself it remains throughout a service industry. It is committed to the service of that which it evaluates and those for whom it evaluates, or else it should not go by the name of criticism at all.

A literary criticism that seeks to be of service focuses on the actual nature of the text through which reader and writer encounter each other, especially when that text has the nature of a promise. That is why criticism develops such unified fields of study as biblical criticism, or Shakespearian criticism, which call upon a variety of skills – linguistic, literary, historical – to be of service to the readers and writers of particular bodies of literature. The biblical critic, despite the inescapable historical interest, belongs to the company of those who deal with literature. We may refer to the culture that aids reading as literary criticism; the interpretation of what is written is known as hermeneutics, and the paradigms that provoke and guide the discussions of critics are provided by literary theory. Historical criticism (which is unavoidably part of evaluative literary criticism) assesses the text from its situation in life. Hermeneutics incorporates on the one hand exegesis (close attention to the meaning of the language used) and on the other exposition (the explanation and application of the material being read). But these and the many other technical terms are misleading if we do not remember the fundamental point: that we are reflecting on the primary activity of reading itself, and our thought must serve the end of reading. The purpose of criticism is to help us to read, to assimilate the content of what is read, to improve our understanding of the process of reading, to delight in the word and to see that language is used effectively. And the first task of the critic is respectfully to discern and accept the actual nature of what he or she is reading: in this case the nature of the Bible.

The nature of the Bible: three key features

Having considered the purpose of criticism, we now turn to our second theme: the nature of Scripture. If we think of the Bible as the book of God's covenant, three of the key features discussed in previous chapters are determinative in our reading of it. The first is its language, because it is a book. The second is its authority, because it is God's book. The third is its unity, because it is God's covenantal book. Acknowledging these features allows us to understand the nature of appropriate biblical criticism and of fruitful reading.

The first feature: biblical language

The Bible functions as the word of God in and through its own language. We encounter God neither apart from nor despite the humanity of Scripture. Our approach must therefore take the text itself with utmost seriousness. This commitment shows itself in four major ways: the first two in our stewardship of the text, and the latter two in our reading of it.

First, there is 'the text of the text' – that is to say, what was originally written. It is perfectly clear that God has not saved the Bible, by some continuous miracle, from textual corruption. Its transmission is guarded by his providential but not his miraculous care. The textual critic aims to restore the text of any work to its original state. It is important to note that the source is often notional, in that the first manuscript (given that there may be such a thing, when some authors leave several manuscripts) may not have survived physically. This, of course, presupposes a moral priority in the original, and therefore a priority for the writer, that may be inconsistent with the role some assign to authorship, but is a necessary assumption concerning God's text. A corrupted text may be more beautiful, precise or significant than the original, but it is to the original that we assign God's authority.

Secondly, there is the presentation of the text. We are seeking a fruitful mode of reading, and the process of reading is affected by the manner in which a text is prepared. There are aesthetic considerations here, as well as the obvious point of accessibility. The appearance of a text on the written page has a significant bearing on interpretation. In the case of the Bible itself this is plainly so. The conventions of Bible printing followed for so many years, in which the text was reproduced in columns, and divided into verses not present in the original, encouraged its readers and teachers to understand it in a gnomic way, succumbing to the difficulties inherent in following the natural unfolding of sense in an ancient text. It is worth noting too that the first printed Bibles were frequently accompanied by extensive marginal notes offering commentary and interpretation. The mere presence of such notes suggests that the text is difficult to read on its own. In the critical task of the evaluation of texts, considerations of presentation, although perhaps of secondary importance, can hardly be neglected. Since we believe that the Bible is to be read, the presentation must serve the goal of reading – not, for example, ornament. Modern versions that mirror its style and sense in their presentation do justice to the nature of the Bible and effectively promote the business of reading it.

Thirdly, the language of a text must engage attention. Biblical readers will rightly continue to concern themselves with the use of language and the business of commenting on the felicity or otherwise of style. But since language is that which carries the text, there are more issues at stake than style alone. Indeed, the evaluation of style leads through such matters as the use of metaphor and irony to the critical review of the manner in which the text reveals itself: to considerations of plot, of story-telling technique, of structure, patterns and rhythm, and of rhetorical devices. Crucial decisions must also be made about genre. Some of the most valuable critical functions are associated with such evaluation; in listening to the critics talk about texts in this way we may gain important hermeneutical insights. Furthermore, evaluating style forces a reassessment of the nature of the connection between language and history; some of the earlier historical critics of the Bible displayed a lamentable grasp of how good literature may be written and stories presented. But there are also linguistic issues to be considered, such as the various functions performed by words and sentences.[7]

Fourthly, there is the issue of the source of the text. Since texts are not self-creating, it may be taken for granted that words on a page demand authorship, and it is also generally – although not universally – believed that knowing the text's authorship (where it may be ascertained) assists in the use to which the reader may put it. (On this point more will be said in due course.) Equally, an individual text may be anonymous or the product of multiple authors. Ancient texts in particular have passed through various hands. The author may well have been joined by an editor who exercised freedom in the task of recension. Considerations such as these have led to endeavours such as source, form and redaction criticism. These labours have their place, but their importance can be overestimated. No-one need doubt that several biblical books have a pre-history; indeed they bear witness to it themselves in various ways. This history may be instructive, and may even lead to the detection of unauthentic texts, masquerading as, for example, Pauline letters. Certainly the apostle himself was very concerned about just such a possibility (2 Thess. 3:17). But our great interest is with what has been called the canonical form of the Scriptures, with the text as it now presents itself to us. Here, not in some text behind the text, or in reconstruction of the history of the text, in where we encounter the authoritative word of God.

Here, then, is the first of the Bible's key features – that it is a book, God's word written in human language. However we read it, we cannot bypass its human linguistic form to get to a revelation beyond. God's revelational mode is not silence, but the Word made flesh, whose way and words are accessible to us in their inscripturated form. The second feature, to which we now turn, is the Bible's authority, because it is not merely a book, but God's book.

The second feature: biblical authority

The authority of the Bible is God's authority. In what follows I shall refer to him as the Author, in contrast with the human writers, because he is the originator of the Bible, the one whose book it is. It is the Author who has made this book authoritative. There is no doubt that it is a wonderful book or that it also speaks with human authority. But it would not merit the esteem we give it if it were not also in a unique way God's word, and hence authoritative. It is singular in the sense that it stands without peer, although it is related positively to other sources of authority such as the church or human reason. Criticism falls into the latter category; it is an exercise of human reason. Like reason in general, it must serve the Bible, not rule it; though it is by no means alien to the Bible, since the Bible is literature.

But a telephone directory also has immense authority in its field. Where does the Bible differ? The authority of the Bible is the authority of the Lord who has entered into covenant with his people, and rules them by his given word. The covenantal idea reminds us that the authority of God begins with certain promises accompanied by stipulations through which he has established his lordship over us, and has bound us to himself as obedient people. The promises relate to particular events, places and

212

persons with real and historical existence, and yet are wide enough to touch all the families on earth. They bind into a relationship the one who gives the promises and the one who receives them. It is not possible to separate a covenant from the one who makes it. Our very relationship with God depends upon trust in his promises and hence also in his commands. Thus the authority of God is the authority of a Lord.

The nature of the Bible's authority means that a proper reading of it must involve the reverence and humility that marked Josiah (for example) when the Book of the Covenant was found in the temple: 'your heart was responsive and you humbled yourself before the LORD' (2 Kgs. 22:19). This is the spiritual point of the doctrine of inerrancy. This book is to be read as the truth and trustworthy. Proper reading demands a humble attitude. While it is true that much of value can be said about the Bible by those who do not believe its message (and much nonsense by those who do), nevertheless, as far as the task of reading is concerned, given that the Bible stands as God's covenantal book, we do not read it adequately unless it also reads us and holds us in submission. Even at a human level this is true. A letter, for example, speaks to its intended recipient in a way it cannot speak to others, no matter how learned or sympathetic they may be. The Bible mediates the very presence of God to those who have entered his covenant.

The authority of the Bible resides in its Author. But what if the whole idea of the author becomes problematic? That is certainly the case in modern literary studies, and it poses new questions about the use of the Bible as the word of God.[8] Characteristic issues for authorship (and hence for authority) are raised about three matters: the process of authorship, the meaning of the text and the role of the reader. When applied to the Bible, all three create a danger that the Author may be overshadowed or even replaced by other realities. Conversely, consideration of these points may offer assistance in the reading of Scripture. We shall now examine some aspects of such criticism as we consider the art of reading the authoritative Bible.

The process of authorship: the Author replaced by the writer
How and why do written works come into existence? What motivates and inspires the author, especially the author of such

material as poetry and prophecy? Enquiry on this topic calls on sources both ancient and modern. One of the chief areas of interest lies in the distinction between what may be called 'inspiration' and 'perspiration'. Are literary works in some sense a gift, received from outside the author, or are they the result of his or her hard labour? This distinction arises from the actual experience of authorship; it is part of the raw material relevant to a discussion of the sources of literature. It is observed by all that the creative process involves hard work, determination, concentration and revision. Yet many authors feel that the work is 'given', and that their best writing is done effortlessly. Experiments using drugs or occult techniques have been conducted in order to arouse the literary gift. Ancient theorists spoke of this arousal as 'inspiration', meaning work done at the behest of a god or spirit, with the human writer being simply an instrument of the divine will. It was sometimes compared to the wind blowing through a pipe, for instance, or to a musician playing a harp.

In modern times the same tensions have been reinterpreted. Freud and others have paid attention to the psychology of authorship. The mysterious 'inspirational' features of human creativity have been explained in terms of the projection of inner conflicts. Others have been interested in the social forces that contribute or even determine the significance of a document. The individual author may matter less than the society or class from which he or she comes. In any case, the sense of discovery, of gift, of being swept along or away by a powerful force, is explained in terms of humanity's own inner life rather than as any intervention from without.

The same shift is discernible at an earlier but equally significant moment of history. According to Alan Jacobs, the work of Samuel Taylor Coleridge (1772–1834) marks the development of a new theory of literary origins that switched the focus from God to humanity. Coleridge exalted the role of imagination in the poetic, breaking free both from the rather prosaic account of his immediate predecessors (who stressed the part played by judgment) and from the older idea of divine inspiration. 'Coleridge's imagination performs a number of functions formerly reserved for God himself: from now on, we will hear nothing of the old poetic *inspiration* in the sense that Plato and, later, the Christian

214

poets up to Milton's time spoke of it – that is, a divine source breathing power into the poet. After Coleridge, if the term *inspiration* is used, it refers not to some external source of poetic authority but to the energy inherent in the poet's own mind.'[9]

Coleridge's view has had an important bearing on nineteenth- and twentieth-century accounts of biblical inspiration. It seemed to allow room for the 'givenness' of literary invention without tying God too closely to the text as its Author. There are, however, two fundamental difficulties with it, or with any attempt to use introspection and induction to arrive at a theory of literary origins totally applicable to the Scriptures.

First, such an attempt is reductionist. The capacity, whether by Coleridge or Freud, to explain how texts originate in the soul of the writer, does not exhaust the possibility of divine inspiration. Admittedly, if we think of divine inspiration merely as the playing of a harpist, an equally valid charge of reductionism may be launched to the contrary; the human writer is given too little to do. But the notion of inspiration is not confined to such direct influence as is suggested by that analogy. Indeed, leaving the production of Scripture out of account for a moment, the distinction between 'perspiration' and 'inspiration' with which this discussion began is overdrawn. As K. K. Ruthven observes, 'Inspirational moments are generally unfit for publication in their raw state.'[10] When it comes to the inspiration of Scripture, the same critic observes, 'The prophetic influences induced by the dynamic Hebrew God are made all the more turbulent by the rugged individuality of those chosen to transmit them.'[11] Thus, to put the matter at its most extreme, there is no inherent reason why the inspiration of God should be vitiated by the unlikely discovery that (say) John wrote the Revelation under the influence of a hallucinatory drug. Inspiration is compatible with the processes of perspiration, meditation, imagination or even unconscious projection. These are merely the human methods, superintended by God, by which his word was written.

The second problem is a theological one. There is no reason why the non-Christian Freud should exempt the Scriptures from his account of the wellsprings of creativity. In the case of Coleridge, however, his move from inspiration to imagination is flawed. As Jacobs observes, 'Coleridge's theory of the imagination is perhaps the most powerful myth of poetic freedom ever devised, for it defines the imagination as immune to any outside force.'[12] Freud was later to attack it on the grounds that the imagination itself is subject to the inner conflicts of the human heart, but we must also question it in the name of God's freedom. A commitment to human autonomy that discards God's autonomy has been smuggled into the Coleridgean account and into the trend of this subject in theology ever since. So much attention is now given to the human writer that the authority of the divine Author is denied. The Author is replaced by the writer. I shall return to this point in due course.

The meaning of the text: the Author hidden by the text

The second major problem to be considered is whether the author matters in interpretation. The New Criticism that developed in the United States after the Second World War made the point that too much attention has been paid to the author rather than to the text itself, and that what we work with is not the author but the artefact.[13] It is useless to prefer what we think that the author may have meant to what he or she actually wrote. Even if we have the advantage of possessing the author's explanation of the meaning, we should not give it a privileged position when we analyse and interpret the document. The author may intentionally or accidentally misinterpret; he or she may also write more profoundly than he or she is aware. To accept only the author's interpretation may well be to miss significant truths that emerge from his or her work, and to give him or her too great an influence over the reader.

Interestingly, a similar problem is raised by legal hermeneutics. In the interpretation of statutes, the interpreter must decide whether the views of the legislature responsible for the Act should be taken into account. Is it right to examine the speeches made when the Bill was proposed in order to discover the mischief it intended to remedy and the aim of the mover? The problem here is that the legislative body may have had many reasons for passing a Bill, which were not necessarily in the mind of the mover. The interpreter has simply the actual legislation that was adopted; if Parliament does not like the interpretation offered by the judiciary, it may amend the legislation to clarify the point. Some believe that this approach is far too restrictive, and that judges must consult any available information about the passage of a statute.

216

Variations of the same issue were prominent in discussion of the interpretation and use of the Bible long before the 'intentional fallacy' (as the question of the author's intention has come to be known) was raised in literary criticism. There is, for example, the problem of the relative importance of background information for the interpretation of Scripture. Since the Bible's writers belong to specific times and places, a knowledge of the political and social issues and of the givens of the particular culture is extremely illuminating. At the most basic level, for example, the languages of the Bible are an indispensable tool for interpretation. The background, however, must not be allowed to overshadow the foreground. Our knowledge of ancient history and culture is very limited, and we may be far too confident about the way we think a text reflects or speaks to its culture. In any case, as with legal hermeneutics, it is what the text says that counts, not what we think the writer may have intended to say in the course of a conversation that we think must have been taking place in the culture.

Useful as these insights are, however, they cannot be allowed to dominate our treatment of any text, let alone the Bible. It is true that what we have is the written text rather than access to the writer's mind by some empathetic or even mysterious route. It is true, furthermore, that a writer may say more than he knows. Yet there are two senses in which access to the writer's mind is essential to the very act of reading. First, the reader must regard the author's act of writing as purposive, especially when it comes to a document inspired by God. The very fact of a text carries with it the idea of purposiveness. Since we rightly assume that there is an intended meaning, however obscure to us, we cannot dismiss the author in our search for it. In this respect at least, we claim to have some access to the mind of the author; we assume that it is a coherent and sensible mind, interested in meaning at some level and in communicating that meaning. Of course, a 'text' may deliberately lack any of these things, but then we should ask whether perusing such a document is the same as reading (except in the mechanical sense). Secondly, and even more importantly, we may rightly conclude that we have access to the mind of the reader via the language of the text. We cannot start with the mind and work to the text, but we can certainly start with the text and work to the mind.

217

To say that God's relationship with the Bible is incidental is to fail to recognize its essentially promissory nature. A promise has two ends; it cannot dangle in empty space disconnected from reality. Suggesting that the Author does not matter for the process of interpretating it denies the Bible's capacity to relate us to God; that is, of the gospel to save us. If any promise relates us to the one making it, how much more the divine promises! Any theory of literature that denies the capacity of language to relate us to the truth or to the persons beyond the text must be resisted as being inconsistent with the very nature of such a basic human activity as making promises, and indeed with the book God has given us. God's promises are embedded within, and explain, a certain history. Literary criticism that simply ignores the historical does not do justice to the nature of the text it purports to be handling; it may reflect the fact that so much contemporary criticism arises in consideration of works of fiction. The Bible contains fictional elements, such as parables, but its temper is historical rather than fictitious.

The giver of the promises that make up the gospel cannot be ignored. Promises are received by faith, and bind us in relationship to the one who utters the covenant. Such a response is mandatory in the biblical piety. Furthermore, the promises tell of a kingdom and a king that are to come. They do not merely inculcate a promise, they delineate the historical reality of the future. The Author is also the inescapable Judge. Even the strictest legal hermeneutics cannot isolate a document from its legislative source; the intentionalist fallacy is itself fatally deficient, especially in the case of the Scriptures. Both source and content tell us that relationship with the Author, indeed union with the Author, can be avoided only by unbelief.

We do not need a naïve form of the correspondence theory of truth to convince us that the language of promises at least gives us some hope (and experience) that words may attain a very strong 'purchase' on reality.[14] A conviction that words have this power, however, leads us to attend closely to what they actually say and do not say – to what we call 'exegesis'. The very significance of these words draws forth an intense effort to understand them in their original form and setting. Thus it involves a determination to acquire the original languages in which the texts were written and a capacity to understand them primarily in the context

218

of their own day and culture. The so-called historico-critical method arises from the impetus of all human hearers of promises (and commands) to know what is being said so that it may be trusted. The method itself may be abused (as when it does not begin by acknowledging that we are dealing with the word of God), but it is of a piece with the reality of the Bible. Indeed, it is demanded by its reality. That is why a true evangelical theology will always demand the rigorous task of going back to the sources in their original languages and settings. What was really said and meant matters.

It is again important to note the theological implications of the 'intentional fallacy' and its denial. In so far as the concept of the fallacy itself arises from a desire not to allow the Author to have the last word about the text that emanates from him, it illustrates once more the tendency to personal autonomy that is such a marked emphasis of the present age. When the Bible is the text in question, it signals even more emphatically the critic's desire to liberate the reader from the Author. Such thoughts lead back, therefore, to the issue of the authority of the text. It is worth remembering that the words 'author' and 'authority' are cognate, suggesting (for a start) that many texts purport to lay claim on us because of the nature of their origin. Among the functions of language, whether written or spoken, is the creation and sustaining of human relationships. Integral to this is the control and direction of others. When such a function is prominent, the authority of the text is very much bound up with its author. But the authority of a document may also be measured against the standard of reality, by its truthfulness in connecting us with the world. Even the least reflective reader brings to the assessment of a text ideas about how we measure truth and error; even the most sophisticated has made certain judgments about the reality of truth and error in our world. In any case, we cannot escape the possibility that a text may very well speak with such authority as to annihilate the distance between text and reader and shape the reader permanently and fundamentally. That, for good or ill, is inherent in language and hence in literature. The authority of the text confronts the autonomy of the reader.

But an even more radical proposal will now be discussed: that the reader becomes the Author.

The role of the reader: Author replaced by reader
In a celebrated literary hoax, Max Harris, then the editor of the Australian journal *Angry Penguins*, was duped into believing in the existence of a brilliant modern poet called Ern Malley. The poems that beguiled Harris and others were in fact arbitrary concoctions of lines, half-sentences and words chosen more or less at random and strung together in what sounded very much like meaningful collocations of words. Certainly the hoaxers were the classic missing author; we need not read any authorial intention into these poems, for there was none, unless we think that potent subconscious factors were at work in the compiling of the material.

Of course, the victims' reputations were greatly harmed, but this should not be overstated. The episode gives us an excellent example of the reader being the author, in that he elicited meaning from the texts before him. It may be that the permissible meanings of a text are manifold, and that the reader has considerable freedom to blend his own experience with its voice in order to achieve a satisfactory interpretation. Indeed, one observation made about the Malley affair was that Harris's interpretations were far from ludicrous, and that there does seem to be a meaning close to the surface of the texts themselves. They are not as arbitrary as they appear.

The emphasis that has fallen on the reader in some types of criticism is appealing. It reminds us that text and reader, however close they may be in time, culture and sympathy, nevertheless engage across a distance, and that the reader inevitably brings a clutch of presuppositions to the task of appreciation. Failure to recognize the importance of the reader and of the act of reading will lead to a false objectivity in evaluation. But there is a more profound relational dynamic at work too. A focus on the reader enables that reader to challenge the author's power and the text's authority in the name of human freedom. In more extreme forms it also enables the writer to abandon responsibility for what he has written. When accompanied by a commitment to hermeneutical 'suspicion', it can be a powerful ideological tool for uncovering the unpleasant commitments of texts, and for drawing forth that which, in a text, will turn it against itself, or bring forth from it what has been suppressed. 'Reader-response criticism' has been developed by biblical interpreters in ways that

220

have produced significant new readings of the ancient texts. Yet there remains the question whether satisfactory controls are in place to test the validity of such readings and to guard against criticism by inspired guesswork. Susan Gillingham remarks, 'Using reader-response theory, one text can produce infinite readings.'[15] This is an ominous observation.

No era has been more conscious than our own of the part played by the observer in interpretation. Even in science, once regarded as the very bastion of objective knowledge, there is now widespread agreement that the observer's perspective is very significant, and, indeed, that the observer becomes a crucial part of what is observed. How much more is this the case when it comes to matters of human relationships, especially where language is involved! What we say is measured against our possible reasons for saying it; awareness of the depths of the human personality, with all their contradictions, mysteries and motives, is a contemporary commonplace. This affects not only what is said, but also, and to an even greater extent, what is heard or read. We are prone to listen selectively, with prejudice and prior understandings that block out the information being conveyed to us. The mixing of the languages at the Tower of Babel afflicts even those who speak the same tongue.

It is these observations, as well as others about the nature of language itself, that have led to the shift of the focus of criticism away from the author and the text towards the reader. Unless we become far more aware of the subjectivities of reading, it is argued, we shall always be victims of our own unconscious prejudgments. But to be aware of the difficulties posed by our own prior commitments is one thing; to turn this into justification for a radically subjective approach to reading is another. Proclaiming that 'the reader is the author', some wish to make the reader the absolute master of the text. Texts are to be treated with suspicion, and to be read 'against the grain' and 'between the lines'. At one level this is enough to highlight the utterly self-defeating nature of such criticism, in that it depends for its own efficacy on the critic's straightforward communication of ideas to the reader. Even such critics resent being misunderstood. But since the dismissal of the author is also intended to free us from the author's authority and influence, the problem with which we are dealing goes deeper than mere logic. It has ramifications for human relationships as a whole, not only for the relation between God and humanity. Once again we are confronted with the theological problem of grace and human autonomy.

The death of the author, especially when the author is God, is all too obviously part of the human desire for independence. We can refute the idea at this point by considering the human experience of love. Love is committed and promises fidelity; the drive for autonomy refrains from commitment, and even from accepting commitment from the other.[16] Commitment is seen to be claustrophobic and entangling. As a result, individualism has triumphed as never before, and the whole question of how to love another has become problematic. Such feelings are especially evident when we come to God himself. The roots of unbelief are to be found not so much in the intellectual life but in the affective. The love of God is so all-encompassing that we do not want to live with it. As is clear from the piety of the Bible, God's gracious approach involves not the diminution of his authority but the restatement of his complete authority over us, and of our submission to his word.

Even theology finds it hard to cope with this thought. When theologians consider God's love, they treat it in all too human a way. In our hopes for love, we want the intimacy and support that love brings without the loss of individuality it entails; in marriage, we want the two to remain two fleshes and not one. Theologians speak, therefore, of the love that 'lets be', the love whose greatest gift to the beloved is autonomy. Indeed, it is common to define human maturity in terms of independence, the ability to stand without others. In particular, the feminist movement has challenged women to give up the ethic of service, which is regarded as leading to bondage, and to declare for a healthy independence. Feminist theologians therefore regard the chief sin of women as dependency rather than pride.[17]

In the midst of such a cultural mood it is easy to see why the death of the author is popular, especially the death of God as an Author. If indeed God is the Author of Scripture, he gives the words an intrinsic authority that is not always welcome. Not only so, but the content of the words themselves create exactly this situation, with the imperious gospel message that God is Lord, and the explication of the consequences of that lordship in human life. It is no accident that promises lie at the heart of the biblical rev-

222

elation and that trust is the saving virtue. It is true that the salvation proffered in the Bible does not involve the union of the soul with God as a drop of water is united with the ocean. We remain ourselves in the union that trusting in the promises brings about. But we are united to him and to one another in an indissoluble bond, which marriage itself merely foreshadows. Furthermore, the biblical pattern is of self-forgetting love that serves even to death. It is in living such a life that we find ourselves, that we become what we were intended to be, and that we discover the freedom to be our God-intended selves, a vague shadow of which the world is so desperately pursuing. 'The man who loves his life will lose it, while the man who hates his life in this world will keep it for eternal life' (John 12:25). This is the stern word of Jesus that defies the wisdom of this present age. Thus the second key feature of the Bible, its authority as God's book, demands a reverent and submissive spirit if it is to be properly read.

The third feature: biblical unity

The third key element in reading the Bible is the unity that arises from its covenantal nature. The prominence of story in the Bible has often been noted. The stories are not fables or moral tales. They arise from the covenant itself; the very backbone of the Bible is a series of stories that constitute a central story. The historical books follow the story of the promises and give the basis for that discriminating commentary on it that we find in the prophetic literature. Indeed, the biblical history is typically 'prophetic'.

Since the advent of printing and literacy it has become common for the Bible to be read by individuals. This obscures the corporate significance of Scripture as the instrument by which Christ rules his church. The narrative element in Scripture, indeed, the narrative line, is of fundamental significance in revealing not merely the person of God, but the identity and nature of the church. It provides the language by which the church connects with its past dealings with God and understands the significance of those past dealings for the present and the future. The narrative constitutes the special language of the church. The repetition of God's story is a vital reminder of the gospel; the variations and differences in the telling of the story are integral to its true application to the present; without the agreed substance of the story there could be no significant variations. This means that criticism cannot be merely historical, but must be sensitive to the literary elements of the material it is reading. The absence of literary criticism as such has been a marked weakness of biblical studies through much of the post-Enlightenment era, but attention is now being paid to this vital aid to effective reading. More will be said about this in what follows.

The unity of Scripture depends on its connection with God, that is, on the divine authorship. I have already pointed out that this unity is consistent with a diversity of time, place, language, genre, experience and outlook. The biblical unity is a unity of source (in God), of function (covenantal rule), of narrative (the fulfilment of promise), and of message (the gospel of Jesus Christ). If there has been a tendency in some circles and at some stages of the history of interpretation to overemphasize the biblical unity at the expense of its diversity, the present mood is the opposite. As a result, the Bible is being treated more and more as a diversity that cannot be reassembled. The Bible is not regarded as an integrated whole. This is a far worse result, since it makes it impossible to give a clear message about what God is saying concerning himself and the world and human behaviour. Nothing destroys the authority of Scripture more effectively than this.[18]

As I noted in chapter 8, the unwillingness to see the Bible as a whole is intellectually suspect in any case. The creation of a canon presupposes a perceived unity. But the real unity of the Scriptures is based on the truthfulness of God. It was for this reason that the Protestant Reformers incorporated as a key interpretative principle the comparison of scripture with scripture. The point, however, was well understood by earlier commentators, who were also loath to accept that there were contradictions in the Bible, and compared scripture with scripture in order to understand Scripture. It is only by seeing Scripture as a whole, and allowing the texts to modify one another, that it is possible to arrive at the doctrine of the Trinity. The fault of the Arians lay in their selectivity; the orthodox were aware of the need to listen to the testimony of the whole Bible. Another way of making the same point is to say that every text has a context, and that the final context for the biblical words is the entire biblical corpus.

I have noted that acceptance of the authority of Scripture encourages close exegesis and both historical and narrative criticism. Now we must go further: acceptance of the unity of Scripture encourages the creation of an integrated biblical theology.[19] Such a theology has used different methodologies over the years, and is now much discounted. When the diversity of Scripture is overemphasized, the project of biblical theology becomes almost impossible. Indeed, if the Bible is treated as a merely human production, an integrated biblical theology is of little interest. But the acceptance of the gospel necessarily leads to the wholeness of Scripture, since our acceptance of Christ depends upon his fulfilment of the Old Testament in the New. If we accept the gospel for the right reasons, we inevitably develop a biblical theology. Furthermore, this biblical theology is of crucial importance to the genuine reading of Scripture. It is essential to what Wolterstorff calls 'reading the Bible to discern what God said or is saying by way of the text'. Without a biblical theology we are not reading the Bible in accordance with its true nature. That unbelievers should reject this is a tragedy; that biblical critics professing to be Christian do so is astonishing.

Such a biblical theology has two facets, and both must be studied and brought into use if we are to read the Bible effectively. First, we need to give what may be called a thematic account of the unfolding revelation, following the themes of Scripture as they are handled by the different authors, and enabling the reader to locate each text within the wider whole. Such an approach is rather like the study of a theological history of the Bible, delineating what used to be called 'salvation history'. But it is more than that. It involves the business of discovering how the individual books contribute to the developing whole, and it also seeks to follow through themes such as the temple and the priesthood as treated in both Testaments. The structure provided by the covenants of Scripture is an integral part of this understanding. The basic principle arises from the comparison of scripture with scripture: how does the New Testament read the Old? Or, to put the matter differently, how does the Bible in its different parts proclaim God's kingdom?

The second aspect of biblical theology follows logically from the first, although when we come to know Christ it may precede it chronologically. When the themes of the Bible are established, we also need to study its topics, the subjects the Bible itself deals with. Just as it is perfectly proper to ask what a particular author may say about a subject across all his or her works (as in the question, 'What does Bertrand Russell have to say about war?'), so it is legitimate to ask, 'What does the Bible have to say about war, divorce, the gospel, the Holy Spirit or sin?' A genuine answer can be given, though much nuanced. Indeed, it is only by giving such an answer that we can establish what the Bible as a whole may have to say, and proceed to the business of comparing scripture with scripture. It is the way, furthermore, by which the message of the Bible can be compared with other systems of thought and applied to the present situation. Rather than calling the results of this exercise 'biblical theology', we may prefer to refer to it as 'the doctrine of the Bible' on the various subjects the Bible addresses. In any case, the interlocking of the exegetical, the thematic and the topical reading of the Bible is essential to understanding the word of God. The failure to observe this leads (among other things) to theological education that leaves the recipient with a fragmented and hence unusable text; or at least a text vulnerable to whatever subjective critical and literary methods are in favour.

At the very centre of the Bible's authority and unity is Jesus Christ. It is his kingdom that is exerted through the gospel, and that then leads us to acknowledge the authority of the Bible. Likewise, the fact that 'Christ Jesus came into the world to save sinners' (1 Tim. 1:15) is the central message of the Christian Bible, and the interpretative key for the whole. The entire context enables us to comprehend the meaning of Jesus Christ's entry into the world; Jesus Christ's great work provides our access to understanding the Scriptures. Indeed, when we fail to realize the centrality of Christ in his work of saving sinners, the Bible becomes a mysterious and fissiparous book. The importance that the study of hermeneutics has assumed in modern Scripture debate partly results from an unwillingness to recognize the gospel-centredness of Scripture. Other messages must then be found to explain the importance of the Bible for the church. Hence the significance of the third key feature of the Bible, its unity as God's covenantal book. Without an acknowledgment of such a unity, we cannot grasp and apply its message.

Conclusion: reading the Bible

I have argued that the gospel must shape our approach to the task of reading the Bible, and that, to use Wolterstorff's dichotomy, we must engage in 'reading the Bible to discern what God is saying', rather than 'reading it to discern the literary qualities of the text'. But I have also maintained that discerning its literary qualities is consistent with genuine critical reading. Such criticism must be the servant rather than the master of what we read. As we think of the nature of biblical criticism, furthermore, we can see principles emerging that may have a bearing on the whole critical enterprise, and we may find that something is being said about reading in general that may be useful to the whole culture. Indeed, a number of these observations imply that literary criticism should accept limitations in all its activities, namely that it should show humility before the factuality of any text, and a duty of love towards reader and author.

The point at issue is illustrated through the contrast made by David Kelsey between ancient and modern modes of reading. 'In the third-century AD pagan or Christian academy one might study ancient texts so as to become more deeply shaped by the virtues ...' In a research university one studies ancient texts to discover the truth about them, their origins, their meanings in their original settings, the history of their uses, the history of teaching about them or readings of them, and perhaps the social or psychological dynamics that explain why such texts came to be.[20] Elsewhere Kelsey pursues the theme by discussing the foundation of the University of Berlin, and the major influence that the model of the research institution has had on education, what is studied, how it is studied and why. It has brought about a major difference in the method and aims of teaching, for example. 'Theological education had always involved teaching in the way that *paideia* does – that is, teaching aims at indirectly cultivating capacities for knowing God. In a research university, however, teaching is aimed at cultivating capacities to do research, to engage in *Wissenschaft*.'[21]

We are, however, approaching the end of the period dominated by the research model. The inherent limitations of scientific method, especially as applied to other disciplines, has become clear. Nicholas Wolterstorff observes that 'there has occurred the death of the notion that there is such a thing as *the* logic of *Wissenschaft* and that we know what that is'. He adds, 'If there is not some true logic of the *Wissenschaft*, which has already been well embodied in mathematics and the natural sciences but at best poorly embodied in everything else, then why exactly are those others to be judged inferior?'[22] In the biblical field, there is a re-assessment of the value of the historico-critical method set loose from a recognition that the Bible is the word of God. The moment has arrived to assert once again the value of sitting before a text to listen to it in its own terms rather than to try to master it through our techniques. In the wise words of David Steinmetz, 'Until the historical-critical method becomes critical of its own theoretical foundations and develops a hermeneutical theory adequate to the nature of the text that it is interpreting, it will remain restricted, as it deserves to be, to the guild and the academy, where questions of truth can endlessly be deferred.'[23]

In our culture we are making heavy weather of the business of reading. There is a distrust of words and of our capacity to relate through words. This is not surprising, given the history of the twentieth century. To point to two major issues out of the many that could be mentioned: a new poetic language had to be developed to reflect the horrors of trench warfare in the First World War, and the art of propaganda throughout the century reached unparalleled depths of mendacity. The critic has been given a dominant role in explaining what is meant, and has found it increasingly difficult to ascribe truth to any communication. Indeed, novels are being written that are more like collages than narratives, making the critic indeed the boss of the house of literature, and literature more obscure than revelatory. But the news that one of America's most respected literary critics, Paul de Man, had once been a Nazi apologist, has raised questions about an enterprise that teaches that the author does not matter.[24] It is possible to want to escape the responsibility for authorship in the guise of escaping the author. In reading the Bible, our flight from the Author is an example of our general flight from God, as when Adam and Eve hid from him in the Garden. The gospel shows that we are fooling ourselves into thinking that freedom may lie in such flight. This applies fundamentally to God, but our unwillingness to accept the authority of the human author also leads to the corruption of relationships at all levels. Cynicism and love cannot co-exist; where words fail, love fails too.

Biblical criticism that starts from the actuality of the Bible – that is, that starts with the God whose speech it is – thus has profound implications for reading in general. If God is able to use words that we may trust, and to develop a deep relationship through words, there is hope for human language. We may not be able to do all that he does, but he points to the possibility that there is such a thing as truthful speech, which may be trusted, and through which genuine human relationships may come. In the search for such speech it may be that the form of the promise can provide the basis for the rehabilitation of language. Promises demand an assessment of truth; they serve to relate persons; they initiate a narrative of hope and fulfilment; they evoke commentary, discussion, literature and poetry. When our culture abandoned the Bible as its standard of life it may have done far more damage to its roots than it could have imagined. The way back will be through a commitment to the widespread knowledge of God in his word.

10

___

THE GOSPEL AND
THE SPIRIT

Revelation, prayer and the Spirit

In his powerfully argued book, *Religion within the Limits of Reason Alone*, the great philosopher Immanuel Kant briefly addresses the subject of prayer. There are few things as indicative of individuals' theology – and especially their doctrine of revelation – as their attitude to this topic. Here we may observe what they know of God and what they have made of their understanding. It was a discussion of great cultural significance: Kant's influence on subsequent thought has been immense. Virtually every area of Christian theology had to be re-examined after him, and he has had many theological and spiritual disciples.[1] Whether through his direct influence or not, the Kantian view of prayer has found widespread acceptance in the churches.

The philosopher's remarks are entirely consistent with his moralistic and rational account of religion: '*Praying*, thought of as an *inner formal* service of God and hence as a means of grace, is a superstitious illusion (a fetish-making); for it is no more than a *stated wish* directed to a Being who needs no such information regarding the inner disposition of the wisher; therefore nothing is accomplished by it, and it discharges none of the duties to which, as commands of God, we are obligated; hence God is not really served.' For Kant, true prayer, what he calls 'the spirit of prayer', is a 'heart-felt wish to be well-pleasing to God in our every act and abstention'.[2]

Such prayer, Kant says with reference to the biblical injunction, 'can, and should, be present in us "without ceasing".' In these terms, the only value of explicit prayer is its role in strengthening our own resolve to live in the service of God. For Kant, it may be worth teaching children set forms of prayer to quicken the imagination, but in adults this risks hypocrisy. A religion shaped by the philosophy of his book as a whole is bound to lay strong emphasis on duty without the motive of reward, on the capacity of the human being to choose the good and do it, and on the cool and self-sufficient practice of religious duties. It is the religion of the self-made and self-directed person. Its distance from the religion of the Bible could scarcely be greater.

Unlike the frigid religion of Kant, Christianity rejoices in petitionary prayer. The prayers of Jesus are models of petition – including prayers for forgiveness, which are difficult for Kant to justify, but are the basis of our relationship with God. We have the right to enter boldly into the presence of God because of the atoning and sufficient sacrifice of Jesus Christ on our behalf (Heb. 10:19–22); something, once again, that found no place in Kant's religion. No-one may doubt Kant's moral seriousness or philosophical stature, but in terms of biblical religion he was a man to whom Paul's question directed to the Ephesian disciples would have been aptly addressed: 'Did you receive the Holy Spirit when you believed?' (Acts 19:2). His view of prayer is evidence that the Spirit-given relational heart of the Christian faith was alien to him. The effects are bound to show in attitudes both to prayer and to the fellowship of believers.

In contrasting biblical prayer and Kant's prayer, we have reached a distinct parting of the ways. Kant has no place in his philosophy for the miraculous, and he excludes from conscious human experience the discernible workings of grace in the heart and life. In effect, his teaching encourages that naturalism that reads the world as empty of the immediate presence of God. But the Bible forces upon us the option of believing in God's activity in people's lives through his Spirit. We have to choose between competing visions of the world: the world in which God is a spectator, and the world in which he is involved. But it is more than that. At base, there is also a competing view of human nature: one in which persons are free, and in which their life is a commitment to choose the good impulse over the bad, so that they may meet their Judge with a good conscience; the other in which persons are enslaved, and need redemption so that they may meet their Judge with a sure Saviour.

Kant as the ultimate Protestant?

It may well be said, however, especially in the light of Kant's Protestant antecedents, and also his influence in subsequent theology, that he simply represents the logical outcome of Protestant thinking. It was, after all, the theologians of the magisterial Reformation who repudiated contemporary miracles, preferring to relegate the supernatural to the biblical era. Their attitude helped to desacralize the world. When confronted with Catholic miracles, all they had to put in opposition was the word of God. It is true that they were convinced of the inspiration of the Scriptures by the Holy Spirit, and this more or less ensured a standing revelatory miracle. But surely, it may be asked, is not the religion of Kant only the deistic end-product of Protestantism? The collapse of the doctrine of the inspiration of the Scriptures, obvious to the Enlightenment thinkers, was God's final banishment from a naturalistic worldview that Protestantism had unwittingly brought into existence. According to the neo-orthodox critique of the liberal theology following Kant, the response was to turn the activity of the Spirit into the activity of the human spirit.

Inspiration and illumination

In so far as revelation is the issue, such a response is wrong. The leaders of the Reformation, especially Calvin, accompanied their doctrine of the inspiration of Scripture with the doctrine of the 'inner testimony' of the Spirit. The Bible was revelation, but the revelatory process was complete only when its word was believed by the sinner. Revelation is given in Scripture but fulfilled in the intersection of giving and receiving. And that too was the work of God by his Spirit. The Spirit was not, so to speak, shut up in the pages of Scripture, but was active in testifying to its heavenly origin and authority, and, indeed, in imprinting the gospel on the heart and drawing the sinner into union with the Saviour. And yet he did not speak independently of the Scriptures, but rather through and with them:

> Let this point therefore stand: that those whom the Holy Spirit has inwardly taught truly rest upon Scripture, and that Scripture itself is self authenticated ... Therefore, illumined by his power, we believe neither by our own nor by any one else's judgment that Scripture is from God; but above human judgment we affirm with utter certainty (just as if we were gazing upon the majesty of God himself) that it has flowed to us from the very mouth of God by the ministry of men.[3]

In all this there is no doubt whatever that Calvin had seized upon a highly important strand of the biblical evidence about the Spirit's work. The doctrine of 'illumination' played a key role in the debate with Catholicism, by safeguarding the sole authority of Scripture (as opposed to that of the church in validating the Bible) and the sole contribution of grace (as opposed to the capacity of human beings to turn to God for help). The doctrine of the Spirit as inspirer and illuminator of Scripture functioned to secure the grace and authority of God in the knowledge of God. In the *Institutes* Calvin gives so profound a treatment of the work of the Spirit that he is justly known as a 'theologian of the Holy Spirit'.

It is true, however, that the Calvinistic doctrine proved unstable. A tension between inspiration and illumination was felt in Protestant theology from an early period. On the one hand, there was a stress on the biblical source of revelation, which tended to formalize the process of revelation so that it simply became the knowledge of the Scriptures. Where the idea of illumination was carefully made subservient to the word, the work of the Spirit became 'invisible' and might just as well not have existed. Inspiration became the fundamental category, and illumination became merely a subset of the doctrine of Scripture, functioning as a polemical device to protect the Protestant theology from attack at this point by Catholic theology. By the end of the seventeenth century, John Locke was in fact appealing to the Protestant denial of contemporary miracles as well to as a Pelagianizing anthropology to deny the inner light at all, whether the need for it or the fact of it.[4] At the same time, however, there were those who took the doctrine of the 'inner testimony' and turned it into the 'inner light' and the 'inner voice'; in this way, the doctrine of the Holy Spirit became a special focus in revelation, so that there were two sources of revelation: Scripture and the Spirit. Professor Nuttall refers to 'the Quakers' tendency to contrast and (as it seemed) even to oppose the Spirit in themselves to the Spirit in the Word, and to treat the former, not the latter, as the criterion'.[5]

Conflating inspiration and illumination

Post-Kantian theology has almost abandoned the category of inspiration when it comes to the Scriptures. But the Kantian 'turn to the subject' enabled some theologians to exploit the doctrine of illumination. Or, to be more accurate, inspiration has been conflated with what the older theologians called 'illumination', so that revelation becomes an episode, often connected with the word of God, in which the recipient is addressed by God by the power of the Spirit. Gary Badcock has defended the major liberal theologians from the neo-orthodox charge of making the Spirit the equivalent of the human spirit. In arguing that in Schleiermacher the Holy Spirit is not 'merely a cipher for human religious-ethical feeling', he observes that 'what Schleiermacher sought to do was to react against this barrenness [sc. of Kant's religion] in order to make room for religious experience – to rehabilitate it, as it were – but to do so in a way that built upon Kant's positive achievement'.[6] There has been a long subsequent roll-call of thinkers from Coleridge onwards who have conflated inspiration and illumination. In so doing, they deny that Scripture may directly be called revelation.[7]

John Macquarrie reflects this approach to inspiration, while making the illumination ecclesial: 'the Scripture is not of itself revelation, but testifies to the revelation in Christ; and … it is in the living context of the Church, as the community of the Spirit, that Scripture comes alive, as it were, so that in the human words of Scripture, as read and preached, the word of God addresses us. It is in this sense that we can think of the Scripture as "inspired". It is the vehicle for the divine word, and through it Christ is made

235

present.'[8] Whether in academic theology, in official church pronouncements or in popular piety, the Spirit's ministry has thus been set free from the written word; and the moment of revelation may be found in community, in event, in history, in culture or in experience.

From the point of view of the Reformation, therefore, we are confronted with Kantian rationalism on the one hand, and with an experiential subjectivism on the other. Clearly, however, the Spirit's ministry is integral to any understanding of revelation, and cannot on any account be neglected if we are to do justice to the biblical teaching about God's disclosure to us. Furthermore, I have argued already for the reinstatement of the earlier view of inspiration. But what is the proper way of stating the connection between word and Spirit?

Once again the best vantage point is the gospel. The way word and Spirit are united in the preaching of the gospel is paradigmatic of the total relation, and offers the proper theological 'control' in the discussion. It shows what is at stake from a soteriological point of view. It reveals what is the essential function of the doctrine of the inner testimony of the Spirit, by reminding us of the plight of humanity and the power of God's saving action. Only thus shall we avoid the reductionism that developed in classical Protestantism and the subjectivism that has marked the various alternatives that have been proposed. In the work of the Spirit we see again that God's disclosure is utterly gracious, a self-giving incorporation that teaches us that, while the knowledge of God may be offered in propositions, it is entirely personal. We know him in the communion of the Holy Spirit.

The Spirit of God

The Old Testament depiction of the Spirit of God is both ordinary and surprising. The basic idea of the word appears to be that of the movement of air, and so, quite frequently, the wind. But God not only sends the wind; like human beings he has a 'spirit'. That God may be thought of as possessing a spirit is no more unusual than that he is said to possess eyes and hands and feet. Human beings possess 'breath' or 'spirit' (it is often the same Hebrew word, *rûaḥ*), and the description of God in anthropomorphic terms is a commonplace of biblical language. The fundamental sense of this language when applied to human beings is that they are alive, as opposed to having lost the spirit and being dead (e.g. Zech. 12:1; Ps. 146:4; Gen. 6:17). Hence references to the Lord's spirit suggest both life and the power of conferring life. In keeping with other such descriptions of human anatomy (we may instance the heart, the kidney or the stomach), there is a linguistic shift from the merely physical towards what we may call the 'personal' or 'psychic'. It is slightly misleading to call this a metaphorical use; the level of connection and explanation is too intimate. The 'breaking' heart is a sensation both physical and 'psychic', for example. Likewise it is not unusual for 'spirit' language to embrace such realms as disposition, where 'spirit' stands for something not merely mundane but also 'personal' (e.g. Exod. 6:9). My breath or spirit becomes the indispensable bearer of my speech, and my speech is more than my breath. Word and spirit are thus connected at the physical and at the personal level. A person's spirit speaks by his or her breath.

What is surprising, however, is the way language about the breath or spirit of God begins to differ from other references to God's activities. We read often enough of the 'eye' of God and the 'hand' of God, but it is natural to understand these as vivid ways of saying 'God'. The 'spirit' of God, however, is used in such ways as to make us sense that something else is at work, so much so that translators commonly designate the spirit with a capital: 'The Spirit of the LORD came upon him in power' (Judg. 14:6); 'from that day on the Spirit of the LORD came upon David in power' (1 Sam. 16:13); 'Do not cast me from your presence or take your Holy Spirit from me' (Ps. 51:11). The suitability of 'spirit' language for what God wishes to convey about himself may owe something to the 'invisibility' of the spirit or breath, as contrasted with the physicality of the body (see, too, John 4:24). In the light of the first biblical uses, it may also have to do with the link between spirit and word as suggested by their proximity in Genesis 1:2–3, and the idea of breath and human life as indicated in Genesis 6:17: 'every creature that has the breath of life in it'.

The use of 'spirit' language in the Old Testament leaves the reader convinced that in dealing with the Spirit we are dealing with God himself. We may contrast this with 'angel' language; in some angelic visitations an angel appears to be identified as the Lord (e.g. Gen. 18:10, 13), but by the end of the Old Testament

237

it is clear that 'angel' is not another name for God. The Spirit of the Lord, however, is the Lord acting in certain ways to achieve his ends, so that the Spirit is connected with the life-giving power and presence of God. To be possessed by the Spirit is to be empowered by God; to flee from the Spirit is to flee from the presence of the Lord himself. In particular, we observe a significant link between the Spirit and those who are designated as, or promised that they would be, gifted for the good of God's people.

The three themes of power, presence and gifted persons are illustrated by the biblical citations already mentioned. The coming of the Spirit of the Lord on to Samson fills him with the power needed to fulfil his role as a judge in Israel. It is clear in the end that his strength does not reside in his hair, but in the Lord's Spirit, who comes upon him and empowers him physically for great works. The works done by this gifted person are done on behalf of Israel, used by the Lord to protect and sustain the life of his people from the depredations of the Philistines. But on other occasions the coming of the Lord's Spirit is more clearly linked with the mind, with knowledge and with speech: it is by his Spirit that Bezalel and Oholiab are filled with skill, ability and knowledge to undertake the craftsmanship involved in the construction and furnishing of the tabernacle (Exod. 35:30 – 36:5). Likewise, and frequently, the capacity to speak for God is linked with the Spirit: 'the words that the LORD Almighty has sent by his Spirit through the earlier prophets' (Zech. 7:12; cf. 1 Sam. 10:9–13; 2 Sam. 23:1–2). In God himself, 'the breath of his mouth' is equated with the creative, life-giving word that he spoke when he created the universe (Ps. 33:6–9).

The ubiquity of God is attested by various means in the Old Testament. One such way is by reference to the Spirit, as in Psalm 51:11 (quoted already), or in Psalm 139:7: 'Where can I go from your Spirit? Where can I flee from your presence?' It may seem at first that this is simply the best word to indicate that God is not limited by body, and may be everywhere at once. But, given the frequent link between spirit and life, it is more likely that once more it refers specifically to God's power. In this case it is his creative power to give life and to remove it, to deal at the level of human or animal spirit with his powerful Spirit, his capacity to order and enliven (or slay) every part of the creation continuously and purposively. The point is even clearer if we add to the 'spirit'

238

references of the English translations the allusions to the 'wind' of (or from) God (e.g. Num. 11:31). This leads us to those texts that link God's breath or Spirit to creation; for example:

> When you hide your face
>   they are terrified;
> when you take away their breath,
>   they die and return to the dust.
> When you send your Spirit,
>   they are created,
>   and you renew the face of the earth
>
> (Ps. 104:29–30)

References to the Spirit, then, are intended to say not merely that God is everywhere, but that his confronting, uttering, enlivening or slaying power is precisely anywhere he wishes it to be. The Spirit is the awesome presence of the one whose word gives and takes life (cf. Is. 11:4).

As the chosen texts indicate, one of the chief places where God makes his awesome presence felt is upon, through and within the human person. There are times when the Bible uses the language of the Spirit to underline the Lord's almightiness, his utter freedom of action, unhindered by space or time. Thus Ezekiel finds himself lifted up and transported by the wind or Spirit, an experience he describes as 'the strong hand of the LORD upon me' (Ezek. 3:14). At other times someone filled with the Spirit delivers God's people, or speaks God's word. But a point of great significance is the link so frequently made between the leadership of God's people and the Spirit of the Lord. As the Lord said to Moses: 'I will take of the Spirit that is on you and put the Spirit on them [the seventy elders]' (Num. 11:17). The transfer of authority from Moses to Joshua, from Saul to David and from Elijah to Elisha is marked by similar language (Deut. 34:9; 1 Sam. 16:13–14; 2 Kgs. 2:9, 15).

As is already plain, the three themes of power, presence and gifted persons are interlocking in the Old Testament. We need only observe that the gifted persons are empowered by the presence of the Spirit to do the work of the Lord. But the fourth element to add to this list is the eschatological one. The Old Testament bears witness to the future action of God's Spirit by which his people as a whole will be lifted up and brought to new life, so that they will live once more in their land, one nation under one Davidic king (Ezek. 37). Furthermore, the Davidic king is designated quite specifically as a man of the Spirit:

> The Spirit of the LORD will rest on him –
>   the Spirit of wisdom and understanding,
>   the Spirit of counsel and of power,
>   the Spirit of knowledge and of the fear of the LORD –
> and he will delight in the fear of the LORD.
>
> (Is. 11:2–3)

Through him the word of the Spirit will bring life and death (11:1–9). As in the historical experience of Israel, so in the promised future, the ones endowed with the Spirit are gifted for the sake of the people, and not merely for themselves. Moreover, the special gift of the Spirit will be revelation: the knowledge of God in Isaiah, the outbreak of prophecy in Joel. Furthermore, both in Isaiah 11 and in Joel 2, another eschatological promise of the Spirit, the outpouring of the last day, will not be confined in its significance to Israel:

> for the earth will be full of the knowledge of the LORD
>   as the waters cover the sea.
>
> (Is. 11:9)

> 'I will pour out my Spirit on all people ...
> And everyone who calls
>   on the name of the LORD will be saved;
> for on Mount Zion and in Jerusalem
>   there will be deliverance,
>   as the LORD has said,
> among the survivors
>   whom the LORD calls.'
>
> (Joel 2:28, 32)

The coming of the Spirit will be marked by the life-giving revelation of God and the salvation of the Gentiles.

The Spirit and God's Son

The empowering presence

Jesus clearly falls into the category, foreshadowed by the Old Testament, of an extraordinarily gifted person. Indeed, there is sufficient material in the New Testament to make an adoptionist Christology at least plausible. In regard to Jesus, and not merely in regard to his followers, the Spirit may be thought of as an *empowering presence*. He was 'conceived ... from the Holy Spirit' (Matt. 1:20). His baptism was accompanied by the descent of the Spirit. Mark tells us that he was sent out into the desert by the Spirit (1:12). Luke reports that he 'returned to Galilee in the power of the Spirit' (4:14). John declares that Jesus spoke the words of God, 'for God gives the Spirit without limit' (3:34). Peter says that God 'anointed Jesus of Nazareth with the Holy Spirit and power' (Acts 10:38). Paul affirms that 'he who raised Christ from the dead' will raise our 'mortal bodies through his Spirit' (Rom. 8:11).

Furthermore, there can be no lessening of the Spirit's status. When encountering the Spirit, one is encountering the Lord: that is the clear testimony of the Old Testament. The astonishing development of the New Testament is the equally strong conviction that when one encounters the Spirit one is encountering a person. It is astonishing, but not contradictory. If he is the Lord's Spirit, an encounter with him must be an encounter with a person, not merely with a force or power. The revelation of personhood is consistent with the Old Testament, though hidden in it, so that the reader who knows the truth does not have to contradict the Old. But the language of the New Testament gives such explicit awareness of the 'person' of the Spirit that 'Spirit' becomes a proper noun, not merely a description but a name. It is possible to blaspheme the Spirit, to lie to him, to grieve him, to quench him and to be led by him; the Spirit intercedes for us, fills us, teaches us and assures us. In the end it is no surprise that his name is included as such in the New Testament's several references to a threefold God (e.g. Matt. 28:19; Rom. 1:3–4; 1 Pet. 1:12). He is divine, and a divine person.

Taken together, the personhood of the Spirit and his ministry to Christ would make a case for a Christology of a Spirit-filled

241

man. In the contemporary church there is a tendency in this direction. Some are anxious to see Christ as empowered by the Spirit and hence as an exemplar for those who can also claim the same Spirit. We defeat sin, the argument runs, as Christ defeated sin, in the power of the Spirit. Our lack of power is then the consequence of our unwillingness to be led by the Spirit: 'just as Jesus remained master of his will and consciousness yet nevertheless deliberately chose to subject himself to the guiding Spirit throughout his life and thus lived powerfully and triumphantly, so his followers must do as he did if they would experience the same power and triumphs in their personal experiences'.[9] But there is the nub: why are we at all unwilling to be led by the Spirit? Can we make the choice? Christ's example here seems singularly unprofitable. In fact, the theme of the Spirit's empowerment of Jesus needs to be brought into fruitful relationship with the scriptural exposition of his lordship.

The Old Testament revelation of the Spirit itself yields material for a resolution of this problem. As we have seen, the public figures of the Old Testament, and especially those who spoke the word of God and were the saviours and rulers of the people, were endowed with the Spirit of God. This anointing functioned to identify and to enable them, and as the conduit of the Spirit's blessing of the people. It enabled them to do their work on behalf of the people of God. To that extent the people shared too in the life-giving presence of the Spirit. We also saw that a promised Davidic ruler would be especially endowed with the Spirit for the sake of the people. The Spirit's anointing would identify him as their ruler and equip him as their saviour. Indeed, the Old Testament holds out the promise that all God's people would share in the gift of the presence and power of the Spirit. For this reason, then, the incarnation of the Son is accompanied by the evident fullness of the Spirit, so that he may mediate the blessing of the Spirit to the people of God. In Calvin's words: 'God the Father gives us the Holy Spirit for his Son's sake, and yet has bestowed the whole fullness of the Spirit upon the Son to be minister and steward of his liberality.'[10]

Not surprisingly, therefore, the New Testament provides us with more than enough evidence of the Christological focus of the Spirit himself. The revelation that the Spirit's name is personal, not merely titular, is a consequence of the revelation of the gospel of the Son of God. It is no accident that, at several points in the New Testament, the Spirit is so closely associated with the Son as to share his name. We read of 'the Spirit of Christ' (Rom. 8:9), 'the Spirit of his [God's] Son' (Gal. 4:6), and even 'the Spirit of Jesus' (Acts 16:7). Thus, being focused on the Son, the ministry of the Spirit is overwhelmingly gospel-centred; one could say gospel-shaped. Those who wish to ascribe to the Spirit responsibility for the created order as a whole, for example, look in vain to the New Testament for support. Redemption, not creation, is his sphere. The Spirit anoints and empowers Christ for his ministry, is the agent of his resurrection, teaches and reminds the apostles about his words and deeds, convicts the world of the truth, brings new birth, helps Christians to be like Christ and energizes the church as the body of Christ: 'when he, the Spirit of truth, comes, he will guide you into all truth. He will not speak on his own; he will speak only what he hears, and he will tell you what is yet to come. He will bring glory to me by taking from what is mine and making it known to you' (John 16:13–14).

There has been a reaction in some quarters to presentations of the Spirit that read his ministry through Christ. This is advanced as a significant imbalance when the frequently reiterated charge of neglecting the Spirit is made. There is merit in the charge, and a Christianity neglectful of the Spirit is hardly New Testament Christianity at all. But we are not dealing here with an issue of 'balance', as though all that needs to happen is that we speak more loudly and frequently about the Spirit until it is Christ's 'turn' again. The fact is that Christ is designated in the New Testament as the 'one mediator between God and men' (1 Tim. 2:5), and the ministry of the Spirit finds its own genius in the service of the mediator. When Paul discovered the Ephesian disciples, who had 'not even heard that there is a Holy Spirit', his response was to preach Christ and to baptize them 'into the name of the Lord Jesus' (Acts 19:1–6). Like the Galatians, they received the Spirit through faith in Christ (Gal. 3:1–2; cf. John 7:39).

This reflects the clear New Testament teaching that it is Christ who, with the Father, sends the Spirit. In the final analysis, Pentecost is not so much about the coming of the Spirit as about the lordship of the Christ who sends the Spirit: 'Exalted to the right hand of God, he has received from the Father the promised Holy Spirit and has poured out what you now see and hear' (Acts 2:33). The promised Holy Spirit will come to those who repent and are baptized 'in the name of Jesus Christ for the forgiveness of ... sins' (2:38). John's Gospel is similarly clear about this order. The Spirit is sent by the Father in response to the Son's prayer (14:16); the Spirit comes 'in my name' (14:26); 'the Counsellor comes, whom I will send to you from the Father' in order to 'testify about me' (15:26); 'I will send him to you' (16:7). Finally, 'he breathed on them and said, "Receive the Holy Spirit"' (John 20:22). Not surprisingly, then, the revelatory work of the Spirit of God is dedicated especially to making the Son of God known (1 Pet. 1:10–12).

The vicarious presence

For this reason, the empowering presence of the Spirit in Jesus is matched by his ministry to the disciples, at the heart of which lies a *vicarious presence*. In this role the Spirit becomes the agent of God's revelatory word. As Christians we live in the strange time between the comings of Jesus Christ. The kingdom of God is being exercised through his lordship; we are in 'the kingdom of Christ'. Christ fulfils his role as lord by being the head of our human race, in our place and for our sakes, ruling until 'he has put all his enemies under his feet': all dominion, authority and power that opposes him, and finally death, the last enemy: 'Then the end will come, when he hands over the kingdom to God the Father.' At the end, our representative and head 'will be made subject to [God]' (1 Cor. 15:20–28). Clearly, and especially in the light of the use of Psalm 8 in this passage, it is Christ as the last Adam who is in view here, Christ in his human nature.

Thus the process of our salvation includes as an integral part the rule of the man Jesus Christ. He has not abandoned his human nature, and cannot do so, but is always for our sake true God and truly human. Thus his rule and presence in this interim period are, in our experience, 'indirect'. He has gone (Acts 1:9); he is absent; yet he is present according to the promise of his word (Matt. 28:20). The followers of Jesus live in the present time by faith in his words; his words are the means of his presence to faith. According to his word, the union of Christ and his people will be fundamental to their lives. He is with his disciples (Matt. 18:20);

244

he is in them (John 14:20); they are in him (John 15:4). In the writings of Paul this incorporation language reaches extraordinary richness (e.g. Eph. 1:3–14). The secret of the whole movement of presence in the midst of absence is the vicarious work of the Spirit, who, by being present, mediates the presence of both Father and Son to the believers.

The role of the Spirit as the presence of God is, once again, consistent with what we know from the Old Testament. But it is brought to a specific point in the promises of Jesus recorded in John 14: 'I will ask the Father, and he will give you another Counsellor to be with you for ever – the Spirit of truth. The world cannot accept him, because it neither sees him nor knows him. But you know him, for he lives with you and will be in you. I will not leave you as orphans; I will come to you … On that day you will realise that I am in my Father, and you are in me, and I am in you' (14:16–20). Both the Old Testament witness and John's language enable us to see what is meant by 'presence'. That God and God's Spirit are everywhere present is basic theism. But the promised presence of God and of God's Son is the presence of relationship, the awesome presence of his intentional fellowship, confronting and enlivening, even (literally) slaying (Acts 5:4–5; cf. 1 Cor. 6:19; Eph. 6:17). It is carried by language, otherwise it could scarcely be a relationship; it is language created by and blessed by 'the Spirit of truth'.

The unitive presence

The empowering and vicarious presence of the Spirit is the groundwork, finally, of his *unitive presence*. In this we see the chief inward application of revelation. We have, of course, already been considering this aspect of his ministry in the indwelling of the disciples and their dwelling in Christ. When we turn to the writings of Paul, however, we are given further understanding of the significance of what he calls the fellowship of the Spirit, first in relation to God himself and then in relation to others. In God's bringing Gentiles into his kingdom we see an extraordinary confirmation of his promises and a revelation of himself and his purposes.

Salvation is accomplished for us on the cross of Christ, but it is applied to us by his Spirit. The way of salvation brings us into union with Christ, and hence into the centre of God's work and purposes: 'to bring all things in heaven and on earth together under one head, even Christ' (Eph. 1:10). The Spirit-inspired word of God is the source and norm of the gospel we believe; the illuminating Spirit enables the resistant heart to see the truth of the gospel and respond; his regenerating power brings us into the new sphere of salvation; his revealing work assures us of the love of Christ; the sanctifying Spirit draws us into the likeness of Christ; the relating Spirit enables us to call Christ our Lord, and to call God – wonder of wonders – our Father. By the Spirit, we stand before him in our Head, our Saviour, made bold in our access to him by the knowledge of the love of Christ, and assured of this love by the gift of his own Spirit. And we do not stand alone.

The unitive work of the Spirit unites us to Christ, but unites us also with others in Christ. This communion with others has its foundation in the historical and theological separation of Jew and Gentile, and of its removal in the gospel of Jesus Christ. The division of Jew and Gentile was a notorious fact of the ancient world, based on the observance of the law of Moses, which made strict provision for it. The alienation of Gentiles from Israel left Gentiles, in Paul's words, 'separate from Christ, excluded from citizenship in Israel and foreigners to the covenants of the promise, without hope and without God in the world' (Eph. 2:12). The wall of division to which he then refers (2:14) is division not between humankind and God, but between Jews and Gentiles, with the effect of dividing the Gentiles from God. The wonder of Christ's work is that he abolished the law, ended the hostile division and preached peace, so that 'through him we both [Jews and Gentiles] have access to the Father by one Spirit' (2:18).

For Paul, this was foreshadowed by the revelation in the Old Testament, and was at the heart of the revelation he received when he became a Christian and an apostle. It is a supreme instance of the way God proves himself by announcing beforehand what he is going to do and then doing it as only he can: 'Christ has become a servant of the Jews on behalf of God's truth, to confirm the promises made to the patriarchs so that the Gentiles may glorify God for his mercy, as it is written ...' (Rom. 15:8). It is also the outworking of a revelation that made his ministry vital to God's mission: 'to preach to the Gentiles the unsearchable riches of Christ' (Eph. 3:8; cf. Gal. 3:15; 1 Tim. 2:7;

246

Rom. 15:15–22). It is a mystery now made known: 'the mystery of Christ, which was not made known to men in other generations as it has now been revealed by the Spirit to God's holy apostles and prophets. This mystery is that through the gospel the Gentiles are heirs together with Israel, members together of one body, and sharers together in the promise in Christ Jesus' (Eph. 3:4–6). Even at such a remove of time and space, it is possible to sense Paul's excitement at the recognition of God's abounding grace, not merely to Israel (who, through God's word, may be thought of as the 'natural' recipients of grace), but to the outsiders, to the Gentiles, whose inclusion in the kingdom of God had been foreshadowed in the prophetic writings of the Old Testament, but not understood by those who possessed them.

Failure to see that this is the route along which the gospel has reached the Gentiles has led to misinterpretations of the New Testament. God's method of saving the world has been through Israel, and the explosive nature of the gospel with its universal implications was at the heart of many of the difficulties and debates reflected in the New Testament writings. We have abstracted the sayings of the New Testament from their historical roots, and made them timeless, at the expense of tracing how God historically did his great work in Christ and made it known to us. There are indeed great universalizing truths here, but they emerge from the vortex of prophecy made, debated and acted upon, and bear the marks of these origins. Not least is this the case with what we may see of the Spirit's role.

There is a further aspect of revelation beyond the promises of God and the role of Paul. We note already from Ephesians 3, quoted above, that the Spirit is the agent of revelation to 'God's holy apostles and prophets' (3:5). The New Testament testifies clearly to the Spirit's function in the production of the written promises and witness that we call the Old and New Testaments. But there is more. In Ephesians, Paul speaks of the access both Jews and Gentiles have to the Father 'by one Spirit' (2:18). In the opening verses, he contrasts the position of Jews ('we who were the first to hope in Christ', 1:12) and Gentiles ('you also were included in Christ when you heard the word of truth, the gospel of your salvation', 1:13). It is in addressing the Gentiles that he specifically refers to the reception of the Spirit: 'Having believed, you were marked in him with a seal, the promised Holy Spirit, who is a deposit guaranteeing our inheritance until the redemption of those who are God's possession – to the praise of his glory' (1:13–14).

The possession of the Spirit is the special revelation of acceptance by God, proof that his grace has been extended to the despised and hopeless outsiders. This Pauline insight is not new here. It is one of the chief themes in the New Testament, and a major element of God's saving work. In particular we may see the pivotal role it plays in the story of the book of Acts. It is the coming of the Spirit that marks the extension of the gospel at Pentecost (ch. 2), among the Samaritans (ch. 8), to the Gentiles (chs. 10 – 11) and to the disciples of John the Baptist (ch. 19). It is the very evidence appealed to by Peter at the Council of Jerusalem: 'God, who knows the heart, showed that he accepted them by giving the Holy Spirit to them, just as he did to us. He made no distinction between us and them, for he purified their hearts by faith' (Acts 15:8–9).

It is the unity of Jews and Gentiles in Christ, and therefore the acceptance of the Gentiles through faith in Christ and not through the works of the law, that are fundamental to many of the significant references to the Spirit in the New Testament. The constant tendency to turn these into grids for piety rather than seeing them first and foremost as moments in the unfolding of God's salvation history has distorted both the interpretation of the New Testament and also contemporary spirituality. Thus the delay in receiving the Spirit by the Samaritans is not a template for the second blessing, but a record of that great moment when the Samaritans received the gospel by faith alone in a way the apostles were able to authenticate (Acts 8:14–25).

Responsive human speech is one of the chief marks of the reception of the Spirit. In Acts, the coming of the Spirit is sometimes accompanied by speech in other languages and by prophecy (e.g. 10:46; 19:6). But this does not seem to have been inevitable, and, indeed, the accounts can give no more than uncertain evidence. We know, for example, that not all spoke in tongues or prophesied (1 Cor. 12:29–30). In the final analysis, the evidence for the coming of the Spirit was the confession that Jesus Christ is Lord (1 Cor. 12:2–3; cf. 1 John 4:2–3). It is this confession that saves (Rom. 10:8–9) and leads to the further and most telling evidence of the Spirit's presence, the confession that

God is '*Abba*, Father' (Gal. 4:6). In short, the coming of the Spirit is what yields the deep communion between the believer and God, and between the believer and fellow Christians. Hence Paul's words in 1 Corinthians 12:13: 'For we were all baptised by one Spirit into one body – whether Jews or Greeks, slave or free – and we were all given the one Spirit to drink.'

Hence also, in different language, the words of Jesus: 'I pray also for those who will believe in me through their message, that all of them may be one, Father, just as you are in me and I am in you. May they also be in us so that the world may believe that you have sent me' (John 17:20–21). Not surprisingly, it is the consistent witness of both Paul and John that Christians have a basic responsibility to maintain unity by loving one another. Their unity is a given, but must be exhibited: 'Make every effort to keep the unity of the Spirit through the bond of peace' (Eph. 4:3). This astonishing unity is itself a standing revelation about the nature and power of the gospel, first to 'the rulers and author-ities in the heavenly realms' (Eph. 3:10), but secondly to the world: 'By this all men will know that you are my disciples, if you love one another' (John 13:35). The way God has brought together sinful people, men and women, slave and free, Jews and Gentiles, into a fellowship, is thus in itself a major revelation. He promised to do it; he promised to do it through Paul; he has done it; the consequent fellowship exists for all to see, giving grounds for believing in the power of the gospel.

We have taken this detour before coming explicitly to the rev-elatory aspects of the Spirit's work because these aspects must be understood in the light of his total person and work, and hence especially in the light of the gospel. In dealing with the Spirit, we deal with God himself; we encounter God in his awesome pres-ence; we receive the gift of Christ, whose role is to exalt Christ; we are incorporated into Christ, and Christ dwells within us; we are introduced to a communion of God and his people, a communion of love that will last for ever and reveals God's power and purposes. In thinking about these matters, we observe how vastly different is the account of Christianity given by Kant from that given by the New Testament. In particular, we may note the difference in relationship, experienced especially in our fellow-ship with God in prayer and with one another in the congregation. Here is a powerful evidence of the action of God in the world.

We now turn specifically to the action of the Spirit in our lives, as we become children of the living God by his power. In so doing we draw conclusions about the subject of word and Spirit.

The Spirit and God's sons

On several occasions already, I have observed the severe terms in which the Bible refers to the spiritual plight of those who do not know God. For example, Paul refers to the Gentiles in these words: 'They are darkened in their understanding and separated from the life of God because of the ignorance that is in them due to the hardening of their hearts. Having lost all sensitivity, they have given themselves over to sensuality so as to indulge in every kind of impurity, with a continual lust for more' (Eph. 4:18–19). This solemn indictment is accompanied by three negative elements. First, Paul teaches that such a condition is condemnable, and that anyone persisting in it will come under God's judgment. Secondly, the moral corruption of those described is allied to a spiritual blindness that shows itself in idolatry and other distortions of the truth. Thirdly, the situation, though culpable, is not reversible by any human effort. Not only do those in this darkness refuse to look for the truth; they cannot do so: 'the sinful mind is hostile to God. It does not submit to God's law, nor can it do so' (Rom. 8:7).

This total disempowerment of the human race requires the presence of God by his Spirit to apply salvation and bring the lost home. The Old Testament lays the foundation by associating word and Spirit, and life and Spirit. We have already established the link between inspiration and the Spirit (see chapter 7). But, in accordance with the darkness of the human mind in relation to the gospel, we now perceive that the Spirit accompanies the word of God and, by illumining the mind, brings people to know the gospel and to turn to Christ. That is why Paul can say, 'we live by the Spirit' (Gal. 5:25). The gospel is received by preaching and hearing; but no preaching or hearing is effective unless the Spirit opens the heart to the truth: 'For we know, brothers loved by God, that he has chosen you, because our gospel came to you not simply with words, but also with power, with the Holy Spirit and with deep conviction' (1 Thess. 1:4–5).

The full treatment of the Spirit's work in John's Gospel

testifies to the same double work of the Spirit in relation to the word of God. The Spirit is the 'Spirit of truth', who will teach the apostles and remind them of all that Jesus said (John 14:17, 26). It is on the apostolic testimony to Jesus, the promises made by Jesus and the activity of the Holy Spirit that the authority of the New Testament rests: 'when he, the Spirit of truth, comes, he will guide you into all truth' (16:13). This is said specifically to the apostles in their apostolic role. But there is a further strand of teaching in John that has to do with the subjective work of receiving the gospel. This too is attributed to the Spirit: 'When the Counsellor comes, whom I will send to you from the Father, the Spirit of truth who goes out from the Father, he will testify about me' (15:26). 'When he comes, he will convict the world of guilt in regard to sin and righteousness and judgment' (16:8; cf. 1 John 2:20–27).

The classic text on the revelatory work of the Spirit, however, is 1 Corinthians 2. The apostle's words, he says, were without human wisdom or power; they were only the word of the cross, 'Jesus Christ and him crucified' (2:2); and the human messenger was, by his own account, as weak and unimpressive as his message (2:3). His hearers' faith, then, was engendered not by human wisdom, but by 'a demonstration of the Spirit's power' (2:4). Since he specifically disowned miracles as feats of power in the preaching of the gospel (1:22–23), Paul means here that the mere fact that their faith was founded on the weakness of the gospel was a triumph of the power of the Spirit. In his subsequent exposition of the Spirit's work, he reiterates the point that human wisdom cannot see the truth about God. But the Spirit, precisely as the Spirit of God and therefore as the one who 'searches all things, even the deep things of God', is able to bring us knowledge of the truth about God, 'that we may understand what God has freely given us', namely the gospel (2:6–16). Gordon Fee observes that for Paul 'the Spirit [is] the key to *the proper understanding of the gospel itself*, both his preaching of it (v. 13) and their experience of it as grace (v. 12)'.[11] Thus word and Spirit belong inextricably together; the Spirit persuades by the word of the cross.

If this work were not irresistible it would be futile, so darkened are our hearts. In keeping with the biblical perspective, the reception of the gospel (or, for that matter, its rejection) is attributed to both human and divine power, with the priority accorded to the divine. Thus faith and repentance are both human activities and divine gifts (e.g. Eph 2:8; Acts 11:18). The Lord uses the human nature that he has created. Likewise, the hardening of the heart is attributed both to God and to those who reject his word. Further-more, the Spirit and the word are not divided from each other. To the power of the Spirit, as we have seen, belongs the new life that expresses itself in calling Christ the Lord and God the Father. We know that the gospel is true because the Spirit overcomes our inability to see the truth and brings us to know God. At the same time, however, power is attributed to the word of God itself, so that we read of 'the word of God, which is at work in you who believe' (1 Thess. 2:13), and which is 'living and active. Sharper than any double-edged sword, it penetrates even to dividing soul and spirit' (Heb. 4:12).

By observing how the Bible itself speaks about the process of revelation we may formulate an adequate account of the relation between word and Spirit. We have already observed the danger of simply making the Spirit's activity a subset of reading the Bible, as though illumination were accounted for in inspiration. We have observed, also, a twofold difficulty in contemporary formulations of this relationship. First, the emphasis of modern theology has reversed the earlier tendency by collapsing inspira-tion into illumination. Secondly, the mood of popular piety sees the inner testimony of the Spirit as a second source of revelation alongside the revelation of Scripture itself. But if the starting-point is the gospel, and if we observe the New Testament's distinction between the inspiration of the word and its illumina-tion, the dangers are averted. The Scriptures are not a textbook of theology but the covenantal expression of the gospel through which God reigns over his people. The Holy Spirit is not speech-less or voiceless, but his inspiration in whatever form is directed towards the bearers of revelation, the apostles and prophets. His illumining work is not verbal as such, but, like his work in general, focuses the attention on Christ and his word. The inner testimony of the Spirit is no 'still small voice', but the subjective appreciation of God's voice in Scripture; hence the words of Jesus: 'The Spirit gives life; the flesh counts for nothing. The words that I have spoken to you are spirit and they are life' (John 6:63), and Paul's graphic depiction of the same truth: 'the sword

252

of the Spirit, which is the word of God' (Eph. 6:17).

If we follow the path outlined by the reception of the gospel itself, we can see the way round these dangers. On the one hand, the gospel thoroughly enriches our appreciation of how the Spirit incorporates us into Christ and hence into the body of Christ. The evidence of the Spirit's work is to be found in the relationship he creates for us with the Lord, with the Father, with our fellow believers, with the world and with him. To take the test case with which we began, the experience of prayer is founded on the Spirit's work. The person who cannot call God 'Father', who does not pray through the mediation of the Son, and who knows nothing of the fellowship of believers, is hardly likely to be possessed by the Spirit. Conversely, the undoubted redemptive focus of the Spirit's work saves us from the other danger of regarding the 'inner testimony' of the Spirit as a second source of revelation, an 'inner light'. Word and Spirit belong irrevocably together; but the function of the Spirit, having inspired the normative revelation, is to illumine the gospel so that we may see Christ, not to add fresh revelations.

I have deliberately turned to the gospel first as the paradigm of the word/Spirit relationship. It demonstrates the need for the Spirit's illumining work in the corresponding darkness of the human heart. But do we have grounds for making the paradigm fit Scripture as a whole? Is the inner testimony of the Spirit a factor in apt Bible reading? There are two major reasons for thinking so.

The first concerns the relation of Scripture and gospel. In this area what is true of one is true of the other. They are not antithetical to each other. Both are rightly called the word of God, and neither can exist without the other. Just as the gospel entails kingdom and covenant, so too does Scripture. In fact, we must go further. We rightly apply our findings about the gospel to the Bible because the Bible is the book of the gospel, centred on Christ and his great saving work. Reading the Bible requires the Spirit's illumining work just as apprehending the gospel does. The work of good reading will continue, but it is the Spirit who will make the text read us.

The second reason is exegetical. The illuminating work of the Spirit is a major theme of the passage that runs from 2 Corinthians 3:1 to 4:6. The individual's incapacity to come to God is illustrated by Israel's inability to see the truth, even when reading the old covenant, because 'their minds were made dull' (3:14). But when a person turns to God, the veil is removed by the Lord, who is the Spirit, 'and where the Spirit of the Lord is, there is freedom' (3:17). When we contemplate the Scriptures of the old covenant now, we contemplate the glory of Christ, to whom the old covenant bears witness, and are all 'being transformed into his likeness with ever-increasing glory, which comes from the Lord, who is the Spirit' (3:18).

As Paul and his friends preach Jesus Christ as Lord, they are 'ministers of a new covenant' 'not of the letter but of the Spirit; for the letter kills, but the Spirit gives life' (4:5; 3:6). The 'letter' that kills is not Scripture *per se*, or the old covenant, but the Scriptures read without Christ as their centre, and without the heart enlightened by the active power of God (4:6). 'It was certainly not Paul's intention to suggest that the Old Testament law was merely a human instrument ... But it was easy to misuse it ...'[12] It is the word of God as law, not gospel. Although the Spirit is not specifically mentioned in 4:6, it seems most likely in the context that the Spirit carries out the purposes of God by illumining the hearts of those who are blind captives of the god of this world. And the illumination of the heart leads not to a sight of the Spirit, but, in conformity with the Spirit's Christ-centred ministry, to 'the light of the knowledge of the glory of God in the face of Christ' (4:6).

The freedom given by the Lord who is the Spirit is designated in Galatians as the freedom of sons in contrast to the bondage of slaves. (I use the word 'sons' here rather than 'children' in order to retain the point that it is as the heirs of God that we now stand.) Whether Jews or Gentiles, we were in bondage to what Paul calls 'the weak and miserable principles', the things that by nature are not gods (Gal. 4:8–9). In other words, we are in the grip of ideologies – even the ideology of the law – with which we attempt to come to terms with the world, and find ourselves enslaved instead. The gospel of Christ liberates, by bringing us into a totally new relation with the true ruler of the world, a relationship of adoption: 'Because you are sons, God sent the Spirit of his Son into our hearts, the Spirit who calls out, "*Abba*, Father"' (4:6). With these words we have come to the very heart of what Christianity is all about. It is an experience Paul then describes in the phrase 'now that you know God', but then, conscious that it is all of grace and that we should not know God except for the illuminating work of the Spirit, he adds, '– or rather are known by God' (4:9). But our knowledge of God is not yet perfect. As Christians we remain in conflict with the sinful flesh, and in need of the Spirit (5:16–18). The Spirit remains our teacher in the things of God, illumining the word of God so that we may keep it.

The Spirit and human autonomy

I said at the opening of the chapter that integral to its theme was the competing vision of human nature. Kant saw God as necessary for morality, but he adhered to an optimistic anthropology. His contemporary successors no longer believe in God, but they do believe in humanity and in freedom. I have already quoted one of the great biblical statements on liberty: 'where the Spirit of the Lord is, there is freedom' (2 Cor. 3:17). Not surprisingly, in our culture such a text is thought of as a slogan for personal independence, and certainly for independence of thought. But in the same passage Paul utters one of his most telling descriptions of human bondage, which he sees in spiritual terms: 'The god of this age has blinded the minds of unbelievers, so they cannot see the light of the gospel of the glory of Christ, who is the image of God' (4:4). The freedom of which he speaks comes as the Spirit opens blind eyes so that those who are perishing can see 'Jesus Christ as Lord' (4:5), which is the gospel Paul preached. He never envisages free persons in the sense of independent persons. To him, the believers are slaves of Christ, making it their aim in all things to please the Lord (2 Cor. 5:9), 'and we take captive every thought to make it obedient to Christ' (10:5).

Once more we are reminded of how very different biblical Christianity is from the main cultural values of western society. Gary Badcock observes that 'freedom has become the dominant issue in virtually all aspects of our lives', and suggests that 'the most basic problem we face in modern theology is to find a way to reconstruct an understanding of human nature in which the relation with God has central place'.[13] This cannot possibly be the religion Immanuel Kant placed within the limits of reason alone. However, freedom *is* a biblical word, and the gospel promises freedom. It involves freedom from adverse judgment, from fear of God and from anxiety. But these are negatives; the gospel also offers freedom for relationship, the freedom that so relates us to God, the ruler of the world, that we are released from our bondage to the things of the world. It is a freedom that creates community. And we need to go further than that.

A culture that values human autonomy above all is a culture that is losing the capacity to love. Autonomy and love cannot co-exist. Significantly, the modern penchant for 'living together' has not led to happiness or longer relationships. The commitment of marriage is still the better way for people wishing to find human fulfilment. The home remains the best place in which to nurture human beings and to educate them in love. It is as we centre our lives on others that we experience joy and find true fulfilment. It is no accident, then, that what has been known inadequately as the 'internal testimony of the Spirit' should turn out to refer to the way God, through the gospel, draws his people into the supremely loving relation of the Trinity, into the love of God, the communion of the Holy Spirit. The work of the Spirit, so defined, is his special work in relation to the gospel, and, from the point of view of the saved, it is one of the glories of what God has done for them in Christ.

11

CONTEMPORARY
REVELATION

The hunger for the living God

The argument of the last chapter was that the role of the Holy Spirit in revelation is focused on the provision and reception of the evangelical message of the Scriptures; that is, on revelation and illumination. But, to many, this scarcely seems to account for the evidence of either the Bible or experience. Thus, in an attractive reference to some godly people, the popular author Joyce Huggett speaks of a husband and wife rising at six o'clock every morning for a time of quiet: 'They would read the Bible, pray and listen for God's still, small voice. Whenever they sensed God was speaking to them, they would write down the instruction or challenges or directions they received. They determined to obey to the best of their ability.'[1] She quotes the late David Watson (admittedly a pastor rather than a theologian): 'Since God is the living God, he is constantly trying to speak to us and we in turn need to listen to him ... If we are to keep spiritually alive and alert, we need every word that God is continually speaking.'[2]

Huggett and Watson speak for many people who have become dissatisfied with what their churches have offered them as the word of God. It seems too frigid and remote. In a culture that not long ago boldly announced the death of God, Christian people need more than the words of a book written for all time on a page. They need the voice of the living God. It is not that Huggett and Watson ignore or fail to respect the Bible; just that they see it as needing to be supplemented by fresh revelations relevant to the recipients and their needs. These revelations need to be of God and to be given the status of a word from the Lord, because they are to be obeyed.

At a more studied level, the American theologian Wayne Grudem refers to the way the Spirit 'gives recognizable evidences that make his presence known'. He also argues that the Spirit continues to guide and direct God's people, giving as evidence the fact that 'Scripture gives many examples of direct guidance from the Holy Spirit to various people'.[3] In substantiating this claim, he cites passages that refer to the leading of the Spirit (e.g. Luke 4:1), the speech of the Spirit (Acts 8:29; 10:19–20; 11:12; 13:2), cases of transportation by the Spirit (e.g. Acts 8:39–40) and the general experience of walking according to the Spirit and being led by the Spirit (Rom. 8:4, 14; Gal. 5:16, 18). He adds references to the guidance of the Spirit in the book of Acts (15:28; 16:6–7; 20:22–23). Grudem also has a thesis about ongoing prophecy, which I shall refer to later. His words are more careful than those attributed to David Watson, but his argument is that 'it seems that one of [the Spirit's] primary purposes in the new covenant age is *to manifest the presence of God*, to give indications that make the presence of God known. And when the Holy Spirit works in various ways that can be perceived by believers and unbelievers, this encourages people's faith that God is near and that he is working to fulfil his purposes in the church and to bring blessing to his people.'[4]

Contemporary Christianity has seen an immense interest in, and turning to, an experimental piety that seeks the word of the Lord in prophecy, intuition, discernment, 'words of knowledge', glossolalia and 'words of the Lord'. Indeed, even in areas not directly to do with the words of the Lord, such as healing miracles, there is a sense that here is proof that God is revealing himself as alive and active, despite what the surrounding culture may say. The presenting problem may be illness, but the underlying problem is hunger for the active presence of God. The patient may seek health, but the congregation seeks assurance.

Nor is this surprising. For various reasons there is a feeling abroad that God has indeed absented himself from the world and even from the church. In the mid-twentieth century it began to look as though religion in the West was finished. The death of God was announced by theologians and the obituaries duly appeared in the media. The philosophical climate, in English-speaking countries at least, was still dominated by linguistic analysis and logical positivism, and very few philosophers were prepared to identify themselves as Christians or as possessing any religious beliefs at all. At a popular level, the 'scientific' attitude had triumphed, which effectively meant that naturalism was assumed to be the basis of the success of science, and that science had proved that there was no God. In vast regions of the world the official creed was atheism. It seemed as though the Enlightenment had triumphed and that the state of affairs predicted by Nieztsche in the nineteenth century had come to pass.

Christians therefore faced a new and severe spiritual and moral dissonance in the culture in which they had for so long felt at home. Nowhere was this clearer than in the widespread disrespect for Christian moral teaching about life issues such as abortion, euthanasia, marriage and the use of Sunday. The immediate post-1945 world was still willing to pay lip-service to the Christian ideals in these and other areas. But now, at the beginning of the twenty-first century, there is little respect for the Christian moral stand in such matters, and a certain impatience with the backwardness of the churches. The Bible has lost the authoritative role it once played. The notion that some people attempt to structure their lives in accordance with its teaching as a mark of submission to Christ is beyond the understanding of many, although in the nineteenth century it would have been instantly recognizable as an aim both laudable and plausible.

Bad conscience among the churches on matters such as racism has contributed to an unease about other moral issues, and to a willingness to think that the world rather than the church may have got things right after all. Extraordinary new ethical issues have emerged, about which it would be helpful to have a direct 'word of the Lord'. The tolerance and social liberalism that marked the secular mind in the last decades and beyond have now become leading indicators of liberal Christian thinking, with the inevitable loss of certainty about God and of assurance about salvation. Appealing to the words of Jesus that the Spirit 'will guide you into all truth' (John 16:13), church leaders and synods have essayed advances, changes and innovations in doctrine and behaviour, some of which have been regarded as inconsistent with the teaching of Scripture throughout Christian history. In the modern world, revelation must be contemporary if it is to address the issues facing Christians. I have already referred to the recent words attributed to an Episcopalian bishop. 'the church wrote the Bible, and it can rewrite it'.

In a world beset with such uncertainty, the key pastoral issue has changed. When the world affirmed naturalism and quarrelled with the Christian assertions, the question for Christians and others concerned God's existence. People asked, 'Where is the true God?' and sought the answer in an apologetic arising from evidence. When the churches emphasized God's law, moral standards and holiness, the inevitable question concerned our acceptability to him. People asked, 'Where is the gracious God?' and sought the answer in teaching arising from the Bible. In the new age of dissonance with the culture and uncertainty about truth, the question has become, 'Where is the living God?' and the answer is sought in an experience arising from the Spirit. We remember Grudem's contention that one of the primary purposes of the Spirit is 'to give indications that make the presence of God known'.[5] For large numbers of Christian people the God of the conventional churches has proved too remote and frigid to meet their needs, and they have turned to churches where they may find experiences evidently based on contemporary manifestations of God and revelations of his Spirit. This is evidence of a hunger for the living God, for the reassuring touch of his hand and the sound of his voice. In short, the absence and presence of God form a central issue.

The contemporary mood within the Christian family gives the present study a special importance. What is Christian experience about, and do we judge it as a source or as a norm of revelation? The nature of the Christian life lived by millions of people, not to mention the practice and strategies of the churches, is gravely affected by our understanding of these issues. The possibility of contemporary revelation needs to be studied in the context of the Christian life as a whole, and especially the doctrines of grace and the sovereignty of God. The sort of biblical and experiential evidence then put forward for the idea of continuing revelation can be assessed in the framework of the method God uses to communicate with us and to sustain the Christian life. The commentary on arguments such as Grudem's must be biblical, but fundamentally they are theological; that is to say, they require the witness of the whole Bible. The main argument of this chapter is that contemporary Christians such as those mentioned are giving a misleading answer to a real question, and that, once again, a starting-point in the gospel provides the necessary insight.

The Christian life: living with a gracious God

Many people have all sorts of religious experiences inside and outside the churches. But authentic Christian experience must be founded on the gospel, which is the instrument by which we come to know God.[6] We have seen in the previous chapter that the Christian life begins with grace and by grace, as the Spirit takes the word of God and persuades us of its truth. This persuasion, or 'faith' (to use the normal word) is the point at which we come into fellowship with God, and is the basic disposition in our Christian apprehension of the gospel. That is why the Christian life may be called 'the life of faith'.

What are the basic elements that make up the experience of living this life? The life of faith begins with our confidence in the Son of God, 'who loved me and gave himself for me' (Gal. 2:20). On the basis of his work alone, we are persuaded by the Spirit that God is our Father (Gal. 4:6), and this issues in a life of godly service (Gal 5:5–6). There are three parts to this definition.

First of all, we exercise faith in Christ, especially trust in his ability to save us. Salvation is complete in Christ; or, to put the same truth reciprocally, Christ is the complete Saviour. From one point of view, the work of Christ is not complete, for he must come again to destroy the last enemy and hand the kingdom to his Father (1 Cor. 15:20–28). From another point of view, his work is complete, both in its essence and in its efficacy. His work is essentially final, because his death on the cross is sufficient to take away the sins of the world, and hence is powerfully described as being 'once for all' (1 Pet. 3:18). No work of the law is useful for salvation (Gal. 2:16). So deep is human sinfulness that we can contribute nothing to our own salvation; our assurance can be complete because it is based utterly and radically on another. Hence the New Testament speaks with such notable confidence about the efficacy of our salvation in Christ: 'For in Christ all the fulness of the Deity lives in bodily form, and you have been given fulness in Christ, who is the Head over every power and authority' (Col. 2:9–10). The finality of Christ is underlined by the comparisons drawn in the epistle to the Hebrews between Christ on the one hand and prophets, angels and even Moses on the other (Heb. 1:1 – 3:0). These comparisons also remind us that Christ is the treasure-house of wisdom and knowledge (Col. 2:3), and hence to know him is, in a profound sense, to know all that is worth knowing (Phil. 3:8).

Secondly, faith in Christ necessarily leads us to the Father: 'For through him we both have access to the Father by one Spirit' (Eph. 2:18). Given our utter sinfulness, this is an astonishing truth; it is the case only because of the sufficiency of Christ. On the basis of his death alone, God accepts us (Gal. 2:21). We become his sons (4:6). The knowledge that the one God, who is in charge of all things, is utterly committed to our good is called 'assurance'. It is not separate from faith, but integral to it. At any time it may feel weaker or stronger, but if we lack assurance altogether, we lack faith itself, since assurance is the persuasion that God is our Father. Such confidence has both grounds and means. The grounds are the all-sufficient person and work of Christ. We are not born the children of God; we do not deserve to be the children of God. Our adoption as children is on the basis of our justification, wrought by Christ's death on the cross. The means of our adoption is God's gracious work by his word and Spirit in bringing us to a knowledge of himself.

Both grounds and means together minister assurance to us in the course of the Christian life. Our experiences may make us doubt the love of God. In particular, we may suffer pain and distress. The New Testament promises that, in the midst of such circumstances, the Holy Spirit will assure us of the love of God in Christ: 'we also rejoice in our sufferings, because we know that suffering produces perseverance; perseverance, character; and character, hope. And hope does not disappoint us, because God has poured out his love into our hearts by the Holy Spirit, whom he has given us. You see, at just the right time, when we were still powerless, Christ died for the ungodly' (Rom. 5:4–6). In this passage, the Holy Spirit uses the word of God about the death of Christ to assure us of the love of God in the midst of difficulties. Indeed, it is the initial outpouring of the Spirit that ministers in this ongoing way. And the Spirit's work is not to give independent witness to the love of God, but, as the passage shows, to focus our attention on the once-for-all and sufficient demonstration of God's love in the death of Jesus (cf. Eph. 3:14–19).

Thirdly, the life of faith issues in obedience and the service of God. The consequence of the Spirit's work is that we become the children of the living and sovereign God by faith. That the Father, Son and Holy Spirit have covenanted themselves to us so publicly is the foundation of the Christian life. We do not doubt the immediate and continuous presence and goodwill of God, for the word we trust assures us of these great, though invisible, realities. To doubt the presence of God is to doubt either his truth or his goodwill. We trust the word of God, and it then transforms our lives. The word of God creates, surrounds and sustains our life, providing the assurance, wisdom, guidance, rebukes and encouragements that we need.

Works done from motives other than simple trust in Jesus – in order to justify ourselves or to gain assurance, for example – are no longer the good works of obedience. 'We live by faith, not by sight' (2 Cor. 5:7). That is, the word of God provides the framework of our lives, the fixed points that we need to consult, the charter and glad tidings that rule our earthly existence. To add to it is to risk anticipating the eschaton and walking not by faith but by sight. It certainly endangers the main thrust of the word as it now stands: the centrality for our lives (including our thinking) of Christ himself, God's great Word.

The Christian life: living with a sovereign God

The gospel leads us to put our faith in the one true God, who made and rules everything – the sovereign God. In accordance with the Scriptures, we understand his control to extend to all his creatures, large and small. He created and rules everything; whatever happens stems from him. Both history and nature are his handiwork; we are near him, for he is near us. In this respect, everything that exists or occurs reveals God, for he is in it all. Such a thought is overwhelming, for when we look at the world we see not only grandeur, courage and goodness, but also doom, despair and evil. At best, our experience is ambiguous; at worst, it is horrendous. Faith in a sovereign God would be dire if it were not for the further insight into his character provided by the gospel. The gospel persuades us that this sovereign Lord is well disposed towards us and uses the world for our good; 'indeed, all things must minister to my salvation' (Heidelberg Catechism). Furthermore, he intends to give us all things in Christ; we may fearlessly use anything in the world to show love towards God and neighbour. God's word of grace enables us to interpret what he is doing in human experience.

What is the life of faith in such a Father in such a world? It consists of repentance before God and the struggle against sin. It seeks the path of obedience in behaviour that befits creatures before the Lord God. Instead of being based on fear and ignorance, it is a life of love, because we now know that he loved us. It is a life in which the Spirit of God brings forth his fruit, including joy with self-control. It is a life of fellowship with the living God in prayer, and with our fellow believers in the congregation. We are not relieved of suffering; indeed, Christians may suffer more than others because of the struggle to be faithful. But the pain of those who suffer is the pain of those who know that the heavenly Father remains in charge, and that he has his own good reasons for allowing these things to happen. In this way the happenings of providence are transformed, not by extra and specific information, but by the profound and basic truths that undergird and hence interpret the existence of those who belong to the Father. Grace explains providence; revelation interprets experience.

At a fundamental level, our access to the Father transforms our relationship to the world he has made. In Galatians 4:1–11, Paul makes the connection between the creator God and adoption. The path of the non-Christian, whether Jew or Gentile, is that of bondage to 'the basic principles of the world' (4:3). In the context of the epistle this must include all those religious observances, including, astonishingly, even the law, by which men and women thought they could successfully manipulate the spirits (or even

God) who ruled their earthly environment. Instead of dominating the world through these 'weak and miserable principles' (which Paul then illustrates with reference to 'observing special days and months and seasons and years'), the Galatians were in danger of being dominated by them again (4:9–10).

But the sufficient work of Christ has now transformed their relationship to God, and so to the creation that belongs to God. Instead of being enslaved to an essentially spiritualistic view of the world, in which God must be approached through his own creation in the hope that he may be found and be propitious, they have become the sons of the living and sovereign God. As a result, they are set free to live by faith in fellowship with him, without the world's fear or its religion. They are liberated to enjoy the world apart from these 'religious' involvements that make the world a sort of sacramental universe. Here is the charter for a new and revolutionary piety, in which the world and its works are the arena of piety, not the way to it. In this we see one of the gospel's great gifts to the human race: liberation from all religion that is fixated on the world and its rituals, and the restoration of the image of God in the dominion of the world as the sons of God in Christ.

Something as mundane as eating, for example, can be interpreted in accordance with the gospel. The special revelation of the Bible tells me that 'everything God created is good, and nothing is to be rejected if it is received with thanksgiving' (1 Tim. 4:4). It reminds me that this meal is provided by God's goodwill, and that I should acknowledge his sovereign provision. Thus the arrival of the specific meal is part of that general revelation of God's unceasing care and mighty power. If I meditate on all that has happened to get the food to me, I will be in awe of God's power, and rejoice in his mercy. In this and every other detail of my life he is intimately and immediately involved.

But the word of God does not help me to decide whether to choose fish or pork for dinner. Instead, it tells me that I am free from any religion interested in such worldly considerations, and it certainly assures me of God's goodwill whatever I eat, provided I do so with love to my neighbour. As the illustration itself reminds us, general revelation under these circumstances does not form a separate source or norm of revelation, and, in this as in a million other decisions of everyday life, we neither expect nor receive specific guidance from God other than the general injunction to trust him, thank him and love others. Indeed, to do more would be to revert to that religious bondage from which he has delivered us.

Living with a sovereign God, then, is living in the world conscious that his control and his purposes touch every part of life, and interpreting our experience of his sovereign power through the gospel, which assures me that he is Father.

Where is the living God?

In the first section of this chapter, I referred to three questions Christians have often asked: 'Is God there?' 'Does God accept me?' and (more pressingly in the contemporary church), 'Is God alive?' Our account of the life of faith shows that it is based on an understanding of the God who is both gracious and sovereign, generous and active, accepting and present. And yet there is always a tendency within Christianity, not least at the present, to falter in its grasp of the gospel of God's grace, and therefore to seek answers to questions such as these in the wrong places. In particular, we tend to explain the ambiguities of experience by experience in itself. In answering the questions, we are tempted to give priority to evidential experience or reason. Is God there? We propound proofs. Does he accept me? We perform good works. Is he with me? We seek religious experience.

Take the issue of assurance that we are accepted by God. We have seen that human sin is totally disabling; that grace makes the redemption won by Christ at the cross the central focus of salvation; and that grace makes the special revelation of God through the Spirit centre unerringly on the Redeemer. Consequently, as we saw, authentic biblical piety is the piety of gratitude and wonder at the work of God in Christ. True piety can never get over his mercy, graduate from his cross or forget his lavish grace. But frequently a piety develops that softens the biblical verdict on human sinfulness; the next step is to allow for human co-operation (however small or 'biblical') with God in the work of redemption. Invariably and necessarily, good works or other experiences are then allowed a crucial role in salvation or in gaining assurance of salvation. Often this leads to a most impressive flowering of devotion and spirituality, arising from the necessity to supplement grace with effort. But this devotion is wrongly directed, and retreats to the spiritual bondage from which the gospel offers us freedom. For in the end it will lead either to despair as we realize that we cannot match God's requirements, even in the small things, or to self-deception as we imagine that we can.

In these circumstances, the assurance offered by the gospel, as God's special revelation, is not thought to be enough. The gospel must be supplemented by contemporary special revelation, experiences that demonstrate to the recipient that God has accepted him or her. But this infallibly diverts attention from the word of the gospel, which focuses on Christ, towards religion, which focuses on the person. The gospel that Christ *for* us is our only hope, becomes Christ *within* us as the proof that we are loved. The temptation must be resisted in the name of the gospel. The order is wrong. The first reply and the last must be that of the word of God itself. The typical answer in each case is inadequate for the load it has to bear, and there is a grave danger that those relying on such answers will either falter or become ever more desperate to find the answer in the bizarre. At a more fundamental level, the gospel of God's grace is set at serious risk by the emphasis on human effort; and the actual method of God's revelation, his word, becomes neglected or distorted.

The same result follows from a weakened doctrine of God's sovereignty. In this case the main victim is the sense of the powerful presence of God in the world, and hence the need to ask, 'Is there a living God?' As we have seen, in the biblical account, all things respond to the word and will of God, whether the birds of the air, the flowers of the field, the movements of armies or the natural forces evident all around us. The revelation of God's might referred to in Psalm 19 ('The heavens declare the glory of God; the skies proclaim the work of his hands') is connected to the regularities observable in the universe, not to what may be called the miraculous. The first thing to observe about the Lord's sovereignty is not its surprising nature but its predictability. It was the stable and regular working of the world, together with the freedom of adoption described above, that helped to give humanity a different picture of the physical universe and encouraged the advent of modern science. It is this very ordinary aspect of nature that the psalmist sees as proclaiming God's majesty.

But not all accept this account of God's sovereignty. Human freedom is valued in a way that affects the understanding of God's sovereignty. In a more 'open' account that often prevails at a popular or even a sophisticated level, God's power in the world is less evident. In the words of Richard Rice, 'history is the combined result of what God and his creatures decide to do'.[7] Humanity and indeed nature contribute more, while God has more of a 'guiding' or 'steering' role. In a piety based on the stronger account of God's sovereignty, everything ministers to the believer as being from God. An unusual event, a striking answer to prayer, even a special deliverance or healing, is greeted with great thanks and joy, but is seen as part of the never-ending, gracious providence of God. The absence of such events does not signal the absence of God, since he is just as present in the ordinary or the painful as in the spectacular or unusual. His marvellous power is seen in the rising of the sun each morning; the fact that it occurs so regularly does not lessen his power or our delight.

Understandably, an 'open' account is accompanied by a sense of God's indirect relation with the world, or even his distancing, in order to make room for human and natural forces. Certainly he is seen as distant from unpleasant events, or at least not directly involved in them. In a piety based on this more open view, God's presence seems more irruptive than continuous, and manifests itself more in the unusual and miraculous. Indeed, in popular piety it almost seems that the more bizarre an event is (according to the canons of human taste and judgment), the more clearly it can be identified as from the Lord. Paradoxically, the 'open' account sometimes understands itself to be more attuned to the reality of God's power than the 'strong' account. But what has happened is that a new 'God of the gaps' theory has emerged, to meet the need for assurance that God is truly alive and active. The real difficulty from the point of view of the teaching of Scripture is that the open God is less than the God of the Bible, and that assurance of God's presence is once again being sought in the wrong place.

That is not to say that there is no value whatever in the experiential or the rational. On the contrary, while the proofs for God's existence may not succeed as proofs, they remain, as Romans 1 reminds us, in the sphere of evidence. Likewise, the assurance that comes from seeing the fruit of the Spirit in one's life may be ambiguous or feeble, but it is not without value in reassurance, as 1 John reminds us (e.g. 1 John 2:3–6). Certainly, the absence of such fruit indicates the absence of the Spirit. In the same way, the providential dealings of God with his children, in which his blessing comes upon them in regular and sometimes totally unexpected ways, provide delight, strengthen faith and stimulate hope. It would be a strange and even lax Christian who could not say that the Father never discernibly answered his prayers, or that he had no testimony to God's deliverance or gracious blessing. From such works of God in the world and in our lives, it is right to draw conclusions. We may even say that through them God is communicating to us, that we are learning from him, that we are receiving his guidance. There is biblical warrant to speak of God's revealing something to us (Phil. 3:15). But into what category do such experiences fit? In due course I shall follow the pattern of chapters 4 and 5 and suggest that it may be appropriate to think of them, with some safeguards, as general revelation.

It is significant, in any case, that the issue of the presence of God is a key one in all strands of Christian faith in the contemporary world. If the thesis of this work is correct, and the place God appoints for us to hear him is his inspired word, it is no wonder that the issue of his presence is so important. Christians have retained the Bible, but since the Enlightenment they have been told that, whatever it is, it is not God's inspired word, and therefore cannot be integral to our fellowship with him. Furthermore, although we ought to respect its opinions, we do not have to obey its teachings. Whether the theory of the Bible adopted has been that of the line of Schleiermacher or that of the line of Barth, inspiration has been denied, with the same effect in each case. It is not surprising that God's presence is sought with ever-increasing desperation in the supernatural moment and the event of revelation, whether in the eucharist or in healing miracles. The absorption of some major churches in eucharistic revival since the Second World War is not one of their glories, but rather a sign of weakness. A growth in the interest in expounding and obeying the Scriptures would indicate a recovery of strength.

Assessing contemporary revelation

What are we to say, then, about contemporary prophetic movements, or claims such as those made by Wayne Grudem, Joyce Huggett and David Watson? Do these constitute an additional stream of revelation, available to all Christians and churches, allowing us to receive from God up-to-date messages for direct guidance in everyday life? Several observations need to be made.

First, God may do as he pleases. He is sovereign. It is sometimes suggested that those who resist the idea of contemporary revelation do so because they limit God's power. But there is no need whatever for those with a strong view of God's sovereignty to deny his capacity to do whatever miracles he pleases and to speak as frequently and in whatever way he pleases now. God may do all or any of this. Their problem does not lie in unwillingness to acknowledge the power of God; on the contrary, they believe that God 'works out everything in conformity to the purpose of his will' (Eph. 1:11), and they see evidence of his power and glory around them every minute of every day. In fact, it is those who take a more 'open' view of God (and hence limit his powers) who believe in contemporary miracles.

Secondly, the biblical evidence adduced by Grudem and others is insufficient. The material about the manifestation of the Spirit's presence needs to be read in the light of the gospel, as I have done in the previous chapter: he manifests his presence pre-eminently in the effects of the gospel. The instances of the Spirit's revelatory ministry in the book of Acts fit in with Luke's general report that the ministry of the word in the apostolic church was accompanied by signs, rather than constituting an ongoing scriptural promise of such guidance. Conversely, the scriptural references to being led by the Spirit, which undoubtedly do apply to all Christians in an ongoing way, do not clearly refer to guidance other than the guidance we need in order to live in obedience to the Lord. They may even refer to following Scripture, which is the Spirit's book. At a deeper level, we should note Grudem's concept of one of the prime elements of the Spirit's role: to manifest the presence of God. This indicates what is at stake in the discussion and warns us that we are being diverted from the word of God in which God manifests his presence by the Spirit.

Thirdly, reports of remarkable events are far more common-place than is sometimes realized. Contemporary Protestantism may have its miracles, but so too do contemporary Christian Science and Catholicism and Hinduism. It is easy for the unusual to be inflated into the miraculous when one is personally involved. Glossolalia (as now practised) is a case in point. It is sometimes understood to be a miraculous gift, and it certainly assures people that God is alive and active. But it is not uniquely Christian and not necessarily supernatural. It occurs in other religions, it can happen in the life of an unbeliever, and certainly for many people it is a learned rather than a spontaneous event. Its capacity to assure diminishes the more we know about it. It quickly becomes routine, and when this happens, the temptation is to seek an even greater 'manifestation'. The blossoming of the miraculous is thus strangely self-defeating. As the Bible demonstrates, furthermore, the miraculous is frequently the province of false prophets, and cannot on its own serve to vindicate a message (Deut. 13:1–5; Matt. 7:21–23; 2 Thess. 2:9–10). In short, the apparently miraculous does not in itself tell us about God's approval or God's will.

Fourthly, the contemporary events do not seem to fit directly with their biblical counterparts, even if they have been correctly reported. The healings are less dramatic and less durable. They seem to select certain diseases. The prophecies are often wrong or only partly vindicated, and prophets likewise are sometimes right and sometimes wrong. On examination, the prophecies are often extremely trivial in nature. Where they are not trivial (e.g. prophecies concerning natural disasters, or the birth of children), experience shows that they need to be controlled, as dangerous mistakes have occurred. But if they are both genuine and important, by what right are they controlled? Furthermore, people seldom report failures.

Fifthly, although the so-called cessationist case (that the miraculous signs and wonders ceased with the apostolic age) sometimes makes an unwarranted appeal to 1 Corinthians 13:8–12, it reflects a true insight into the shape of the biblical revelation. God's provision of signs and wonders throughout the biblical era was frequently associated with extraordinary times of revelation, and associated with great prophetic figures such as Moses, Elijah and Elisha, Jesus, Peter and Paul. The miracles of the book of

Acts are connected with the apostles and other preachers of God's word as it made its way out of Jerusalem to the ends of the world. No text in Scripture teaches that contemporary miracles are impossible or have ceased. But the method of revelation employed by God suggests that the extraordinary was used to illustrate and adorn the gospel; that is, it was attached to the word, rather than to a new dispensation of God's kingdom where we may expect such things to be commonplace. The danger that the miraculous would divert attention from the word was recognized by Paul (1 Cor. 1:18ff.). The constant recourse to claims for miracles today diminishes the revelatory significance of those recorded in the New Testament.

Given these observations and the theological analysis that preceded them, we may conclude as follows. Claims about contemporary revelation do not need to be dismissed out of hand. Such events fall within the power of God if it pleases him to bring them about. But, if they are genuine, they come within the category of general rather than special revelation. They are like the general revelation available in the natural order. They are not uniquely Christian, but they may occur fruitfully within a Christian context and bring encouragement and even a measure of assurance. In this respect, they are like answers to prayer, or other providences of God. The recipient is able to interpret them adequately, not out of a knowledge of the event itself, but from the perspective of the word of God.

This conclusion is not altogether inconsistent with the approach to prophecy set out by Wayne Grudem. Defining prophecy as 'telling something that God has spontaneously brought to mind', he contends that the prophetic activity described in 1 Corinthians 14:26–33 (and elsewhere in the New Testament) is in a different category from that of what may be called the classic prophets of either the New Testament or the Old.[8] The word of the classic prophets and the apostles is the direct word of God and may not be disbelieved or disobeyed. But the very nature of the prophecy in 1 Corinthians 14 is open to interrogation, at least, by some of the listeners, and also to being controlled. This prophecy may be partly wrong, or may be wrongly interpreted by the prophet himself. He concludes: 'So prophecies in the church today should be considered merely human words, not God's words, and not equal to God's words in authority.'[9]

272

If Grudem is right in his exegesis, the contemporary phenomenon of prophecy is, in a sense, of little consequence. It is a
species of general revelation and needs to be treated in the same
way. It would be rather like the 'testimonies' given in church,
which tell of the Lord's dealings with us; they clearly rely on all
that we are told about the Lord in the Scriptures, but do not come
with the authority of his word, and need to be assessed and tested
by the hearers. If Grudem is wrong (and I am inclined to regard
Sinclair Ferguson's critique as sound),[10] the phenomenon is
better understood as Calvin does in his treatment of the same
passage: prophetic gift is equivalent to classical prophecy, but
has now passed away. The gospel has been launched, the Scriptures have been completed and the church has been founded.
We have the prophetic gift in abundance in the Scriptures; contemporary prophecy is only a diversion.

Of course, many advocates of contemporary prophecy refuse
to accept even Grudem's constraints. They insist that their words
of prophecy constitute special revelations with the same authority
as Scripture itself, requiring belief and obedience. Not surprisingly, such exponents become anecdotal in their theological and
pastoral method, and unintentionally dismiss the claim of the
Scriptures to be the 'living and active' word of God. They are
committed to a God who guides but does not control, and who is
impotent in the face of human recalcitrance. In the words of
David Watson already quoted, 'Since God is the living God, he is
constantly trying to speak to us and we in turn need to listen to
him … If we are to keep spiritually alive and alert, we need every
word that God is continually speaking.'[11] This is a far cry from
the God who has spoken and still speaks through the Scriptures,
and who makes his voice heard (or not) as he pleases.

The general revelation available to us in nature or in history,
personal or public, remains of some value for communicating
God's mind and will, and hence for assurance. Even the misinter-
pretation of events can provide subjective assurance and hence a
measure of increase in spiritual life for a time. A longer-term gain
is possible, however, only where experience of God's general
revelation of himself is both authentic and interpreted in accordance with the gospel as revealed in the Scriptures.

Listening to God

It is the tragedy of much modern theology, and of whatever church life is influenced by such theology, that it has chosen to follow its culture rather than the word of God. It has accepted the negative verdict on the Bible of movements such as the Enlightenment, and has tried to substitute other revelations or other versions of revelation. These must be doomed to failure. One may declare the religion of the Bible to be totally wrong, but one cannot deny that it is a religion of the word. This has been fully recognized throughout the history of the church, even when the word has been added to by tradition. It is ironic, to say the least, that so many who claim to respect tradition have given up the tradition of the word, which is as firmly based as any of the theological commitments of Christians through the ages. If the word must be abandoned as the locus of revelation, it would be far better to join those who have abandoned the whole Christian enterprise as fundamentally flawed.

God has assigned his word as the listening-post for us. Here we learn about the mediator, Jesus Christ, the one in whom is all wisdom and knowledge, through whom we know God. But this mediator is not simply any 'Jesus'. The apostle Paul was aware of those who preached 'a Jesus other than the Jesus we preached' (2 Cor. 11:4). He feared that the Corinthians might accept such a figure, and that, 'just as Eve was deceived by the serpent's cunning, your minds may somehow be led astray from your sincere and pure devotion to Christ' (11:3). Paul's Jesus was the one defined by the preaching; that is, by the word of God – ultimately, by the Scriptures. If we come to God through Jesus, it is this Jesus to whom we come. If we wish to obey the Lord, it is his word that we must trust and keep, whether as individuals or as the church.

The tragedy of which I speak is played out most sadly in the churches, where ministers trained in sceptical theology no longer have enough confidence in the word of God to submit to it themselves or to call upon the people to do so. But the word is foundational to the church. Consider some of the chief biblical metaphors of the congregation. The flock hears the voice of the shepherd (John 10:3–4). The word cleanses and remains in those designated as branches of the vine (15:3, 7). The bride is 'cleansed by the washing with water through the word' (Eph. 5:26). The household is 'built on the foundation of the apostles and prophets, with Christ Jesus himself as the chief cornerstone' (2:20). Christ gives to his body those who will build it up through the ministry of the word: 'some to be apostles, some to be prophets, some to be evangelists, and some to be pastors and teachers' (4:11). For the same reason, the different picture of the body in 1 Corinthians 12 – 14 tells the same story: 'in the church I would rather speak five intelligible words to instruct others than ten thousand words in a tongue' (14:19). Peter thinks of the church as a temple, a priesthood, a nation and a people (1 Pet 2.5–9); but the once so designated are those who have been 'born again ... through the living and enduring word of God' (1:23); those who do not belong are those who 'disobey the message' (2:8). Not surprisingly, when Paul describes the church as it meets together, he exhorts his readers to let 'the word of Christ dwell in you richly as you teach and admonish one another with all wisdom, and as you sing psalms, hymns and spiritual songs with gratitude in your hearts to God' (Col. 3:16). How does the Lord gather and rule his church if his word is not given its rightful place?

In this connection, an earlier generation spoke of the perfection of Scripture. In this phrase they included the infallibility and supreme authority of God's word, matters discussed in earlier chapters. But there is another characteristic of the word which it is fitting to mention here, since it too belongs to the doctrine of Scripture that needs to be established as we think about the revelation of God through his word. This is that the Scriptures are *sufficient* to enable us to know God, to be saved, to walk as he wishes us to walk, and to know what pleases him (2 Tim. 3:16–17).

We have already noted the common belief of popular piety that we need a continuous revelation of God, contemporary words of God. The same claim surfaces in different ways in theological discourse and ecclesiastical life. Thus, for example, developments in ecclesiastical life that occur in spite of what the Bible teaches are sometimes justified on the ground of the ongoing revelatory work of the Spirit, with a proof-texting use of John 16:13: 'he will guide you into all truth'. The Holy Spirit is appealed to as the special source of these extra words of God,

275

often in a way that betrays the underlying belief that the Spirit, being the Spirit of freedom, endorses the libertarian human spirit. But, as we saw in chapter 9, the Spirit delights in bringing sinners to salvation through Christ. That is what he speaks of through the word: 'the sword of the Spirit ... is the word of God' (Eph. 6:17). Thus, too, the 'message of knowledge' of 1 Corinthians 12:8, trivialized by some, is best thought of as a word about the gospel.

The Scriptures already claim to be contemporary with us. This is indeed how Jesus treated the Scriptures: 'have you not read what God said to you, "I am the God of Abraham, the God of Isaac, and the God of Jacob"?' (Matt. 22:31–32, my emphasis). In this and in many other passages he merely reflects the Old Testament's own view of its nature as the 'Book of the Covenant', and hence as being of ongoing immediate significance: 'the word is very near you; it is in your mouth and in your heart so that you may obey it' (Deut. 30:14). Since we have been brought into a living fellowship with God through these words, we cannot then regard them as out-moded without throwing the whole experience into doubt.

This may be thought of as an Old Testament perspective, appropriate for the period of law, when the people of God was a nation, but not suitable for the new age introduced by the Son of God (see, however, Rom. 10:5–13). Yet it is precisely in this new age that the same conviction is reinforced. We live between the times, between the two great Christological events of Jesus' first and second comings. No matter how long the period of human history that lies between these events – and it may be lengthy – we remain in what the New Testament calls 'the last days', the kingdom of Christ. It is not as if a new age (say, an age of the Spirit) is to be inserted into history before the return of Christ. Hence the significance of Paul's words: 'For everything that was written in the past was written *to teach us*, so that through endurance and the encouragement of the Scriptures we might have hope' (Rom. 15:4, my emphasis); and 'These things happened to them as examples and were written down as warnings *for us*, on whom the fulfilment of the ages has come' (1 Cor. 10:11, my emphasis).

In the final analysis it is because 'in these last days he has spoken to us by his Son' (Heb. 1:2) that the Scriptures remain always contemporary. The revelation in Christ is final and hence both sufficient and perennial. We have not yet left the era ('the last days') in which this revelation was launched. We must observe the structure of the biblical revelation if we are to understand how God continues to speak to us. His word for us is centred first and foremost on the salvation of the world from the wrath to come, provided by God through Christ. The perfection of Scripture both upholds and is upheld by the perfection of Christ. Because he is sufficient, the Bible is sufficient. Additions to one entail additions to the other.

Neither then nor now, neither by promise nor by precedent, did God set up a situation in which believers would be relieved of consulting the word, remembering it and applying it to their individual situations. The covenantal Scriptures abundantly fulfil the role of giving us guidance for daily living, not least in the legal and wisdom literature of the Old Testament. The lacuna which contemporary revelation is intended to fill has been created by neglecting the full riches of God's word, not least such books as Proverbs, Psalms and Ecclesiastes.[12]

Thus, for example, much of the ethical material of the Bible comes to us in the threefold form of axioms ('Love God'), principal commands ('Do not steal') and case law ('In the event of X, Y constitutes stealing'). The application of such material to everyday life is an everyday business: we all do it one way or another. The flexibility that we need to show in new situations does not constitute abandoning the original, but demonstrates the power of the original to shape the present. The new ethical dilemmas that face us, arising, for instance, from remarkable developments in biology and genetics, are not beyond the ethical norms of the Scriptures. But, if the nature of the biblical revelation is to be trusted, the ethical insights will not come in a flash of revelation, but will arise from scriptural teaching carefully, corporately and patiently applied.

The longing for contemporary words of God reflects several needs. We have already spoken of the need of assurance. But people also feel a need for guidance in the dilemmas of life. Although the Scriptures counsel us for salvation in Christ, they do not tell us which career to follow or which bus to catch. Hence the desire for immediate, private revelation. But it is the given scriptural revelation, with the surrounding words of commandment, wisdom and promise, that acts as the health-giving atmosphere of our lives, and enables us to make these and the thousands of other ordinary decisions of everyday life. In whole and huge areas of human existence we have the freedom of not having a direct word except this one: 'Christ Jesus came into the world to save sinners' (1 Tim. 1:15). The idea that God may be continually speaking in the still, small voice may sound 'godly' and relational, but it is a myth. The very passage that (in some English versions) refers to the 'still, small voice' (1 Kgs. 19:12, AV; NIV, 'a gentle whisper') in fact offers us only the counsel that Elijah received: no new mode of revelation, but life under the covenantal commands of God.

As we awake each morning to a new day, however, we do so under the same promises and the same commands as the day before: commands and promises that, because they deal with the very fundamentals of human existence, remain as applicable and relevant as ever, no matter how much time has passed. The promise of Christ's return and of the day of judgment is still powerful; the command to love cannot be surpassed or become outmoded. As we heed the word of God and live for him in this world, he is preparing us to be like Christ. In a culture that imagines that scientific research into the origins or eventual destruction of the universe is tremendously significant, we need to remind ourselves that what really matters is love, faith and hope, and the application of these virtues to the business of life and death. The message of the Son as the Saviour of the world will always be of supreme relevance as long as there are sinful human beings who need to be saved. Human nature and human needs remain essentially the same.

We cannot deny that there is a great cultural gap between the original recipients of the Bible and the modern reader. This is the force in the argument that we live in such a different world that the Scriptures have to be shorn of much of their garb in order to make any sense at all. Hermeneutics offers itself as a bridge between what the Scriptures meant and what they mean. But the case is usually put too strongly. The Scriptures continue to speak powerfully, directly and effectively where their main message is accepted. We have no reason whatever to deny that the Bible's central message is about salvation from the wrath to come, through the death of Jesus. Disbelief in the message of salvation arises not from science, history or reason, but from spiritual distaste caused by the philosophy of autonomy. Thus, if we continue to accept the eschatology of the Bible – to believe in the coming of one who is the Judge of the living and the dead, and that there is a wrath to come – there is little need to clothe the Bible in contemporary cultural garb. This is especially so where the chief hermeneutical strategy remains the task of comparing scripture with scripture. We do not need to master it and make it relevant; we need to serve it and show its relevance.

Conclusion

Both the sufficiency of Christ and the sufficiency of God's word are underlined by the phrase 'once for all', the single word *hapax* in Greek. Jude uses the term, when he speaks of 'the faith that was once for all entrusted to the saints' (3). Even at that early stage in the history of the church, Jude was able to think of the faith as a body of truths, as 'the faith' on which faith is based. It was a faith worth contending for. It was a faith, furthermore, that had been passed on entire, 'once for all'. But the same is said of Jesus, and especially of the cross as the central moment of Jesus' existence: 'Christ died for sins once for all' (1 Pet. 3:18). The two belong together, as unique and irreplaceable parts of God's plan to save the world. To weaken one is to weaken the other; to add to one is to add to the other. The full gospel contains both.

Notes

Introduction

[1] Joseph McCabe, *Selected Works of Voltaire* (London: Watts & Co, 1935). 'Voltaire' was the pen name of François Marie Arouet (1694–1778).

[2] Ibid., p. 113.

[3] Ibid., p. 53.

[4] Ibid., p. 14.

[5] R. Wollheim, *Hume on Religion* (London: Collins, 1963), p. 142.

[6] Ibid., p. 226.

[7] B. Ramm, *The Evangelical Heritage* (Grand Rapids: Baker, 1973), p. 64.

[8] C. E. Gunton, *The One, The Three and the Many* (Cambridge: Cambridge University Press, 1993), p. 1.

[9] For an account of the developments up to 1960, see H. D. McDonald, *Theories of Revelation* (Grand Rapids: Baker, 1979).

[10] Ramm, op. cit., p. 64.

[11] Reprinted as *God, Revelation and Authority*, 6 vols. (Wheaton: Crossway, 1999).

[12] John Calvin, *The Institutes of the Christian Religion*, ed. J. T. McNeill, tr. F. L. Battles (Philadelphia: Westminster, 1960), I.i–v, pp. 35–68. See also Bruce A. Demarest, *General Revelation* (Grand Rapids: Zondervan, 1982).

[13] E. Brunner, *Revelation and Reason* (London: SCM, 1947), p. 7.

[14] J. Baillie, *The Idea of Revelation in Recent Thought* (New York: Columbia University Press, 1956), pp. 30ff.

[15] Avery Dulles, *Models of Revelation* (Dublin: Gill & MacMillan, 1983), p. 117.

[16] A Protestant summary is that by Paul Avis, 'Divine Revelation in Modern Protestant Theology', in idem (ed.), *Divine Revelation* (Grand Rapids: Eerdmans, 1997), pp. 45–66.

[17] Daniel L. Migliore, *Faith Seeking Understanding* (Grand Rapids: Eerdmans, 1991), p. 20 (his emphasis).

[18] For a biblical survey, see James D. G. Dunn, 'Biblical Concepts of Divine Revelation', in Paul Avis (ed.), op. cit., pp. 1–22.

[19] E. Brunner, *Dogmatics 1: The Christian Doctrine of God*, tr. O. Wyon (Philadelphia: Westminster, 1950), p. 26 (his emphasis).

[20] 'The Gospel Story and Talk of Revelation', in G. Santer and J. Barton (ed.), *Revelation and Story* (Aldershot: Ashgate, 2000), p. 173.

[21] Keith Ward, *Religion and Revelation* (Oxford: Clarendon, 1994), p. 258.

[22] Ibid., p. 221.

[23] Thus, although revelation has come to stand at the doorway of much systematic presentation of the Christian faith, it has done so with the hesitation of theologians. Hendrikus Berkhof remarks: 'In the Bible this concept is so much a matter of course that it does not play a central role. And for centuries such was also the case in the study of the faith. The fact that it has now become such a central concept is that it has lost its self-evidence.' Hendrikus Berkhof, *Christian Faith*, tr. S. Woudstra (Grand Rapids: Eerdmans, 1979), p. 43. See also John Webster, *Theological Theology* (Oxford: Clarendon, 1998), p. 10, who describes the rise to prominence of the doctrine of revelation in modern Protestant theology as a 'fairly modern invention' and uses it to illustrate 'the disorder within Christian dogmatics'.

[24] Recently by Keith Ward, op. cit.

Chapter 1: The gospel as revelation

[1] Kyle Snodgrass, 'The Gospel in Romans: A Theology of Revelation', in L. Ann Jervis and Peter Richardson (ed.), *Gospel in Paul*, *JSNT* supplement series 108 (Sheffield: Sheffield Academic Press, 1994). Snodgrass comes to this conclusion at the end of a study of Romans. But his observation is true for the New Testament as a whole (p. 314). See also Markus N. A. Bockmuehl, *Revelation and Mystery* (Tübingen: Mohr [Paul Siebeck], p. 147.

[2] P. T. O'Brien, *Consumed by Passion* (Sydney: ANZEA, 1993), p. 77.

[3] There is considerable debate about whether we can speak of a single 'gospel'. Thus, for example, J. D. G. Dunn concludes that 'Any attempt to find a single, once-for-all, unifying kerygma is bound to fail' (*Unity and Diversity in the New Testament* [London: SCM, 1990], p. 32.) But Dunn also outlines some core features of the post-resurrection gospel, and is willing to see significant continuity between the words of Jesus and those of the first Christians (p. 228).

In my judgment, furthermore, he has overemphasized the diversity of the New Testament. See also Brevard S. Childs, *Biblical Theology of the Old and New Testaments* (Minneapolis: Fortress, 1993), pp. 219–225. For the purpose of this discussion, therefore, I am assuming that there is fundamental continuity (despite much variety of expression) between the New Testament interpreters of the original gospel. See also Martin Hengel, *The Four Gospels and the One Gospel of Jesus Christ* (London: SCM, 2000) pp. 164–168

[4] Hengel, op. cit. Similar definitions of the gospel from a systematic point of view may be found in Wolfhart Pannenberg, *Systematic Theology* (Grand Rapids: Eerdmans, 1991), pp. 454ff., and from John Webster in T. Bradshaw (ed.), *Grace and Truth in a Secular Age* (Grand Rapids: Eerdmans, 1998), pp. 109ff.

[5] For a recent discussion of 'gospel' terminology, see Andreas J. Köstenberger and Peter T. O'Brien, *Salvation to the Ends of the Earth* (Leicester: Apollos, 2001), pp. 271–74.

[6] D. Garlington, 'The Obedience of Faith in the Letter to the Romans, Part I', *Westminster Theological Journal* 52 (1990), p. 203.

[7] See the emphasis on prevenient grace in R. Thiemann, *Revelation and Theology* (Indiana: Notre Dame University Press, 1985).

Chapter 2: The nature of the gospel

[1] On the question of the nature and possibility of divine discourse, see Nicholas Wolsterstorff, *Divine Discourse* (Cambridge: Cambridge University Press, 1995).

[2] Karl Barth, in J. Baillie and H. Martin (ed.), *Revelation*, tr. J. O. Cobham and R. J. C. Gutteridge (London: Faber & Faber, 1937), p. 42.

[3] K. Barth, *Church Dogmatics*, tr. G. W. Bromiley (Edinburgh: T. & T. Clark, 2nd ed., 1975), I/1.4.

[4] Wolfhart Pannenberg, *Systematic Theology* 1 (Edinburgh: T. & T. Clark, 1991), p. 235; see also Wolterstorff, op. cit., pp. 63–74.

[5] Daniel L. Migliore, *Faith Seeking Understanding* (Grand Rapids: Eerdmans, 1991), p. 35.

[6] E. Brunner, *Dogmatics* 1: *The Christian Doctrine of God*, tr. O. Wyon (Philadelphia: Westminster, 1950), p. 27.

[7] C. H. Dodd, *The Apostolic Preaching and its Developments* (London: Hodder & Stoughton, 1963), pp. 76–78.

[8] Ibid., p. 77.

[9] Quoted in Ronald S. Wright, *Fathers of the Kirk* (London: Oxford University Press, 1960), p. 261.

[10] John Calvin, *The Institutes of the Christian Religion*, ed. J. T. McNeill, tr. F. L. Battles (Philadelphia: Westminster, 1960), II.9.4, p. 426.

[11] See M. J. Harris, *Slave of Christ* (Leicester: Apollos, 1999).

[12] Both Keith Ward, *Religion and Revelation* (Oxford: Clarendon, 1994), pp. 302–310, and Colin E. Gunton, *A Brief Theology of Revelation* (Edinburgh: T. & T. Clark, 1995) comment on the theme of autonomy in connection with revelation.

Chapter 3: The gospel and the knowledge of God

[1] J. W. Kleinig, 'The Indwelling Word – Meditation in the New Testament', *Reformed Theological Review* 3/51 (1992) p. 87

[2] Brevard S. Childs, *Exodus* (London: SCM, 1974), p. 76.

[3] U. Cassuto, *A Commentary on the Book of Exodus*, tr. I. Abrahams (Jerusalem: Magnes, 1987), p. 38.

[4] A number of these observations are similar to those of R. Rendtorff in W. Pannenberg (ed.), *Revelation as History* (London: Sheed & Ward, 1969), pp. 38ff. But Rendtorff fails to connect word and event as the Old Testament evidence demands.

[5] Walter Brueggemann, *Theology of the Old Testament* (Minneapolis: Fortress, 1997), p. 146.

[6] W. J. Dumbrell, *Covenant and Creation* (Exeter: Paternoster, 1984), pp. 11–46.

[7] See the discussion of whether God is obliged to keep promises in Nicholas Wolterstorff, *Divine Discourse* (Cambridge: Cambridge University Press, 1995), pp. 95ff.

[8] See e.g. Brueggemann, op. cit., pp. 197, 591–592, for 'Torah piety' in the Psalter and the wisdom literature.

[9] Ibid., p. 198; also pp. 450ff.

[10] P. R. Williamson, art. 'Covenant', in T. D. Alexander and B. Rosner (ed.), *New Dictionary of Biblical Theology* (Leicester: IVP, 2000).

[11] *A Commentary on the Second Epistle to the Corinthians* (London: A. & C. Black, 1973), p. 121. Cf. the comments by S. J. Hafemann, *Paul, Moses, and the History of Israel* (Peabody: Hendrickson, 1996), p. 384.

[12] R. A. Finlayson, art. 'God', in J. D. Douglas et al. (ed.), *New Bible Dictionary* (London: IVF, 1965), p. 474.

[13] E. Brunner, *Dogmatics* 1: *The Doctrine of God*, tr. O. Wyon (Philadelphia: Westminster, 1950), p. 33 (his emphasis).

Chapter 4: The gospel as a pattern of revelation

[1] There is a survey by James D. G. Dunn in Paul Avis (ed.), *Divine Revelation* (Grand Rapids: Eerdmans, 1997), pp. 1–22.

[2] A further discussion of such revelations is found in chs. 5, 6 and 11 below.

[3] For a defence of 'propositional revelation' see P. Helm, *The Divine Revelation* (London: Marshall, Morgan & Scott, 1982). Other authors to offer a more sympathetic account include Colin E. Gunton, *A Brief Theology of Revelation* (Edinburgh: T. & T. Clark, 1995), pp. 7ff. and Keith Ward, *Religion and Revelation* (Oxford: Clarendon, 1994), pp. 225–226. In addition, fresh vistas are opened by 'speech-act' theory. See Nicholas Wolterstorff, *Divine Discourse* (Cambridge: Cambridge University Press, 1995), passim.

[4] E. Brunner, *Dogmatics* 1: *The Christian Doctrine of God*, tr. O. Wyon (Philadelphia: Westminster, 1950), p. 15.

Chapter 5: Revelation and human experience

[1] See E. A. Litton, *Introduction to Dogmatic Theology* (London: James Clarke, 1960), pp. 42–57; R. L. Dabney, *Lectures in Systematic Theology* (Grand Rapids: Zondervan, 1972), pp. 5–78; C. Hodge, *Systematic Theology* 1 (Grand Rapids: Eerdmans, n.d.), pp. 191–237.

[2] R. Swinburne, *The Existence of God* (Oxford: Clarendon, 1979).

[3] For an introduction to these issues, see C. Brown, *Christianity and Western Thought* 1 (Leicester: Apollos, 1990), chs. 14 and 15.

[4] See, in addition to Swinburne, op. cit., A. Plantinga, *God and Other Minds*, (Ithaca: Cornell University Press, 1967).

[5] Jaroslav Pelikan, *Christianity and Classical Culture* (New Haven and London: Yale University Press, 1993), pp. 38–39.

[6] See Bruce A. Demarest, *General Revelation: Historical Views and Contemporary Issues* (Grand Rapids: Zondervan, 1982), pp. 13–42.

[7] Alan J. Torrance, 'Christian Experience and Divine Revelation in the Theologies of Friedrich Schleiermacher and Karl Barth', in I. Howard Marshall (ed.), *Christian Experience in Theology and Life* (Edinburgh: Rutherford House, 1988), p. 94.

[8] F. Schleiermacher, *The Christian Faith*, tr. H. R. Mackintosh (repr. Edinburgh: T. & T. Clark, 1968), p. 739.

[9] Karl Barth, in John Baillie and Hugh Martin (ed.), *Revelation*, tr. J. O. Cobham and R. J. C. Gutteridge (London: Faber & Faber, 1937), pp. 52–53 (his emphasis).

[10] Richard Swinburne, 'Intellectual Autobiography', in A. G. Padgett (ed.), *Reason and the Christian Religion* (Oxford: Clarendon, 1994), p. 2.

[11] Published as J. Barr, *Biblical Faith and Natural Theology* (Oxford: Clarendon, 1993).

[12] Walter Brueggemann, book review in *Modern Theology* 10/2 (1994), p. 220.

[13] Barr, op. cit., p. 115.

[14] Quoted in H. D. McDonald, *Ideas of Revelation: An Historical Study AD*

1700 to AD 1860 1 (London: Macmillan, 1959), p. 85.

[15] Ian Markham, *Truth and the Reality of God* (Edinburgh: T. & T. Clark, 1998), p. 83.

[16] Ibid., p. 123.

[17] R. W. Hood Jr. (ed.), *Handbook of Religious Experience* (Birmingham, AL: Religious Education Press, 1995), p. 3 (his emphasis).

[18] See Barr's discussion, op. cit., pp. 32ff.

[19] John Calvin, *The Institutes of the Christian Religion*, ed. J. T. McNeill, tr. F. L. Battles (Philadelphia: Westminster, 1960), I.iii.1, pp. 43–44.

[20] Douglas Moo, *The Epistle to the Romans*, New International Commentary on the New Testament (Grand Rapids: Eerdmans, 1996, p. 150.

[21] See e.g. G. I. Mavrodes, *Revelation in Religious Belief* (Philadelphia: Temple University Press, 1988); also John Baillie, *Our Knowledge of God* (Oxford: Oxford University Press, 1943).

[22] Frank Tipler, *The Physics of Immortality* (London: Macmillan, 1994), p. ix.

[23] Robert Jastrow, *God and the Astronomer* (New York: W. W. Norton, 2nd ed., 1992), p. 107.

[24] See e.g. F. Hoyle and C. Wickramasinghe, *Evolution from Space* (New York: Simon & Schuster, 1981); Swinburne, op. cit.

[25] Paul Davies, *The Mind of God* (London: Simon & Schuster, 1992), p. 192.

[26] Tipler, op. cit., pp. 309ff.

[27] Ibid., p. 305.

[28] Jastrow, op. cit., p. 9.

[29] Harold P. Nebelsick, *Renaissance and Reformation and the Rise of Science* (Edinburgh: T. & T. Clark, 1992), p. 186.

Chapter 6: The gospel and religious experience

[1] George A. Lindbeck, *The Nature of Doctrine* (London: SPCK, 1984), p. 21.

[2] D. Z. Phillips, *Faith after Foundation* (London: Routledge, 1988).

[3] Richard Swinburne, *Revelation* (Oxford: Clarendon, 1992); W. P. Alston, *Perceiving God* (Ithaca: Cornell University Press, 1991); K. E. Yandell, *The Epistemology of Religious Experience* (Cambridge: Cambridge University Press, 1993); Caroline Franks Davis, *The Evidential Force of Religious Experience* (Oxford: Clarendon, 1989).

[4] See D. W. Bebbington, *Evangelicalism in Modern Britain* (London: Unwin Hyman, 1989), pp. 5ff.

[5] R. W. Hood (ed.), *Handbook of Religious Experience* (Birmingham, AL: Religious Education Press, 1995), pp. 72ff.

[6] Richard Swinburne, *Is There a God?* (Oxford: Oxford University Press, 1996), pp. 133–134.

[7] W. R. Matthews, *Memories and Meanings* (London: Hodder & Stoughton, 1969), pp. 42–43. Matthew's account could be supplemented copiously. Both

the author Vera Brittain and the actor Alec Guinness record religious experiences in their autobiographical writings, for example.

[8] See e.g. the discussion in David Hay, *Religious Experience Today* (London: Mowbray, 1990).

[9] E.g. John Hick, 'Jesus and the World Religions', in idem (ed.) *The Myth of God Incarnate* (London: SCM, 1977), p. 181.

[10] George A. Lindbeck, *The Nature of Doctrine*, p. 16: he argues that a 'cultural-linguistic' approach is more fruitful.

[11] Arnold Dallimore, *The Life of Edward Irving* (Edinburgh: Banner of Truth, 1983), p. 159.

[12] See e.g. Alister Hardy, *The Spiritual Nature of Man* (Oxford: Clarendon, 1979), and David Hay, *Exploring Inner Space* (London and Oxford: Mowbray, 2nd ed., 1987).

[13] 'Freudian Theory and Religious Experience', in Hood (ed.), op. cit., p. 201.

[14] Classically, K. Thomas, *Religion and the Decline of Magic* (London: Weidenfeld & Nicholson, 1971).

[15] See my 'Calvin, Charismatics and Miracles', *The Evangelical Quarterly* 51 (1979), pp. 131–144.

[16] D. W. Dockrill, 'Spiritual Knowledge and the Problem of Enthusiasm in Seventeenth-Century England', *Prudentia*, Supplementary Number (1985), pp. 147–171.

[17] Details in Kenneth Clark, *The Other Half: A Self-Portrait* (London: John Murray, 1977), and David Marr, *Patrick White: A Life* (London: Jonathan Cape, 1991).

[18] See the discussions in Daniel Cohn-Sherbok and Christopher Lewis (ed.), *Beyond Death* (London: Macmillan, 1995), chs. 12 and 13.

[19] John Hick, *God Has Many Names* (London: Macmillan, 1980), pp. 6, 59ff. For a recent Roman Catholic account, see Gavin D'Costa, *The Meeting of Religions and the Trinity* (New York: Orbis, 2000).

[20] Keith Ward, *Religion and Revelation* (Oxford: Clarendon, 1994).

Chapter 7: The authority of Scripture

[1] Quoted by Gertrude Himmelfarb in *On Looking into the Abyss* (New York: Knopf, 1994), p. 76.

[2] Ibid., p. 77.

[3] Ibid., p. 103.

[4] D. N. Livingstone, 'Situating Evangelical Responses to Evolution', in D. N. Livingstone et al. (ed.), *Evangelicals and Science in Historical Perspective* (New York: Oxford University Press, 1999), pp. 193–219.

[5] Himmelfarb, op. cit., p. 84.

[6] Ibid., p. 88.

[7] P. R. Williamson, art. 'Covenant', in T. D. Alexander and Brian S. Rosner

(ed.), *New Dictionary of Biblical Theology* (Leicester: IVP, 2000).

[8] See the discussion by Nicholas Wolterstorff in his *Divine Discourse* (Cambridge: Cambridge University Press, 1995), ch. 3.

[9] The phrase comes from the famous essay by Benjamin Jowett, 'On the Interpretation of Scripture', in *Essays and Reviews* (London: Longman, 1863), p. 338.

[10] Paul Avis, in idem (ed.) *Divine Revelation* (Grand Rapids: Eerdmans, 1997), p. 50. Avis is summarizing Barth's approach, but his point is applicable in other discussions.

[11] Edwyn Bevan, *Symbolism and Belief* (Boston: Beacon, 1957), p. 291.

[12] See e.g. Gabriel Hebert, *Fundamentalism and the Church of God* (London: SCM, 1957), pp. 138ff.

[13] Rafla Zaluuriu, *Muhammad and the Quran* (London: Penguin, 1991), p. 4.

[14] Lawrence S. Cunningham, *The Catholic Faith: An Introduction* (New York: Paulist, 1987), pp. 27–28.

[15] See his article in Alan Richardson (ed.), *A Dictionary of Christian Theology* (London: SCM, 1969); also his *Tradition in the Early Church* (London, SCM, 1962), pp. 237ff. Cf. H. E. W. Turner, *The Pattern of Christian Truth* (London: Mowbray, 1954), pp. 482–492.

[16] *Dogmatic Constitution on Divine Revelation*, p. 10.

[17] Ibid., p. 11.

[18] Ibid., pp. 9–10.

[19] Ibid., p. 12.

[20] Ibid., p. 11.

[21] Ibid.

[22] See, for example, H. R. McAdoo, *The Spirit of Anglicanism* (London: A. & C. Black, 1965), pp. v–vi.

[23] Bernhard Lohse, *Martin Luther's Theology* (Minneapolis: Fortress, 2000), pp. 196ff.

[24] See Paul Helm (ed.), *Objective Knowledge* (Leicester: IVP, 1987).

Chapter 8: The nature of Scripture

[1] *Shorter Oxford English Dictionary* (Oxford: Clarendon, 1977).

[2] For an introduction to narrative criticism and its relation to revelation, see Gabriel Fackre, *The Doctrine of Revelation* (Edinburgh: Edinburgh University Press, 1997).

[3] Michael Welker, *God the Spirit*, tr. J. F. Hoffmeyer (Minneapolis: Fortress, 1994), p. 273.

[4] At an even more basic level of the unfortunate divisions assumed in biblical criticism, see Francis Watson, *Text and Truth* (Grand Rapids: Eerdmans, 1997), pp. 1–32.

[5] See Susan E. Gillingham, *One Bible, Many Voices* (Grand Rapids:

Eerdmans, 1998).

[6] See Roger Beckwith, *The Old Testament Canon of the New Testament Church and its Background in Early Judaism* (London: Fontana, 1986), and Bruce M. Metzger, *The Canon of the New Testament* (Oxford: Clarendon, 1988), pp. 251–54.

[7] Frederick W. Norris, *The Apostolic Faith* (Collegeville: Liturgical, 1992), p. 53.

[8] See Kevin J. Vanhoozer, 'The Voice and the Actor', in J. G. Stackhouse (ed.), *Evangelical Futures* (Leicester: Apollos, 2000), pp. 61–106.

[9] *The Chicago Statement on Biblical Inerrancy*, published in Norman L. Geisler, *Inerrancy* (Grand Rapids: Zondervan, 1979), pp. 493–502. The citation is from p. 500.

Chapter 9: On reading Scripture

[1] Nicholas Wolterstorff, *Divine Discourse* (Cambridge: Cambridge University Press, 1995), p. 17.

[2] Anthony Thiselton, *New Horizons in Hermeneutics: The Theory and Practice of Transforming Biblical Reading* (Grand Rapids: Zondervan, 1992).

[3] Kevin J. Vanhoozer, *Is There a Meaning in this Text?* (Leicester: Apollos, 1998.

[4] Ibid., p. 30. Vanhoozer's work is a powerful full-scale treatment of the issues addressed in this chapter.

[5] M. H. Abrams, *A Glossary of Literary Terms* (Orlando: Holt, Rinehart & Winston, 1985), p. 38.

[6] *The Idler*, 9 June 1759; cf. Vanhoozer, op. cit., p. 22.

[7] I am thinking here of the extensive use being made of the work of J. L. Austin.

[8] See Vanhoozer, op. cit., pp. 43–97.

[9] Alan Jacobs, 'Psychological Criticism: From the Imagination to Freud and Beyond', in Clarence Walhout and Leland Ryken (ed.), *Contemporary Literary Theory* (Grand Rapids: Eerdmans, 1991) p. 99 (his emphasis).

[10] K. K. Ruthven, *Critical Assumptions* (Cambridge: Cambridge University Press, 1979), p. 53.

[11] Ibid., p. 57.

[12] Jacobs, op. cit., p. 99.

[13] 'The poem is not the critic's own and not the author's (it is detatched from the author at birth and goes about the world beyond his power to intend about it or control it).' W. K. Wimsatt and M. C. Beardsley, 'The Intentional Fallacy', *The Sewanee Review* LIV (1946), pp. 468–483; quotation from p. 470.

[14] For an allied theme see David Carr, *Time, Narrative and History* (Bloomington: Indiana University Press, 1986).

[15] Susan E. Gillingham, *One Bible, Many Voices* (Grand Rapids: Eerdmans,

1998), p. 242.

[16] A remarkable illustration of this clash may be found in a self-justifying letter of Oswald Mosley to his first wife, in which, having stated that 'our love and alliance is all things', he makes a claim for 'individual happiness', without which 'and a sense of all-pervading freedom we cannot be complete people'. Nicholas Mosley, *Rules of the Game/Beyond the Pale* (London: Pimlico, 1998), p. 136.

[17] See e.g. Judith Plaskow, *Sex, Sin and Grace* (Lanham: University Press of America, 1980).

[18] See Gillingham, op. cit. Her extraordinary treatment of Psalm 8, illustrating the approaches of different types of criticism (pp. 232–244), is a telling (if unintended) commentary on the futility of much that passes for criticism.

[19] See especially T. D. Alexander and Brian S. Rosner (ed.), *New Dictionary of Biblical Theology* (Leicester: IVP, 2000), and the bibliographies therein.

[20] David H. Kelsey, *To Understand God Truly* (Philadelphia: Westminster, 1992), p. 85.

[21] David H. Kelsey, *Between Athens and Berlin* (Grand Rapids: Eerdmans, 1993), p. 14.

[22] Nicholas Wolterstorff, 'The Travail of Theology in the Modern Academy', in Miroslav Volf et al., *The Future of Theology* (Grand Rapids: Eerdmans, 1996), pp. 44–45.

[23] David C. Steinmetz, *Memory and Mission* (Nashville: Abingdon, 1988), p. 163.

[24] David Lehman, *Signs of the Times* (New York: Poseidon, 1991).

Chapter 10: The gospel and the Spirit

[1] Note the references to Kant in the survey edited by P. C. Hodgson and R. H. King, *Christian Theology* (Philadelphia: Fortress, 1989).

[2] Immanuel Kant, *Religion within the Limits of Reason Alone* (New York: Harper Torchbooks, 1960), pp. 182–183 (his emphasis).

[3] John Calvin, *The Institutes of the Christian Religion*, ed. J. T. McNeill, tr. F. L. Battles (Philadelphia: Westminster, 1960), I.vii.4, p. 78.

[4] D. W. Dockrill, 'Spiritual Knowledge and the Problem of Enthusiasm in Seventeenth-Century England', *Prudentia*, Supplementary Number (1985), pp. 147–171.

[5] Geoffrey F. Nuttall, *The Holy Spirit in Puritan Faith and Experience* (Chicago: University of Chicago Press, 1992), p. 30.

[6] Gary D. Badcock, *Light of Truth and Fire of Love* (Grand Rapids: Eerdmans, 1997), pp. 113, 116.

[7] See H. D. McDonald, *Theories of Revelation* (London: Allen & Unwin, 1963), pp. 218–287.

[8] J. Macquarrie, *Principles of Christian Theology* (London: SCM, 1977),

p. 454.

[9] Gerald F. Hawthorne, *The Presence and the Power* (Dallas: Word, 1991), p. 236.

[10] Calvin, *Institutes* III.i.2, p. 238.

[11] Gordon D. Fee, *God's Empowering Presence* (Peabody: Hendrickson, 1994), p. 100 (his emphasis).

[12] C. K. Barrett, *The Second Epistle to the Corinthians* (London: A. & C. Black, 1973), p. 112.

[13] Badcock, op. cit., pp. 258, 263.

Chapter 11: Contemporary revelation

[1] J. Huggett, *Listening to God* (London: Hodder & Stoughton, 1986), p. 21.

[2] Ibid., p. 93.

[3] Wayne Grudem, *Systematic Theology* (Leicester: IVP, 1994), pp. 641–642. See also idem, *The Gift of Prophecy* (Eastbourne: Kingsway, 1988).

[4] Ibid., p. 641 (his emphasis).

[5] Ibid.

[6] See ch. 6 above.

[7] R. Rice, 'Biblical Support for a New Perspective', in Clark Pinnock et al., *The Openness of God* (Downers Grove: IVP, 1994), p. 16.

[8] Grudem, op. cit, p. 1049.

[9] Ibid., p. 1055.

[10] Sinclair Ferguson, *The Holy Spirit* (Leicester: IVP, 1996), pp. 214–221.

[11] See note 1 above.

[12] I owe this observation to a former student, Rev. Tim McMahon.

For further reading

Paul Avis (ed.), *Divine Revelation* (Grand Rapids: Eerdmans, 1997)

John Baillie, *The Idea of Revelation in Recent Thought* (London: Oxford University Press, 1956)

Karl Barth, *Church Dogmatics*, tr. G. W. Bromiley (Edinburgh: T. & T. Clark, 2nd ed., 1975) I/1.1

Emil Brunner, *Revelation and Reason: The Christian Doctrine of Faith and Knowledge*, tr. O. Wyon (London: SCM, 1947)

John Calvin, *The Institutes of the Christian Religion*, ed. J. T. McNeill, tr. F. L. Battles (Philadelphia: Westminster, 1960), I.i–x

Bruce A. Demarest, *General Revelation: Historical Views and Contemporary Issues* (Grand Rapids: Zondervan, 1982)

Avery Dulles, *Models of Revelation* (Dublin: Gill & Macmillan, 1983)

Colin E. Gunton, *A Brief Theology of Revelation* (Edinburgh: T. & T. Clark, 1995)

Paul Helm, *The Divine Revelation: The Basic Issues* (London: Marshall, Morgan and Scott, 1982)

Carl F. Henry, *God, Revelation and Authority*, 6 vols. (Wheaton: Word, 1976–83; repr. Wheaton: Crossway, 1999)

H. D. McDonald, *Theories of Revelation: A Historical Study, 1700–1960* (Grand Rapids: Baker, 1979)

G. I. Mavrodes, *Revelation in Religious Belief* (Philadelphia: Temple University Press, 1988)

J. I. Packer, *'Fundamentalism' and the Word of God: Some Evangelical Principles* (London: IVF, 1963)

————, *God Has Spoken: Revelation and the Bible* (London: Hodder & Stoughton, rev. ed., 1993)

Keith Ward, *Religion and Revelation: A Theology of Revelation in the World's Religions* (Oxford: Clarendon, 1994)

B. B. Warfield, *Revelation and Inspiration* (New York: Oxford University Press, 1927)

Nicholas Wolterstorff, *Divine Discourse: Philosophical Reflections on the Claim that God Speaks* (Cambridge: Cambridge University Press, 1995)

Kevin J. Vanhoozer, *Is There a Meaning in this Text? The Bible, the Reader and the Morality of Literary Knowledge* (Grand Rapids: Zondervan, 1998)

Index of Scripture references

Genesis *203*
1 *48*
1:2–3 *237*
3:1 *74*
6:17 *237*
12:1–3 *77*
15:6 *77*
18:10, 13 *237*

Exodus
2:24–25 *70*
3:14 *69*
6:9 *237*
14:14 *159*
19:6–7 *158*
23:7 *192*
24:3–4 *155*
24:4 *158*
24:7 *77, 82, 154–155*
32:15–16 *158*
34:6 *194*
34:6–7 *58*
34:27 *158*

35:30 – 36:5 *238*

Numbers
11:17 *239*
11:31 *239*
22:21ff. *140*

Deuteronomy
4:15–40 *69*
4:15–16 *163*
6:4–9 *71*
13:1–3 *131*
13:1–5 *186, 271*
18:9–22 *69*
30:2 *166*
30:14 *164, 191, 276*
34:9 *239*

Joshua
22:5 *166*

Judges
7 *156*
14:6 *237*

1 Samuel
10:9–13 *238*
16 *140*
16:13 *237*
16:13–14 *239*

2 Samuel
23:1–2 *238*
7 *78*
7:16 *78*

1 Kings
18:39 *70*
19:12 *163, 278*

2 Kings
2:9, 15 *239*
18:19–25 *157*
22:19 *213*

2 Chronicles
34:14 *155*
34:14–31 *82*
34:15 *154*

293

Index of names

298

Index of subjects

302